ALEX AND THE HOBO

ALEX AND THE HOBO

A CHICANO LIFE AND STORY

JOSÉ INEZ TAYLOR AND JAMES M. TAGGART

 UNIVERSITY OF TEXAS PRESS AUSTIN

Requests for permission to reproduce material
from this work should be sent to Permissions,
University of Texas Press, P.O. Box 7819,
Austin, TX 78713-7819.

⊗ The paper used in this book meets the minimum
requirements of ANSI/NISO Z39.48-1992 (R1997)
(Permanence of Paper).

Library of Congress Cataloging-in-Publication Data

Taylor, José Inez, 1937–
    Alex and the hobo : a Chicano life and story /
José Inez Taylor and James M. Taggart.
        p.   cm.
Includes bibliographical references and index.
    ISBN 0-292-78179-2 (alk. paper)—ISBN 0-292-
78180-6 (pbk. : alk. paper)
    1. Taylor, José Inez, 1937–   2. Taylor, José Inez,
1937– —Settings.   3. Mexican Americans—
Colorado—Antonito—Biography.   4. Mexican
American authors—Colorado—Antonito—Biogra-
phy.   5. Political activists—Colorado—Antonito—
Biography.   6. Labor movement—Colorado—
Antonito—History—20th century.   7. Mexican
Americans—Ethnic identity.   8. Antonito (Colo.)—
Biography.   9. Mexican American children—
Fiction.   10. Tramps—Fiction.   I. Taggart,
James M., 1941–   II. Title.
F784.A58T39 2003
305.868'720788'0092—dc21

                                    2002015454

 **To our grandchildren**

Contents

Preface   xi

1. Introduction   1

PART I: THE STORY   13

2. *Alex and the Hobo*   15

PART II: THE LIFE   71

3. The Valley   73

4. Awareness   89

5. Social Structure   104

6. Anastacio Taylor   118

7. Beatriz Mondragón   136

8. Women in Peril   149

9. Conclusion   162

Appendix:
Juana's Witchcraft Testimony   167

Notes   177

Bibliography   189

Index   199

Illustrations

1. Joe Taylor talking in his kitchen 9

2. Rock formation in the llano 22

3. Sociedad Protección Mutua de Trabajadores Unidos (S.P.M.D.T.U.) in Antonito 38

4. Bridge over Rio Grande 47

5. Map of San Luis Valley 74

6. Joe Taylor and James Taggart on Kiowa Hill 78

7. Train headed north out of Antonito 80

8. Great Lakes Carbon (GrefCo) perlite processing plant 95

9. John Mansfield perlite processing plant 97

10. Main Street in Antonito looking south 108

11. Anastacio Taylor's *zapatería* 119

Preface

We have written this book for the people of Antonito and for anyone with an interest in a good story. We present one man's view of history in his work of fiction and in his account of how he wrote about his experiences. Readers from Antonito who occupy a different position in the social structure may have another view of their town. We hope they will have the chance to add their own stories to this one. For readers from other places, we aim to convey what it meant to grow up as a Spanish-speaking boy in a railroad town in a corner of the Southwest.

Our joint writing project came about when we met in Joe Taylor's secondhand shop on Antonito's Main Street in 1998. Joe Taylor tells and writes stories about the San Luis Valley in southern Colorado. Since our first meeting, we have had many conversations about stories as expressions of ethnic identity. We explored the meaning of ethnic similarities and differences by first discussing our own ethnic heritage. We have fathers with Anglo-Saxon surnames and mothers with Spanish surnames. One of our first discoveries was just how paternal surnames yield misleading impressions of ethnic identity. Anastacio Taylor and Richard Taggart were different in many ways, not the least of which was their language. Anastacio could not speak English, and Richard could not speak Spanish. When discussing our mothers, we recognized the enormous difference between the words "Mexicana/o" and "Mexican." Joe Taylor's mother, Beatriz Mondragón, was a "Mexicana," a Spanish speaker born and raised in the Southwest, but not a Mexican. The term "Mexican" when uttered by an English-speaking Anglo-Saxon is an insult tantamount to a racial slur in the San Luis Valley. Jim Taggart's mother, Carmen de

Lara, was a Mexican national who was born in Mexico City to a Mexican father and a Canadian mother, and she immigrated to the United States in 1911. Always proud but sometimes ambivalent about her national heritage, she did not consider the term "Mexican" to be offensive.

We found stories a way to organize and convey experience across ethnic lines, particularly if placed in their historical and cultural context. We present one of Joe Taylor's most autobiographical written stories in the first part of this book. In the second part, he recalls how he wrote out of his experience. This is based on many hours of recorded conversations in Spanish and English. Jim Taggart edited, translated, and organized Joe Taylor's spoken words, and Joe Taylor read and offered suggestions for further revision.

Scholars interested in how we edited and translated our conversations may write Jim Taggart for copies of the original transcriptions. We included only the English translations of conversations in Spanish to reduce the length and cost of this book and because we are still working on the best way to represent the Antonito dialect of spoken Spanish. Scholars will find in our appendix a lightly edited transcription and translation of a conversation in Spanish with a woman we call Juana. Her words are crucial for our argument.

We have woven our words together with the help of several people who supported our project, read earlier drafts of our book, and made constructive suggestions for revision. Mary Romero and Kathy Figgen introduced Carole Counihan and Jim Taggart to the San Luis Valley. Leonard Velazquez read an early draft of our book and gave us encouragement when we needed it most. Phil Jaramillo told us how to keep the reader's attention on what really matters. Carole Counihan combed through two drafts and pointed out, with her fine editorial skill, rough transitions and places where readers needed more signposts. Miguel Díaz Barriga gave us excellent suggestions on how to organize more effectively the chapters following Joe Taylor's story. A second reviewer encouraged us to be very precise with our facts and our use of languages, Spanish as well as English. Beatrice Taggart once again contributed her great artistic skill, this time by making the map of the San Luis Valley. We owe special thanks to Theresa May for her faith in our project and her support over the years. Funds from the Lewis Audrenreid Professorship in History and Archaeology at Franklin and Marshall College generously supported all phases of this project. We thank manuscript editor Jan McInroy and copyeditor Sue Carter for their careful and thoughtful reading of our book. We extend our gratitude to our neighbors in Antonito, who gave us their friendship and their support.

José Inez Taylor and James M. Taggart
Antonito, Colorado

ALEX AND THE HOBO

 **INTRODUCTION**

Alex and the Hobo is a work of fiction about a nine-year-old boy's loss of innocence and transition to manhood. The author, José Inez "Joe" Taylor, created the story out of his own coming-of-age in the San Luis Valley of southern Colorado. The tale is set in 1942 in Antonito, a small railroad town in the valley's southwestern corner. Alex Martínez loses his innocence as he befriends a mysterious hobo and learns about evil in his community. This book presents *Alex and the Hobo* and describes how the author wrote his story out of his experience.[1]

Joe Taylor turned to writing in the 1990's after a lifetime as a farmworker, a union man, a roofer, a construction worker, a heavy-equipment operator, a jailer and sheriff's dispatcher, and a Chicano activist in his community. His body, like his story, is inscribed with his experience: he lost a finger in a sawmill accident; he has no cartilage in his left knee from an old football injury; his arm trembles from a pinched nerve; he has chronic back pain from when he fell from a truck.[2] *Alex and the Hobo* is one of the many works of fiction that he wrote and stored in dust-filled boxes in his backyard shed. He showed his manuscripts to Carole Counihan and me a few years after we settled in his community for a long-term fieldwork project in anthropology.

Joe Taylor explained why he wrote by referring first to his deep connection to the San Luis Valley. **I've lived in this valley and I've slept, I've eaten, I've seen the harsh winters and the bad springs and the years of drought and the dust storm that flew over.** He explained that he had read and heard a lot about the Anglo-Saxon pioneers but very little about the Mexicanos who inhabited the valley before them. **The pioneers came in the wagons, but the mountains were already**

named, the rivers were already named, the families that helped them out were Mexican families so that tells you they were already here way before them.

He remarked that many have come into the valley and written about their own or others' experiences, and he had experiences of his own to write about. He mentioned the time he cut off his finger in a sawmill accident the year he graduated from high school. **I cut my finger off at ten o'clock in the morning. They didn't attend to me in the hospital until about nine-thirty, ten o'clock that night. I had it wrapped and everything, and they did give me a shot in between. But that's how long it took from the time I had my finger cut off until the time the doctor attended to it and finished amputating it.** On the basis of our many hours of conversation, I think he made several points by recounting this event: he suffered great pain as a worker; he was invisible to his Anglo-Saxon employer and the doctor for what seemed like a very long period of time, and he was invisible because he was a Mexicano from a humble family. He wrote *Alex and the Hobo* and other stories to be seen and heard.[3]

On many occasions, he referred to the relative position of the Spanish speakers from the south and the Anglo-Saxon pioneers from the east. **Manifest Destiny was the battle cry of the Anglo when he was pioneering or supposedly pioneering the West. "We dominate. The Indians have no rights. The Mexicans have no rights. We have the rights."** The "Mexicans" to whom he refers are the Spanish speakers like himself whose ancestors settled along the banks of Culebra Creek and the Conejos River in the Upper Rio Grande basin during the early 1850's.[4] He used the word "Mexican" deliberately to draw attention to the prejudicial attitude of Anglo-Saxons toward the Spanish-speaking residents of the San Luis Valley. "Mexicanos" is the preferred term for the descendents of the settlers of the Culebra Creek and the Conejos Rivers communities. A reader unfamiliar with the San Luis Valley may find the difference between "Mexicans" and "Mexicanos" difficult to grasp because, after all, "Mexicans" is the English translation of the Spanish word "Mexicanos." However, the negative connotation of "Mexicans" developed from the way the Spanish-speaking residents heard English-speaking Anglo-Saxons use the term to imply social and racial inferiority. "Mexicanos" carries a very different meaning because it rarely passes the lips of English-speaking Anglo-Saxons and appears in the speech of the Spanish speakers who observe rules of respect in polite conversation.

The terms "Mexicans" and "Mexicanos" may imply to some readers that the descendants of the Culebra Creek and Conejos River settlers came from Mexico. In fact, they came from what is now northern New Mexico, which belonged to the country of Mexico for only twenty-seven years, from the conclusion of the Mexican War of Independence in 1821 to the Treaty of Guadalupe-Hidalgo in 1848. Many of the Spanish-speaking settlers of northern New Mexican communities came directly from Spain and had children with Native American women—"mestizos," or offspring of mixed ancestry. They moved north into what is now Colorado, settling along the banks of the Conejos River and Culebra Creek in the early 1850's, after the Mexican government created the Conejos and Sangre de Cristo land grants in 1833 and 1843–1844. When Joe Taylor said that "the Mexicans have no rights," he was referring to the precarious position of the "Mexicanos" or Spanish-speaking settlers who were under the jurisdiction of a conquering government after the Treaty of Guadalupe-Hidalgo in 1848, which concluded the war between Mexico and the United States. The U.S. government "disallowed" the Conejos Land Grant in the 1860's, and Anglo-Saxon settlers from the East took advantage of the conquering country's legal and political system to nullify land grants and acquire much of the valley's best land and water during the last quarter of the nineteenth century.[5] Anglo-Saxon settlement came with the railroad, which reached Joe Taylor's town of Antonito in 1880.[6] The arrival of the Anglo settlers set the stage for the creation of a highly stratified society based on the commercial agricultural production of sheep, potatoes, cauliflower, and peas.

Writing *Alex and the Hobo*

Joe Taylor wrote *Alex and the Hobo* from his particular perspective as the son of a Mexicano cobbler and as a worker on the commercial farms and in the mining industry around Antonito. Although a native speaker of Spanish, he wrote his story in English. In school, Joe

Taylor and other Mexicano children were discouraged from and even punished for using Spanish, and he only learned to write English. *Alex and the Hobo* may remind some readers of the stories Tomás Rivera wrote in Spanish about his migrant labor experience in south Texas.[7] Both writers were born in the 1930's—Tomás Rivera in 1935 and Joe Taylor in 1937—and they both wrote about the hardship of working in the fields, the marginal and precarious social position of the field-worker, and Anglo-Saxon prejudice. The two men are also different. Tomás Rivera grew up in the lower Rio Grande, became a schoolteacher, went to graduate school at the University of Oklahoma, and published stories after studying literature.[8]

Joe Taylor wrote in comparative isolation from the intellectual currents that have shaped nineteenth- and twentieth-century Spanish American fiction. He completed Antonito High School, served in the U.S. Army, and then returned to his hometown. There, he worked for the perlite mine and was active in the union for nearly twenty years. Without knowing how to read Spanish, he lacked access to Spanish American literature and had little exposure to Chicano writers until he took advantage of the G.I. bill and enrolled in a Chicano studies class at Adam State College in 1977. Work and family kept him from completing the class, but he read Rudolfo Anaya's *Bless Me, Última,*[9] about another young boy's loss of innocence, and found a model for his own writing. Joe Taylor's Alex and Rudolfo Anaya's Antonio both lose their innocence as they learn about evil. Antonio learned about corruption as he entered the spiritual world of Última, a curer. Alex came face to face with secular officials who abused their power and betrayed the public trust.

Alex and the Hobo is an important cultural document because it is an insider's view of a culture, something that anthropologists desire but rarely find.[10] The story went through no censorship before he turned his manuscript over to me for typing and light editing. Although he is a well-known and highly respected man in his community, almost no one in Antonito has read *Alex and the Hobo*. Joe Taylor penned his story several years before Carole Counihan and I arrived in his community, and so he created it beyond the reach of our "anthropologist-informant" relationship, which might have carried the baggage of Manifest Destiny. Chicano scholars have justifiably criticized the work of anthropologists and folklorists who have entered or perhaps intruded into the Upper and Lower Rio Grande basins and written with ethnic and class prejudice, which I have tried to avoid by keeping the focus on Joe Taylor's words.[11]

Joe Taylor's story is a very personal account of his town's history. He created all of the characters, including the corrupt officials, out of the composite characteristics of people he actually knew. His story is a product of his particular "historical imagination," a phrase that John and Jean Comaroff use to describe historical narratives, including those written by academic historians as constructions of the past.[12] The difference between Joe Taylor's narrative and that of an academic historian is one of perspective. *Alex and the Hobo* and Joe Taylor's account of how he created it offer a valuable perspective that is complementary to that of Sarah Deutsch in her comprehensive description of southern Colorado and northern New Mexico history from 1880 to 1940.[13] Deutsch presented an exhaustive account of the economic, social, and political forces affecting gender relations for Spanish-speaking women and men like Joe Taylor and his ancestors. *Alex and the Hobo,* set in 1942, presents the meaning as well as a recollection of past events. As a work of fiction, the story conveys what it means to be a Spanish-speaking boy at the economic margins of a class-stratified and Anglo-dominated society.[14] Such statements are comparatively rare in the historical record.[15]

Allusion in *Alex and the Hobo*

In our conversations as well as in his story, Joe Taylor frequently resorted to allusion when presenting his meaning of the past. Understanding his allusions makes *Alex and the Hobo* a much richer experience, particularly for readers who came of age at a different time and in a different place. His allusions take several forms—cultural, social, and historical—which are laid out in more detail in the chapters following his story. His cultural allusions refer to beliefs that he inherited as a member of a Spanish-speaking community and that he took for granted and did not always make explicit. His social allusions are to the specific people he knew in the past. His historical allusions are to his understanding of how Anglo-Saxons have transformed his valley.

Cultural, social, and historical allusions converge in the core meaning of *Alex and the Hobo.* Joe Taylor explained that his story is about a boy who loses his innocence as he finds out about corruption in his community. The term "innocence" has many cultural connotations that did not become apparent until late in our dialogue, when we discussed his religious beliefs about innocence and sin. He said that innocence is a time in childhood when everything is **pure and simple and beautiful and wonderful.** He explained: **if you're innocent, you cannot commit a sin.** To lose innocence means gaining awareness of sin and understanding that one lives in a world of corruption.

He spoke in the second person when he explained what he meant. **Well, you learned a lot out in the field. As far as innocence is concerned, one part can be lost pretty quickly while another takes a little longer. You were there with a bunch of girls and a bunch of boys. You were left alone. You had no supervision except what they told you at home. And there were older girls trying to explore sexuality. A few men took their bottles to work. When you befriended one of them, which I did a lot of times, he'd give me a drink of wine. You would go on over there and you'd say: "Well, I'm going to take a basket of peas back home. I'm going to hide it under all these clothes." So you'd hide a basket of peas under all these clothes, and everybody would help you, and that's stealing. The Ten Commandments were being broken little by little.**

Alex likewise lost his innocence by witnessing sex, drinking, stealing, and the abuse of power. Losing innocence is an important step in making the transition from boyhood to manhood. Alex takes the next step by standing up to corruption when he foils the plot of the marshal, the judge, and the bookkeeper/insurance man to blame the hobo for a crime he did not commit. I asked Joe Taylor why he wrote about corruption, and he said he saw it as part of the class system. He defined corruption as **the abuse of power. I do not like that. I hate that.** One example he brought up on several occasions was an employer who abused his power by exploiting his workers. He said: **I would hate, for my own greed, for my own benefit, to use somebody else's sweat, somebody else's work** to become rich.

He linked corruption to sin in a clear moral vision that he traced to his religion and to his family. Despite the clarity of his vision, he also described a morally complicated world, conveying moral complexity in *Alex and the Hobo* and in his life story. Alex, he said, went through great anguish as he decided what to do after he learned of the plot to kill the hobo to cover up a crime committed by one of the powerful members of the community. Alex suffered great anguish because he knew his parents liked and supported the town marshal, one of the co-conspirators in the plot. Alex worried about what would happen to his parents if he went against the marshal, and he felt nausea in the pit of his stomach as he acted to prevent an injustice.

Alex and the Hobo as an Act of Resistance

Alex's moral dilemma is an example of what Antonio Gramsci meant when he said that resistance is "hard to think." [16] However, resistance is not *impossible* to think: Alex did act to save the hobo, and Joe Taylor did write his story. [17] He is a good example of what Antonio Gramsci meant by the term "organic intellectual," [18] a person who may lack formal academic training but who can articulate the interests of his class. Two sources of Joe Taylor's resistance are his class and ethnic consciousness. As our dialogue and friendship developed, I became increasingly aware that he, like men and women in other parts of the Southwest, was critical of the class system because it was destroying his culture. In this respect, he resembles the elders of Córdova, New Mexico, who lament the erosion of their culture as their children and grandchildren become more individualistic, embrace commodity fetishism, and turn away from the Mexicano community. [19] Joe Taylor took me to interview men and women in the area who told how they were experiencing economic and cultural pressure. They couched their experiences in terms of witchcraft, a system of thought used to explain evil. One man told of how a diabolical Anglo miner, described as a "psychological vampire," tried to bribe him into giving up his daughter by offering him a gold mine. He spoke in terms of devils and vampires, but he was also talking about larger issues of colonialization and domination. One woman believed a witch had caused her husband to drink heavily, her son to attempt suicide, and her daughter to run wild. At the time, she was struggling with great economic hardship because her husband had just lost his job.

These "informants" were among the visitors to Joe Taylor's secondhand store, now located in his home in Antonito. Some had spent time in the Conejos County jail when he worked for the sheriff's office as a jailer and dispatcher. He had taken them under his wing, given them advice, and they reciprocated by giving him their trust and loyalty. Many regard him as a father figure and value his advice because of his clear but complex masculine moral vision, his perspective on being a man in his culture and community.

Interpreting the Creation of *Alex and the Hobo*

Our dialogue began when I walked into his secondhand shop on Antonito's Main Street in June of 1998, looking for someone who knew folktales like those Juan B. Rael had collected in the same area in 1930.[20] Joe Taylor obliged by telling me several Spanish folktales he had learned from his father, Anastacio Taylor, and his mother, Beatriz Mondragón. Our dialogue has continued through the final stages of preparing this book for publication. I recorded and transcribed all of our conversations, and the transcriptions reveal how we gently struggled with each other as we pursued our own, sometimes quite different, aims. I wanted him to be what anthropologists call a "key oral informant," who would explain his culture to me so I could write a scholarly paper (an ethnography). For his part, he persuaded me to take his writing seriously.[21]

Our dialogue yielded a wealth of information on the creation of *Alex and the Hobo,* all of which had to be organized so readers would not get lost in the details. In organizing this material, I ran the risk of imposing an alien meaning on another man's life and story.[22] However, readers of the first draft of this manuscript, who included some in Antonito, asked for more direction, more interpretation. Joe Taylor and I developed a more coherent framework by practicing

Joe Taylor talking in his kitchen.

what Elaine Lawless has called "reciprocal ethnography."[23] I gave him all that I wrote about him, and he diplomatically and thoughtfully offered his critiques. I found that short papers worked well to gauge his reactions to my interpretations of what he had written and told me in oral interviews. He found some more convincing than others, and I tried to incorporate what he liked best when organizing the chapters that follow his story. He expressed the most enthusiasm about a paper that examined food symbolism to describe how Alex made the transition to manhood by moving from the world of his mother to that of his father and other men. That paper combined the approach to masculinity I used for Spain and Mexico with the method of food-centered life history that Carole Counihan applied to understanding the subjective experience of being a woman in Italy and the United States.[24]

The approach to masculinity for interpreting *Alex and the Hobo* begins with Joe Taylor's verbally expressed meaning. One strand in his "web of meaning"[25] is his class and ethnic consciousness. He echoed Marx when he asked me to ask him if he was a rich man. I obliged, and he replied: **I am rich in my own way. I am rich because I'm at peace with myself. I'm at peace with the community. I'm at peace with nature over here.** His words resemble those of Marx, who described the human condition without estranged or wage labor as a time when humans will be at peace with themselves, with each other, and with nature.[26] Joe Taylor said that he never read Marx, although he could have learned about Marx's critique of capitalism while working to establish the Raza Unida Party in Conejos County, while taking the Chicano studies course at Adam State College, or while working for the union.

As our conversations continued, Joe Taylor turned to the influence of his family and his religion on the moral vision that guided writing *Alex and the Hobo.* I asked him why Alex took his first step toward manhood by standing up to corruption, and he replied: **That's the way his parents wanted him to be raised, and that's the way the Church wanted him to be raised.** We talked at great length about what these words meant, first discussing his father, who died in 1983, and then his mother, who died in 1950, when Joe Taylor was only thirteen years old. It became clear that the particular form of his masculine moral vision developed as he made his first steps toward manhood. As in the case of many boys, taking those steps involved moving from the world of his mother to that of his father, a transition that took place around the time that he and his family moved across the San Luis Valley to Antonito.

Culturally sensitive studies of masculinity reveal that boys become men by moving from the mother to the father in many different ways, depending on a number of variables: the prevailing conception of manhood; the boy's relationship with the mother; the role of the father; the social structure in which the transition takes place; the historical forces impinging on the lives of the boy, his parents, and other actors in his social field.[27] We spent a great deal of time delving into the recesses of his memory to discover just how he made that transition. He provided many recollections of his father, his mother, and his church, and I gradually realized that the moral vision he conveyed in *Alex and the Hobo* was heavily based on the concept of sin that he learned as a child. Joe Taylor was raised as a Catholic, he served as an altar boy, and he takes his religion very seriously. He and his sister revealed that his loving mother and grandmother laid the foundation for his concept of sin during his early infancy. His father, a more remote emotional figure, nevertheless played a complementary role, adding to Joe Taylor's moral education by providing him with tools for standing up to corruption.

Our dialogue about his childhood provided many clues that enable us to see how *Alex and the Hobo* is an intimate verbal portrait of Joe Taylor himself. The story contains his memory of how he formed the core of his masculinity, which is a convergence of the concept of sin that he learned from his mother, the moral examples set by his father, and the class and ethnic consciousness he acquired from bitter experience throughout his life. We used several approaches to unlock his memory to discover that core. He recalled his mother's love when talking to Carole Counihan and me about food, sometimes in our kitchen and sometimes in his. He spoke about food from the perspective of a man who consumed food prepared in the kitchen by women, and he associated feeding others with expressions of love. He spoke about his transition from the world of his mother to that of his father by recounting his experiences of producing food in the fields around Antonito. Some of his memories of working in those fields when he was the age of Alex contain the seeds of his ethnic and class consciousness.

In the chapters that explain how Joe Taylor created his story, I shall describe how he developed his masculine moral vision as he moved from the world of his mother to that of his father. As in the case of many men, that move took place over his entire life and involved many dimensions of experience: the meaning of manhood, his historical experiences, his position in the class structure, the organization of parental labor in his family, the particular personalities of his father and mother. The chapters following his story will explore each of these dimensions of his life in reverse chronological order, beginning with the moment he wrote *Alex and the Hobo* and ending with his relationship with his mother. In between are his participation in the Chicano movement, his work with the union, his proofs of young manhood on the football field and in the streets, and his boyhood moral education in his father's cobbler shop.

PART I THE STORY

CHAPTER 2

➤ *ALEX AND THE HOBO*

A young boy stood inside his father's barbershop looking out a large window. He could see the building directly across from him but could not make out anything more than a block away, up or down the street. Gusts of wind rattled the plate glass, and for five days, gales had howled day and night, turning the sky a chocolate brown. A street lamp whirled on its pole, and Alex thought it would tear loose from its socket at any moment. The world from end to end seemed covered by a massive cloud of dust blocking out the sun. Endless balls of tumbleweed rolled down the street, snagging in doorways and under parked cars.

"Papá, is this what the end of the world is like?" asked the boy, with a worried look on his face.

"No, but it sure seems like it," his father patiently explained. "Does this scare you?"

"I guess, but will the sun ever shine again?"

"Oh, I'm sure it will, Alex. But I must agree with you, this is the worst dust storm I've ever seen."

A lone man fought his way through the back alley and on to Main Street not far from where Alex stood watching from the window. The man faced his head into the wind and tried to walk, but tumbleweed snagged his feet. He stumbled, nearly fell, and struggled to regain his footing only to feel the wind tear a sack from his grasp and carry it down the street. The man disappeared as if swallowed by the cloud of dust. March had come in like a lion, bringing winds that blew away tons of badly needed topsoil. The spring winds, showing no mercy, had dried the mountain snows, battered roofs, torn off shingles, and rattled loose sheets of galvanized iron, scattering them for miles around. Alex spotted the Fire Department bell, jarred loose from its cage across the street, and he watched as some volunteers climbed up on the roof and put it back in its place. The wind blew down their ladder, and other members of their company set it back up so the volunteers could climb down from the roof.

The year was 1942, and Alex and his family had left their ranch so his father could find work and a better school for his children. The new town needed a barber, and Alex's father was a good one. Their ranch only had a one-room schoolhouse and a single teacher for all the students, from first to eighth grade. Their new town had a high school with a football field, a railroad station, and a main street with stores and saloons. Still, Alex could walk just a few blocks in any direction and be out in open country teeming with jackrabbits.

Alex was nine years old and the third in a family of five children. His father fought an uphill battle to provide for such a big family. A barber did not earn a lot, and there was little money floating around anyway. The country had just come out of the Great Depression, and some employers paid their workers with vouchers. The rationing and shortages that came with World War II meant that even those with money could not buy many items. A person had to have ration stamps for gasoline, tires, coffee, sugar, and cigarettes. Car companies made Jeeps, army trucks, tanks, and airplanes to fight the war.

The hardships facing the nation didn't affect Alex much, but he did have to go out to work in the fields. The war had taken the best men, and so Alex, like many boys and girls his age, would soon hire out. New farm machinery slowly replaced old. Alex and his family struggled to get by. Their work was hard, and the hardest work came in the spring when the fields started to turn green.

By the end of May, the winds had died down, and Alex was excited when school let out on the 25th. He was a curious boy and was allowed to roam the streets during the day. With his school friends, he played near the old flour mill or walked the rails and watched the big steam engine switching cars from one track to another. Sometimes, he would stand near the shipping yard and watch as sheep or cattle were loaded onto the stock cars headed for the high-mountain summer grazing. Alex liked being out in the open and missed living at the *rancho*, even though he could walk seven blocks in any direction and be out of his new, adopted town.

His father and mother insisted he work hard and be polite, particularly to the elderly members of his community. He heeded their advice, and had heard his mother say more than once, "Son, I know that what I tell you is hard for you to understand. But I think you have the makings of a good man in you."

"Like what, Mamá?"

"Just things I see in you, son. For one thing, you're not lazy or disrespectful with your friends. But you are a boy yet and you have to grow into manhood. For now, we'll just let nature take its course."

He did not really understand what she meant. He had heard his mother say he got his red hair and the freckles dotting his cheeks through the Martínez blood line on his father's side. Still, when picking someone on whom to model himself, he was sure he was not going to be a barber like his father. He had seen his father stand on his feet for hours at a time and thought there was more to life than just standing in one place hour after hour. Plus, there was not much money in it— at least that's what his mother always said.

"There's never enough left over. How can I feed a family of seven with what you make?" he had heard her complain.

Many times, Alex had fallen asleep on the bench in his father's shop, waiting for customers.

"Papá," he asked, "why don't more people come in for haircuts?"

"It's the times, son. If people don't have jobs, they don't make money. If they don't make money, they can't spend it," his father, Tomás, answered as he read a magazine.

Alex had an older brother and sister, and they liked to spend time with their own friends. Alex also had his own friends, with whom he often got into mischief. He did not know how, but his parents always found out and they gave him the strap. One of his friends was Gilbert,[1] and, although Alex considered him a know-it-all, he liked him anyway. Gilbert did not take "no" for an answer and always convinced Alex to go against his better judgment.

"Where to, Gil?"

"Wanna go to the river and smoke puff wood?" Alex recalled the last time they went to the river to smoke the hollow roots of willow and cottonwood trees as if they were tobacco.

"No, can't, Gil. My dad said the river is too high now, and I can only go with him, like on a picnic, but not alone."

Gilbert was hurt by this answer and let Alex know it.

"You're not going alone, Alex! I said with *me*, guy."

"Last time I went with you, you got me lost and what happened? Papá found out, and I had a sore butt for a week."

"OK, OK! Then let's go ride Mr. Jaramillo's goats. He don't mind."

That sounded like fun. He liked Juan Jaramillo's big red barn. It was sort of spooky, and he liked spooky places. They played there until they were caught by old Juan and run off.

"I thought you said he didn't mind!" Alex said after running for several blocks.

"He didn't use to. Maybe he changed his mind."

From there, they went to the stockyards and played in their fantasy world until Alex realized it was getting late and he had to get home. His mother only served a meal once. If he missed it, he missed it for good. He could hear his mother saying, "I don't run a restaurant here, you know. You're late for dinner, you go hungry!" She always kept that rule except for her oldest son, Lupe, who could skip a meal and still get fed. He always found an excuse that worked.

As Alex headed for home, he spotted the hobo. He had seen him before and was fascinated by the man. Yet he could not explain why. He decided to follow him. He would find out who he was, where he lived, where men like him come from, and what being a hobo was like. Once, when they still lived on the ranch, a tramp had come by to ask for a handout. His father was not at home at the time, and his mother was scared to death. She fed the tramp but would not let him inside the house. When he left, she warned her children never to go near tramps. She had heard stories of tramps and gypsies stealing little kids. Alex was not sure if the stories were true. "Why would my mother lie?" he wondered. "Mothers don't lie, but fathers do."

Every time his father took a drink, his mother asked, "Tomás, have you been drinking?"

His father always said no, even though Alex saw him sipping from a bottle in his shop. Alex was not crazy enough to tell on his father.

He figured the hobo to be his uncle's age, even though he had white hair. He was maybe five feet ten inches tall with a stocky build, weighed one-eighty or so. His clothes were old and baggy, but he kept himself neat. He was not sloppy and dirty like the hobos Alex had seen before. His complexion was ruddy and his eyes were blue with a white circle around the pupil. There was nothing outstanding about his nose, and his lips were fuller than most. Alex had never seen any man before who looked quite like this hobo. There was nothing odd about him, but he had a look all his own.

Alex played cat and mouse with the hobo, trying not to look obvious as he followed him about town, keeping his distance. He watched the hobo pick up empty beer and pop bottles, tin foil, and egg cartons and put them into his sack. The hobo went through the alleys and rummaged through discarded piles looking for anything of value. When his sack was full, he walked to a nearby store and turned in his bottles and egg cartons for their deposit. Alex had two pennies in his pocket, and so he went into the store on the pretext of buying some penny candy. He watched the clerk count out the bottles and egg cartons and then give the hobo some change. The hobo headed for another store, where he turned in the cans and scraps of tin foil. Alex was shocked to see the hobo slip a can of food into his bag. The boy considered stealing a sin, and many thoughts raced through his mind. Should he tell the store owner? What would happen if the hobo was caught? Would they put him in jail? He decided to say nothing and then realized he had missed the evening meal and would have to go to bed hungry.

The next day was Saturday, and Alex again stood near the front window of his father's shop. A man was sitting in the barber chair and two other men waited their turn for haircuts. Alex spotted the hobo across the street with his sack full, headed for a nearby store.

"Papá, who is that man over there?"

All of the men turned to look.

"I don't know, *hijo*. I see him around quite often."

"That's Milo," the man in the barber's chair said.

"Milo who?" asked Alex's father.

"Just Milo is all I've heard him called."

"Has he always lived here?" Alex asked.

"No," the man responded. "I've lived here most of my life and I've only seen him in the last two years. But he comes and goes."

Another man chimed in: "Some say he's a hobo or a tramp. They follow the railroad and, since the war started, quite a few have passed through here, but they never stay. Only old Milo has stuck around."

Alex remembered his mother's warning that tramps steal children, and he asked, "Are they bad people?"

"No. At least not this one. He's a quiet man and stays pretty much to himself. I've never seen him looking for trouble."

A fourth man spoke up, "You know, some of the town's bullies tried to run him off, even tried to beat him up, but that old goat gave them a run for their money. They got the worst of it, and the old goat stayed on." He paused before he continued, "I guess he never sleeps, either. Day or night, rain or shine, he's always out."

"That's right," the first man agreed. "He lives in an old abandoned house with only a small wood stove."

"That's all?" Alex's father asked in surprise.

"Yeah, and from what I heard, he's never sick, either. Tough old goat."

"Is he really old?" Alex asked.

"No. His white hair makes him look old, but he isn't young, either. I'd say he's up in his forties. Yet nobody knows where he came from," said the man.

"It makes a person wonder about men like him," remarked the man sitting in the barber's chair.

"There's only one person he talks to," the second man said. "That's the postmaster. He says the man isn't dumb, he's well educated. But then he won't say anything more about him. I find that kind of strange."

Alex's father finished with the haircut, and the men continued wondering why the hobo only talked to the postmaster. Then they changed the subject, and Alex did not hear any more about Milo that day. The conversation in the barbershop changed like the phases of the moon and the weather.

Outside, the strong winds of spring abated, leaving scars all over the prairie. This dust storm was the worst some had ever seen. Still, plowing and planting went ahead, and the town's people hoped for a good harvest. The long storing sheds next to the railroad tracks would open up soon and bustle with activity as workers made crates and loaded freight cars to ship wool and pelts out of the valley. Alex and his older sister would soon be among the women and children working in the fields. Meanwhile, he enjoyed the outdoors and filled his lungs with the scent of lilacs in full bloom. Nearly every house had a lilac bush in the yard, and he presented his mother with a special bouquet every day.

One Sunday after Mass, as he was wondering what to do, his father came up to him and said, "I bought an old ewe to butcher. I'm going out to the Sánchez ranch to get it. I'm taking your mamá and the kids. Do you want to come?"

"Boy oh boy! Yes!" Alex shouted. "What are we going in?"

"I borrowed a pickup from Tony."

"Can I ride in the back?"

"Going and coming. That way you can keep an eye on the ewe for me."

Alex and his father walked two blocks to get the truck and drove it back to their house. He climbed down from the cab to make room for his mother and younger sister, Linda, and jumped into the truck bed. His younger brother, Tommy, and his older sister, Olivia, joined him. Lupe insisted on staying behind because it was beneath his dignity to be seen with his parents. The day was perfect for the five-mile drive to the ranch. The sun was shining brightly, the fields were green, and the trees and willows lining the lane were alive with their new leaves. They drove down a road that rambled between two rivers, the Conejos to the north and the San Antón to the south. The two rivers met each other several miles to the east and then emptied into the Rio Grande, flowing south to New Mexico and into Texas. Red-winged blackbirds chirped their cheerful tunes in a cattail swamp. Alex's father pulled in at the ranch, and the Sánchez family met them with a warm and friendly greeting. Alex's mother, his sisters, and his younger brother were invited into the house. Alex went in the truck with his father and Mr. Sánchez to the corral to fetch the ewe. He spotted an old man sitting under a big shade tree. He thought of his grandfather as he walked over to the old man.

"Good morning," Alex greeted him.

"The same to you, young man. And who might you be?"

"I'm Alex, Señor. And you, what's your name?"

The old man acted friendly, Alex thought, so he felt comfortable talking.

"I like your ranch. Were you born here?" Alex asked.

"Yes, I was, and so was my father."

"There in that house?"

"No, son. Over there, next to those hills," said the old man, pointing to a barren rise in the east.

Alex spotted a rock formation that looked like some prehistoric animal looming at the foot of the hills. It reminded him of something he had seen in a schoolbook.

"Have you ever been to those rocks over there?" Alex asked as he pointed in the direction of what looked like an ancient creature.

"Yes, and did you know those rocks are strange? They hold a mystery. The Indians considered them sacred."

"Are they sacred and that other word you said: myster . . . ?"

"Mystery."

"Is it a mystery, Señor?"

"I'm not sure. Maybe not to everybody, but to me they are. Maybe not sacred, but strange in a way."

Alex looked at him, confused, not sure of what he meant, but the old man had a serious look on his face, as if recalling something that had happened in his past. He waited for the old man to continue.

"I was there several times, but not alone. Then one time I had to go by myself. I was only a boy. Not much older than you are now."

"Was it scary for you?"

"Not at first, but then it was late in the day. We had a flock of sheep

Rock formation in the llano.

grazing over there, and I had to go herd them home. Well, the sun was down, and it was close to dark. I remember it was during Lent. Matter of fact, it was Wednesday of Holy Week. I got to the flock about a half-mile from there. That's when it happened."

Alex stood in silence, wide-eyed, waiting for the man to continue.

"There behind me, but to my right, I saw this big ball of fire rolling over the prairie. I stood and watched it as it rolled right into those rocks. For a while, flames shot up into the sky and they lit up the whole prairie."

"Wow! I bet you were scared!?"

"*Jito*, I was scared, all right. I've never been as scared as I was then. I even cried from fear."

"Holy Moley. What did you do then?!"

"I left the sheep, ran for home, and told my father."

Alex wondered what he would have done in the same situation.

"What did he say? Did he believe you?"

"No, he didn't that night. He thought I was making it up just to get out of herding the sheep. He got mad at me and made me go with him and bring them home."

"Was that the only time you saw them?"

"No, *jito*. We saw them the next night. Both my father and I did." The old man nodded his head. "He believed me then, and every year since I've seen them during Lent and Holy Week. Every year I sit and look for them and I see them. This last Holy Week I saw them again."

Alex had not known about the lights by the rocks because he was new to this part of the valley. Legend had it that these lights or balls of fire appeared often. Many a traveler going through had seen them, cowboys and shepherds among them, but few came right out and spoke to just anyone about what they had seen.

"Does anybody ever go over there?"

"Oh, yes. Some do, but I've never gone near them again. Not right up to them, like some have."

"But why do they go there if they're mysterious?"

"Well, son, some say there's a treasure buried there and they go looking for it."

"Have they found it?"

"No, *jito*. Not that I know of, but they did find treasure in these parts. That I'm sure of."

"Are you the only one in your family who has seen these balls of fire, Señor?"

"No. My mother, my son, and his wife have, and many of our neighbors have too. But only during Lent and mostly in Holy Week."

"That's scary. I'd like to see them someday."

"As I live and breathe, you will."

As they talked, Alex saw his father and Mr. Sánchez load the ewe and drive the short distance to the house. Olivia, who had climbed into the truck bed, called out, "Come on, Alex! We're going."

"I have to go now, Señor."

"Good-bye, *jito*, but come back and visit again."

"I will. I will."

On the way back, Alex told Olivia what the old man had said.

"Rolling balls of fire?" she sassed. "And you believe him?!"

"Yes, I do, but what do sissy girls know?"

"Alex," she countered in disgust, "you're such a phony."

They were silent the rest of the way home.

Lupe helped his father butcher the ewe, and the rest of the family pitched in to make use of nearly every part of the animal. They used the blood for sausages, they cleaned and scraped the tripe for *menudo*, they ground the liver, lungs, and kidneys. To prepare *burruñates*, they cleaned the ewe's intestines and colon, which was always loaded with fat, cut the fatty colon into strips, and wrapped the intestines around each strip for baking in the oven. They reminded Alex of a coiled spring, and he always found them to be very tasty. They removed the tongue and brains for eating later, they skinned the head to bake in the oven, and they dried the pelt for sale, leaving only a small pile of waste to throw away. Their work done, they settled in for a hearty meal.

Alex kept up his daily routine of spying on the hobo, and one day he followed him to the coal bins. He had to scurry to keep up as Milo disappeared around a corner and then ran smack-dab into him. The hobo was waiting for him, and the sudden impact of their collision shocked Alex, whose face turned white as he stood staring wide-eyed with his mouth open.

"What is it you want, boy?" asked Milo with an accent. "Why do you follow me wherever I go?"

"I . . . I . . . I . . ."

"You what?"

"I . . . I . . . just wanted to be your fr-fr-friend."

"Well, I don't need a friend, especially not a brat like you."

By then Alex, halfway composed, felt hurt by the remark. "I'm-mm, not a brat."

"Do you stutter like that all the time?

"N-n-n-no, Señor," Alex replied, close to tears. "Only when I'm s-s-scared."

"Scared of what? Me?"

"Well, yes, no, no, yes," replied Alex, who felt his freckles dance on his face.

"What is it? Yes or no?"

"No."

"What's your name, boy?"

"Alex."

"Is that all, just Alex?"

"No, Señor. Alex Martínez. My father is the barber," Alex said, hoping the mention of his father would help him.

"Is that a fact! Then why doesn't he keep you at home where you belong?"

Milo was not a bad person. He did not bother anybody, and he expected the same in return. He had not lived an easy life, and he had never married. He liked children, but he had not really been around them enough to understand them. Once he tried to befriend some in another town, but the townspeople had taken offense and run him out at gunpoint. From then on, he had never again tried to befriend a child. Still, somehow this lad touched him.

"I'll tell you what, Alex. Follow me if you want, but don't get in my way."

"OK, I promise I won't."

From that day on, Alex was his constant companion. Milo was a quiet man, and when Alex wanted an answer to a question, he would practically have to pry it out of him.

Milo did not expect to get something for nothing. He would not accept handouts and food, and he scavenged for bottles and cans and also did yard work for money or payment in junk. Sometimes Milo gave Alex a few pennies for helping him. For Alex, it was a treat to help, although he never refused the money.

Late June was the time to cultivate some of the crops, and farmers would need extra help for hoeing, weeding, transplanting lettuce, and irrigating their fields. Only women, children, and some older men were available because so many younger men were away in the army. Workers piled into trucks with high racks and went out to the fields, some of which were over twenty miles away. Drivers would pick up the workers in their crews as early as 6 A.M. and would not return until after 6 P.M. Members of the same family usually worked together, and Alex and Olivia were on one of the crews headed for the fields to help harvest the crops. The valley typically did not get much summer rain except for an occasional downpour, and so farmers used water from melting snows, high in the mountains, to irrigate their crops. Irrigated rows of crops stretched for three-quarters of a mile, and Alex and the others in his crew were paid by the row rather than by the hour. Workers had to return the next day to earn the money for crops they had picked on the unfinished rows from the day before. Some field bosses were crooked and gave the unfinished rows to their favorite workers so they could earn pay for rows they hadn't picked the day before.

Alex found field work hard and uncomfortable. His ride to the field started in the cold morning at the grain elevators. The wind blowing through the truck racks made the ride seem even colder. Then came the hot sun, shielded only by an occasional cloud. Field hands not only worked long hours, but they also had bad water and no toilets. The crew chief brought water in a ten-gallon milk can, and by the end of the day the water, heated by the sun, was unfit to drink and made some of the workers sick. When rains came up in the afternoon, only a few trucks had a tarpaulin to protect the crews on their ride home. Even with a tarp, rain blew through the cracks in the sideboards, soaking Alex and the rest of the crew through to the bone. Some field bosses had little consideration for the workers, regardless of their sex or age, and were downright mean, shouting in foul language, making passes at the women, patting them on the butt and looking down their blouses. Alex saw one of them try to touch Olivia's breasts. Olivia was a blossoming young girl who was considered very pretty. Feeling shocked and enraged, Alex tried to jump him, but the man slapped him hard across his face. He and Olivia both tried to put up a fight and got hurt trying to defend themselves against their field boss. He just laughed them off, but he did leave them alone and did not try to pester Olivia again. Alex did not tell his parents what had happened because he knew they would be upset, even angry, and yet they needed Olivia to continue working.

The trucks returned to town and dropped off the workers at the same spot near the store, where they bought food for the following day's lunch and then drove home or hitched a ride with family, friends, or neighbors. Few could afford an icebox, and so their lunchmeat only lasted through the cool night and into the middle of the next day. Alex often spotted Milo near the drop-off, collecting empty pop bottles left by workers in a hurry to catch a ride home.

Work ended at noon on Saturday, and Alex collected his pay from the field boss, who kept a record of the number of rows completed by each member of the crew. Alex and the other workers kept their own tally to double-check the field boss's record. Some used their wages to pay their charge accounts in stores, but Alex turned what he earned over to his father, the head of his family, who gave out spending money for a movie or a carnival.

Many let off steam by drinking on Saturday night and showing their worst behavior. Dances and taverns attracted crowds from miles around even though gasoline was rationed and only a few could afford to drive. Many got to town by sharing rides in the cars that lined the streets. By seven in the evening, the town was packed. The stores stayed open late; only the post office kept regular hours, closing at the usual time. This particular Saturday, Alex had permission to go to the movies, but he could not go alone. Lupe did not want him tagging along, and so Alex had to go with Olivia, who had invited two of her "goofy" friends to go to the movies with her. Alex protested to his mother, "Mamá, why do I have to go with a bunch of girls? I see them all day long. Boys, boys, boys is all they talk about. Why do I have to go with them now?"

"Well, young man, either you go with them or you stay home."

Olivia butted in. "Look, mister big shot, all you have to do is walk with us. Once there, we don't want you sitting with us anyway. That's all Mamá is asking."

"I suppose she gets to hold the money and buy the tickets," said Alex in disgust.

"Why not?" Olivia declared. "I'm older and more responsible."

"Oh, yeah! Who lost her money the other day? Huh! And who found it? Huh!"

"I didn't lose it. You and your fat friends hid it from me, rusty face."

"That's enough," their mother, Nena, scolded. "I've had just about enough of you two."

Olivia changed the subject out of respect for her mother, who was getting angry.

"Where are you and Papá going?" Olivia asked.

"We're invited over to the Romeros'."

"What's at the Romeros'?"

"I told you, didn't I? The wedding is next Saturday. Their daughter is getting married. I was sure I told you."

"Maybe you did, but I don't remember. Are you taking the kids with you?"

"We have to."

"I'll stay and watch them, if you want."

"No, we won't stay long, *hija*. Besides, you and your brother work too hard during the week. You need your own time."

"Are you going to be part of the wedding party?"

"In a way, I think so. I guess that's why they want to see us, to tell us what part we'll take."

"Who is she going to marry, Mamá?"

"Damián Domínguez."

"But isn't he going to join the army?"

"Yes, that's the sad part, Olivia. I think they should wait until he comes back."

"Why, if they love each other?"

"I think it's very important for a couple to spend the first part of their marriage together."

"When I get married, I'm not going to marry a soldier."

"Who'd want to marry you?!" Alex sassed. "You're too ugly."

"You shut your trap, rainbow face."

"Oh, I know who. It's that guy you kissed on the truck today."

"I said shut your trap, you tattletale, or I'll slap your face silly," Olivia yelled, turning red.

"Sticks and stones may break my bo—" Alex started to say before his mother cut him off sharply.

"I said enough out of you two! You stop it right now or neither of you is leaving this house."

Alex noticed that Olivia blushed at his remark, and he figured she hoped their mother had not noticed. She was saved by a knock at the door and sighed with relief. Alex knew she would get even with him for his wisecrack. She gave him a look as if to say, "You just watch it, boy! Your time is coming."

Tommy, the youngest of the boys, ran to answer the door as his little sister, Linda, tagged at his heels. Olivia's two friends stood in the doorway, looking into the house.

"Is Olivia ready?" one of them asked.

"In a minute. Come on in," her mother invited.

The girls came in and sat down. One was chewing gum a mile a minute. Nena gave Alex and Olivia a quarter each, just the amount of money they would need to go to the movies. "Now don't go running all over the town after the show. You come straight home," she warned.

"We will," Olivia promised.

"And don't let Alex out of your sight. I don't want him around that tramp."

"Oh, Mamá, he's not a tramp," Alex protested.

"I don't know why you can't pick someone better than a beggar as a friend," his mother scolded.

"But Mamá—" Alex started to protest.

"You heard me!" she cut him off. "If I hear of you running off, you'll have to deal with your father. Do I make myself clear?"

"Yeah, yeah."

The theater was only a block away, and they were on their way by ten to seven. A nickelodeon played in one bar they passed, and crowds gathered in the others. Stores stayed open to accommodate the late shoppers, some wearing military uniforms. Olivia and her friends giggled as they passed a young soldier on the street. A long line waiting at the ticket window was doing a brisk business. Saturday was kids' night at the movies. Almost everybody knew each other from school or from working together in the fields. Alex spotted some of his friends and walked over to them, separating from Olivia so that no one would think he was in the company of girls. He heard someone calling out his name. The neon lights flickering on the marquee announced a serialized Western, the fifth chapter of *Jungle Man*, and *The Little Rascals*. There was laughing and yelling, pushing and shoving, and games of tag. A couple of boys were locked in wrestling holds. The girls found the boys' behavior disgusting, and they went by themselves, but Olivia kept Alex in her sight at all times.

By seven most had purchased tickets, and the theater doors opened, starting a stampede. Olivia lost sight of her brother but was confident he was with his friends. She and her friends were in the wave pushing to get into the theater. Alex waited for the moment when he saw Olivia swallowed up in the crowd and then ran down the street in the twilight toward Milo's place. He slowed to a fast walk and headed toward the railroad tracks. A freight engine had been switching cars and was waiting on a siding to let a passenger train pass. Alex stood watching the lighted coaches and heard the passenger locomotive blow its whistle for the crossing ahead. He listened to the growing rhythm of the click-clack of the big wheels rolling over the cracks in the iron rails. The air was filled with black smoke, billowing out of the stack as the steam engine chugged its way north. Alex watched a black man, dressed in a white coat, waiting on tables in the diner, the last car on the train.

He darted across the tracks and headed for Milo's shack, hoping to find his friend. He did not find any lights on inside the house, and so he figured Milo must be nearby, perhaps down an alley or in the parking lot, where he was sure to find empty bottles on a Saturday night. Alex headed back to Main Street, kicking a tin can in front of him. Ahead were the chutes where the steam engine took on coal, and he spotted a small group of men drinking out of a wine bottle. One wore a soldier's uniform. They were all talking at the same time and their loud voices carried in Alex's direction. The soldier was the drunkest, and he swayed back and forth like a willow in the wind. Frightened, Alex shied away from them and headed through the growing darkness toward Main Street. The hair on the back of his neck seemed to stand on end, his heart beat a mile a minute, chills ran down his back, and goose bumps covered his whole body. He was having second thoughts about his back alley search when he spotted a man about a half a block away. No mistake. It was Milo.

29

"Wait!" he muttered to himself. "Something strange is going on."

It was Milo, all right, but where were his sack and his baggy clothes? This Milo was neatly dressed. Alex was about to call out and ask him to wait up, but the hobo's clothes made Alex pause and then change his mind. "Where," he thought, "could he be going, especially at this time of the day?!" Wherever it was, Milo walked straight ahead and did not seem to notice him standing in the dusk, giving Alex the chance to satisfy his curiosity by following his friend. What was he up to? He trailed the hobo through several dark streets to a house where a woman lived alone. Alex had seen this woman many times and only knew her as China, a nickname she acquired because she had curly hair.[2] Alex remembered seeing Milo work in her yard. Although China did not dress in the latest fashion, she was not bad-looking for her age. Alex thought she wore too much makeup, but she was jolly and liked company, particularly the company of men. That is where she got her reputation as a *vagabunda*. Could it be that she and Milo were going dancing? But he couldn't picture Milo in public with a lady friend. From what Alex had seen, drinking and dancing go hand in hand, and Milo was one of the few men no one had seen take a drink.

Alex saw Milo knock lightly on her door. After a few seconds, China answered and let him in without a word, evidently because she'd known he was coming. Alex was puzzled about why his friend was with a woman like her. He figured Milo was a hobo with just one ambition in life: to survive by collecting junk. He waited to see if Milo and China would appear on their way somewhere and, when they did not come out of the house, he crept into the yard and hid behind a lilac bush. The bushes had lost their flowers and were covered with green seed clusters. After the suspense had built up, curiosity got the better of him and he decided to peer into the house and spy on his friend. He crept further into the yard and peeked in through the kitchen window. He could not see anyone, but he noticed a light coming through a doorway from another room. Alex eased his way along the wall until he came to another window with the shade down to an inch or so from the bottom sill. Alex peeked in but could not make out anyone at first. Then his eyes adjusted to the faint light, and he saw the outline of two people sitting very close together on a couch. Alex pressed his nose against the glass and got the shock of his life when he saw his Milo and China in a passionate embrace with their hands all over each other, touching shameful parts of their bodies. Alex was disgusted and figured he was seeing sin, but he could not help from peering in. He was lost as if in a trance until the lights of a passing car revealed his hiding place, and he quickly dropped to the ground under the lilac bush. When the car passed, he picked himself up off the ground and peered into the window again. He saw Milo and China heading into another room after leaving their clothes lying all over the couch. Alex felt sick to his stomach and lost some of his admiration and respect for Milo. He knew people did this kind of thing, but he did not like to think of Milo doing it because he placed his friend in the same category as his parents.

There was only one thing left to do, since his plan for the night was shot full of holes. He would go back to the theater, make use of his ticket, and watch the movie. He found the theater packed with people and spotted his friends in the very front. He decided not to join them. He found a seat at the very back near the exit sign, and sat down alone. The last part of the serialized Western was on the screen. The hero was chasing the bad guy on horseback, and the kids watching the movie were yelling and screaming, drowning out the sound. Alex could see the puffs of smoke coming from the cowboys' guns, firing at the bad guys on the run. The movie had a happy ending, as most Westerns do. The bad guy finally ran out of bullets after he shot at least twenty times from a "six-shooter." The hero fired as many rounds, but he still had some bullets left in his gun and he shot and killed the bad guy to end the movie. Then this week's chapter of *Jungle Man* came on. Alex had watched the preceding episode, during which lions chased Jungle Man and cornered him at the edge of a high cliff. Jungle Man had two choices: he could either fight four lions single-handedly or jump off the cliff to his death. At the very end, just as he was about to make up his mind, he slipped and fell. This week's episode showed that the hero had managed to grab hold of a vine. He swung himself out of one danger and into another as he landed in the cave of the vicious Jungle Queen, without even losing his hat. Alex heard loud applause but could not get into the mood of the crowd because the scene of Milo and China stuck in his mind and ate at his insides. "Maybe by now," he thought, "they have finished their disgusting and sinful act. But why go back?" Alex was not sure he wanted Milo as his friend anymore. He left his seat and walked the short distance to the small lobby, where he noticed the aroma of fresh popcorn filling the air. He spotted the light of the projector shining through a small opening high in the wall, near the ceiling. For a moment, Alex thought of going through the swinging doors into the projection room to see how a movie appeared on the screen, but he thought better of the idea because he did not want to create a problem for himself. The popcorn smelled good, and Alex was tempted to buy a bag, but he wanted to save his money to buy firecrackers. He heard the screams as the crowd inside thrilled to a new scene in the serial, and Alex wondered what he was missing. He decided to check on Milo because he really wanted to see his friend again. He walked toward the exit door, and the ticket taker, a stern man of about fifty years of age, stopped him.

"Where are you going?"

"Just outside. I don't feel good. I think I'm going to throw up," Alex lied.

"Well, I'll let you out this time, but don't take too long or I won't let you back in."

"I won't," Alex promised. "I'll be right back."

Once outside, he began to change his mind. He fought the urge to run over to China's house, and then the commotion across the street attracted his attention. Alex could see at least ten people—men and women—arguing in loud voices outside of a tavern. Although it was dark, the light from the doorway revealed two men in the group pushing and shoving each other. Then two more jumped into the fray. A woman, seeing her man pushed, swung her purse by the strap and hit his attacker hard on the head. The next thing Alex saw was the woman flying backwards and falling on the cement walk with her legs up in the air and her skirt opening like a parachute and coming down over her head. Alex heard a man whistle a wolf call when the woman's bare legs and underwear were exposed, and he saw her man help her get back up on her feet. Then all hell broke loose as men and women threw punches at each other, and couples ran up the street to join the brawl.

"A fight! A fight! There's a fight!" someone yelled. Alex saw two more men heading toward the commotion and recognized them as the town marshal and his deputy. The brawl had become a free-for-all. A jacket was ripped off and papers from the pockets scattered onto the street. Then a bystander gave the alarm, "Cops! Cops!" The bystander fled in the opposite direction, and a couple of soldiers followed him into the dark street. When the marshal and his deputy got there, they found only a handful still slugging it out. They tried to stop the fight, but one of the men came at the deputy, who pulled out his billy club and hit the man on the head. The guy went down in a cry of pain. Other men came out of nowhere and jumped into the brawl. Alex saw the marshal fall as he was overpowered by several men. As the brawlers kicked and slugged the marshal, Alex could see bottles flying out of dark corners.

One hit a man in the back, and others smashed against the walls and shattered on the cement sidewalk. Alex could not figure out why people who lived and worked together were beating each other up. Even soldiers were in on it.

He was staring so intently that he did not see James standing next to him.

"Some fight!" James commented as he watched with excitement, swaying back and forth like a boxer. "Look! Look! They're beating the shit outta the cops!"

James was a little older than Alex, and he worked only when he felt like it. He was thirteen going on thirty. He smoked, and he hung around bars and pool halls. Some considered him a "bad seed." James did not have to answer to anyone, but Alex did not think he was as bad, deep down inside, as some said. He just acted big. Alex sensed that James liked him for some reason. Every chance he had, James would chum up to him, and sometimes he would come to Alex's aid when other kids picked on him. James was never without money. One day, for no apparent reason, he handed Alex a handful of change: forty-two cents, to be exact. That was a lot of money! Alex had to keep the friendship a secret because his parents did not like James.

Alex lost track of time and forgot about Milo. There seemed to be no end to the fight until a car with a red light on the roof drove up.

"That's the sheriff," said James. "He's a bad man to mess with."

The sheriff got out of his car, followed by four of his deputies, who fired their guns in the air to get the attention of the brawlers fleeing in many directions. Two of the deputies chased after them, and the sheriff and his other deputies rounded up the ones who did not get away. The sheriff, seeing the marshal beaten to a pulp, shouted to those who escaped, "I know who all of you are. There's going to be hell to pay. I'll get every damned one of you. You damn better believe I will!"

The fight ended with as many arrests as the sheriff and his deputies could handle. They crammed some into their car and walked others to the city jail.

"You wanna make some money?" James asked Alex.

"How? Where?"

"Hell, over there, where they were fighting. Didn't you hear the quarters hitting the ground?"

Alex had not even thought of it. All he had seen were men and women in a big brawl.

"Come on! Let's go take a look," James insisted.

At first Alex was reluctant to go, but he did not want to act like a sissy in front of James and so he followed him across the street and started searching the grounds.

"Not bad, huh, kid?"

Alex was there in body but not in spirit, dreading being recognized and fearing that word would get back to his parents that he was with James at that time of the night—and picking stuff up from the street, after a fight. For James, it was second nature to be out late because he was street-smart. Nothing seemed to bother him. Ending their search, they walked back across the street and passed under the neon lights, where they pooled their haul. They had a woman's wristwatch, a man's ring, two knives with the blades open, and a man's billfold. Alex only wanted the money and refused the rest. James did not care; he played it square or maybe was overly generous. Alex got eight dollars in bills plus some change and finally accepted a knife he put into his pocket.

"What I made tonight in a few minutes is more than what I make in a week," James sounded off.

Alex did not say anything. He wanted to get away from James, who appeared jittery and nervous, and return to the movie house.

"I have to go back into the picture now," Alex announced, hoping not to hurt his friend's feelings.

"That's OK, kid," James answered agreeably. "I'll see ya tomorrow."

Alex headed back to the movie house, feeling surprised that James was so friendly and also feeling excited and scared about finding so much money. He imagined what it would be like trying to explain to his parents how he had acquired his newly found wealth, and he decided it would be better not to tell them about it. The ticket man was not around, so Alex went straight to his old seat, where he watched the last part of *The Little Rascals*. But his mind was not on the movie. A loud cheer filled the building as the movie ended. The lights went on, and Alex rushed out the exit with the other kids, hearing but not sharing in their laughter and shouts of excitement. He waited outside, and Olivia and her two friends soon appeared, one of them holding a half full bag of popcorn.

"Where were you sitting?" Olivia asked. "I couldn't see you anywhere."

"I saw you," he lied. "I even waved at you once."

"Oh, I think I saw you," Helen said. "That was you waving at us!?"

"Boy, that girl definitely needs glasses," Alex thought. Thanks to her, the subject was dropped. Outside, Alex saw kids scatter like a flock of sheep. The ones who lived in town had only a short walk home, and those who lived farther had to wait until the dances were over to find their rides. Alex felt sorry for the kids who lived out of town, and he noticed that every bar and dance hall was in full swing, spewing music into the street. He saw some kids going from place to place, looking in through the big plate glass windows of the bars and dance halls searching for the person who could drive them home. He saw a man stagger out of a tavern, fall flat on his face, and try to get up but then fall again. A woman followed right behind him shouting insults, and then she tried to help him get up. Just when she almost had him on his feet, he stumbled and fell again, taking her with him, and they both lay on the ground cursing each other. Alex figured she too had had one drink too many, and he did not pay her much mind because he had seen many drunks on the street before and he expected to see them on Saturday night. He just kept out of the drunks' way if he saw them walking toward him on the sidewalk.

"I'll be glad when I'm old enough to go to a dance," Helen said. "Won't you be, too?"

"I won't be," Alex butted in.

"Who asked you, creep?!" Helen snapped back. "What do you know about dancing?"

"Maybe more than you think."

"Oh, Alex, why don't you shut up!" Olivia said in support of her girlfriend.

The girls' laughter hurt Alex's feelings, but he did not sass them back. He listened to them talking the rest of the way home about the top ten songs of the weekly Hit Parade.

Sunday morning his mother tried to get Alex up and ready for the early Mass. He had forgotten about the money until he started to put on his pants and heard the coins rattle in his pocket. He shared a bed with his younger brother, who was half asleep and did not notice. He knew he had to hide his money outside the house and was not sure where. He dressed in a hurry, went out into the yard, and walked over to a storage shed, where he found a small jar. He placed his money and knife inside of it and then hid the jar. He would find a safer place for it later, he thought, and then went back inside to wash and get ready for church. His father never used their car to go the four blocks to Mass unless he had to take the long way. He always walked to church, even on the coldest days of winter. The family walked together, all except for Lupe, who said he would attend a later Mass with his friends. They passed the bar where the fight had taken place the night before. A town drunk had the job of sweeping up the broken glass to pay off his fine, and the marshal was combing the area of the fight. Alex saw the bruises on the marshal's face and the big patch on his forehead, and noticed that he was walking with a limp.

"What happened here, Sam?" Tomás asked the marshal.

"All hell broke loose last night," the marshal replied. Then he saw the barber's wife and children.

"I'm sorry for the language," he apologized. "I didn't see your wife and kids."

"No offense taken," Tomás assured him.

The marshal took off his hat as a gesture of respect for the women present. Alex could see fresh blood around the patch, evidence that his cut was deep and nasty.

"We had a big fight here last night, Martínez."

"Were they the usual bunch?"

"No. Some were soldiers on furlough, and most were outsiders."

"You look like you got the worst of it."

"Yeah. My deputy and I did. I also lost my gun. At least I think I lost it here. I didn't miss it till after the fight."

Alex was about to tell what he had seen, but he caught himself. He had not noticed any gun on the sidewalk, but he knew there would be "hell to pay" if he were caught disobeying his parents.

"Well, Sam, I hope you find it," said Tomás, shaking his head in disgust and in sympathy with the marshal.

"Thanks, Tomás, and if you hear of a stray gun around, let me know."

As they walked toward the church, they talked about the fight.

"What makes people act that way?" the barber asked his wife.

She answered him with a tinge of anger, "It's the liquor. Liquor is the devil in a person. What person in his right mind would strike an officer of the law? Did you see the cut on that man's head?!"

"Yes, and it was still bleeding," Tomás noted. "I think Sam is a good cop. This town needs a man like him, and he should be respected."

"You mean there is a devil in a bottle of wine?" little Tommy asked his mother.

"Yes, *hijo.* That's why when you grow up, you should never touch that poison."

Alex had asked the same question before and knew his mother hated alcohol. Her father, Alex's grandfather, had died of drink, and her mother had worked herself to the bone trying to raise the family he had left behind. Alex thought of the previous night, when he and James scoured the streets for money. He had not seen a gun, but he wondered about James. He had lost sight of him several times, and later he noticed a bulge inside James's pocket but thought nothing of it at the time. He wondered why James had been so generous. How come he had not tried to persuade Alex to stay with him? Was he anxious to be alone? It was not like him to let Alex get away so easily. Whatever happened, Alex was determined to keep a tight lip over the whole affair. He was not about to make trouble for himself by saying anything to his parents. He had heard his mother mutter critical remarks about James's behavior. He would also be putting his sister in a fix if he said anything, because she would have to explain why she had not kept an eye on him.

The four children sat between their parents during the sermon, which the priest delivered in Spanish, a language Alex understood better than English. For that Sunday's sermon, the priest came down hard on drinking, stealing, and lying. Alex felt that the priest was speaking directly to him and was accusing him of wrongdoing in front of the whole congregation. In his mind, he felt the eyes of a hundred people on him. Was the priest directly condemning *him*? Did the priest really have the power to know what he had done? He sneaked a side glance at his parents and then at the people sitting around him. They all looked ahead and listened to the sermon. Alex felt a great burden of guilt, but then examined his conscience; he only came up with the sins of lying and disobedience. They were bad enough, and he promised God never to sin again.

Back home, Olivia and her mother fixed a big breakfast. Lupe was up by the time they returned home. Alex was free for the day. He went out into the shed; he needed to find a better place to hide his money. He wandered into the alley hoping to find James or Milo. Most of the businesses were closed on Sunday, a day of rest, except for the bars, pool halls, and the drugstore, the only place not off limits. He began to have misgivings about meeting James because he might want some of the money back. He combed the streets and alleys looking for Milo and came upon Lupe and his friends smoking in back of the S.P.M.D.T.U. hall.[3] Lupe seemed surprised to see him, but called him over anyway.

"What do you want, Lupe?"

"I don't want you to tell I was here or that I was smoking," Lupe requested with a hint of pleading in his voice.

Sociedad Protección Mutua de Trabajadores Unidos (S.P.M.D.T.U.) in Antonito.

"Do you want me to lie for you?"

"No. I don't want you to lie for me. I just don't want you to tell on me is all."

"Why didn't you go to church, Lupe? You know it's a sin," Alex said.

"We are going. Weren't we just leaving, Fred?"

"Yeah, Lupe, if you say so," Fred shrugged.

Lupe dug into his pocket, pulled out some change, and asked his friends to do the same. They pooled their coins and handed them to Alex.

"What's that for?"

"For nothing. Buy yourself a pop or some firecrackers."

The money was a payoff, but Alex accepted it anyway. He searched in vain for Milo. He passed the large grain elevators and went into the rail yards near Milo's house. He called out his friend's name, but he heard no answer. He approached the shack and knocked on the door. Pushing it open, he heard the hinges squeak as the door gave way. He called out his friend's name again and, hearing no response, he eased his way inside and found a very simply furnished room and a door nailed shut with slats. Milo apparently used just one room as a kitchen, front room, and bedroom. Alex spotted a cot in one corner, a table and two chairs in the middle of the room, and a wood-burning cook stove against a wall. He remembered the men in his father's barbershop talking about that stove. A small dresser sat against the sealed door, and curtains of flour sacks decorated the only window. His eyes fell on a shelf with six or seven neatly stacked books, and he wondered what his friend read. So he walked over and took one down very carefully, so as not to place it out of order. He opened it and leafed through it, but he could not find a word he understood. At his age, he was not able to pronounce big words, much less understand their meaning. Carefully, he put the book back and reached for another one with a red cover. This one was different because it had some English words in it, but they did not make any sense to him. The postmaster had said that Milo was an educated man. "That's it," he thought. "These books are for smart people."

As he put the book back, the whole bookshelf moved forward and opened up like a door on hinges. In the opening behind the shelf was a radio, or what looked like a radio, but it was not hooked up to a socket. It had a key like the ones he had seen at the freight office in the train depot. After all, what did Alex know? Milo was an *educated* man. Alex did not want Milo to catch him snooping, and he figured he had overstayed his time. He closed the secret door, leaving everything the same way he found it. He followed the railroad tracks south into town, and headed toward the shipping yards, where Milo spent a lot of time. As he walked along the tracks, he thought of the many times freight trains had passed through town. Sometimes they pulled as many as fifty cars, some covered with heavy canvasses, and Alex recalled very vividly seeing two steam engines pulling them. The engines stopped in the freight yard to take on coal and water, and just about every time, even before Milo became his friend, he had seen the hobo walk over and look under the tarpaulins. Even now, he did not feel he could ask Milo what he was looking for. Their friendship had taken too long to develop, and he did not want anything to break it up. Milo had already warned him not to get in his way, and one warning was enough.

When he passed near China's house, he strained to see his friend. As he looked, he lost his footing and fell from the rail he was walking on, landing on his hands and knees. He quickly got up and dusted his bibbed coveralls. Embarrassed, he looked around to see if anybody had seen him fall, and then he saw James, who had spotted him and now ran in his direction.

"Hey, Alex, wait up."

He did not really want to be seen with James, but he felt that he did not have a choice. He sat on a rail and tied his shoe as James came over to him. Out of breath, James seemed to be in a good mood, as always, and said, "Been looking for you, kid."

"Why? What's up, James?"

"Nothing, kid. Just wanted to see you, that's all," he said as he sat down on a rail next to him.

"What did you think of the fight last night, kid?"

"I guess bad." Then, without wasting time, he added, "You know, James, the marshal lost his gun last night."

James faked a surprised look and said, "He did? Who told you?"

Alex went into detail about what the marshal had said on the way to church.

"Did he find it?"

"No, he didn't. You wanna know why, James?"

"Yeah, kid. I wanna know why."

"Because you have it."

James looked as if he could have been knocked over by a feather. "Hey, kid, how did you know I took it?"

"I saw you," he lied. "I saw when you found it and put it under your jacket."

"You gonna tell on me?"

"Don't know yet. My father says he's a good man. This town needs him, James. You think I should tell?"

"Hell's bells, no, kid! That's all I need to get sent to reform school. That marshal don't like me. You wanna see me go to jail?"

"No, I don't. I don't wanna see you go to jail. But I won't tell if you give it back."

"Finders keepers. Like the money we found. You gonna give it back, are you?"

"I would if I knew who it belonged to," Alex lied.

"But you don't. You don't know, do you?"

Alex had been trying to make a point, but he could not get it across to James.

"Look, kid, don't say nothing, OK? I promise I'll return it first chance I get. Cross my heart and hope to die."

"OK, but you promise?"

"I crossed my heart, didn't I? And I'll give you eight quarters if you won't tell."

Alex took the money and put it in his pocket. Before James left, he made Alex promise again not to tell on him and to seal his promise by crossing his heart. Alex did not know if he was doing the right thing. He was taught to be honest, and that morning in church he had promised God never to sin again. Yet James was not honest, and Milo had committed a mortal sin with China. Even his own brother smoked, and Alex was sure Lupe had not gone to church. His sister Olivia kissed a boy while working out in the fields. Now he was committing a sin by covering up for all of them and he wondered if it was worse to sin on Sunday. While deep in thought, he spotted Milo rummaging through a nearby trash bin. Alex decided to forgive his friend, and then, as he stood up, he heard the sound of the change rattling in his pocket. Ashamed and guilty, he tried to reassure himself that he had not done anything wrong. He figured the worst he had done was cover up for someone else's sins.

Milo stopped briefly upon seeing Alex and then continued digging through the trash. Alex made small talk by asking some questions, and Milo answered without stopping what he was doing. No longer distracted by Alex, Milo was becoming accustomed to the boy tagging along and even enjoyed the "brat's" company.

"Where were you yesterday?" Alex asked.

Milo said he had gone fishing early that morning. The sound of the word "fishing" was magic to Alex's ears.

"Fishing! Did you catch anything?"

"I caught nine," said Milo as he walked over to another pile of trash. Sometimes the hobo answered with "*ja*" and "*nein*," but to Alex it was great conversation, and he followed his friend around until it was time to go home for the noon meal. When he said he had to go, Milo stood up and said, "If your parents don't mind, next time I go fishing, you want to come along?"

This was the greatest invitation anybody could have given him.

"You promise?"

"*Ja.*"

"OK!" he yelled, and ran home like a kid who was promised the world.

The next morning, he and Olivia were up and ready to go to the fields. Lupe was about to head off to the warehouse, where at just fifteen he would be doing a grown man's job, hoisting heavy bushel baskets of peas and sacks of wool, potatoes, and cauliflower. Their mother had their lunch bags ready, and their father called Olivia over.

"What is it, Papá?"

41

"I want you to tell your boss you will work only until Wednesday."

"Why, Papá?" she asked as she put on her coat.

"Because it's the Fourth of July and we're going to spend it with your grandparents, but we have to be back by Saturday for the wedding."

Olivia let out a shout of joy, but Alex had mixed feelings about the surprise. What if it was the weekend Milo had in mind to take him fishing? He did not dare question his father's authority.

"Be sure and tell your boss."

"I will."

She ran out to meet the truck that took them to the fields, and Alex followed behind her like a puppy. The day started out hot, but clouds were building up over the western mountain range, a sure promise of rain. The field hands did not all come from the same community. Four trucks arrived from separate towns; there was a total of two hundred workers in four groups. Each group lined up in a row and started toward the opposite end of the field. Women and girls wore sunbonnets, and the men and boys wore hats. Some of the younger workers were smaller than the hoes they were using, but as small as they were, they managed to keep up with the adults.

At noon they were given an hour to eat. It took them half that time to walk to where they had left lunch at the edge of the field and back again. They ate in groups, and the lunch hour was their only time to use the toilet, which was only a figure of speech. All the workers wore slacks and had to find a safe place to answer their call of nature. The men had an easier time than the women. Then it was back to work until quitting time. On the way home, they heard the warning to bring a raincoat the next day. That is, if they owned one.

Tuesday started out with just a few scattered clouds over the valley, but they had become thick and black by midday. Alex could see lightning toward the west, and then he felt a breeze rapidly cool the valley floor. The truck drivers knew rain would soon follow, and the driver of Alex's crew drove out of the field and tied a heavy tarpaulin over his truck. He looped the rope through the racks and then returned to the main body of workers. Max, Alex's driver, asked the contractor if he wanted to leave before the rain came, but was told no. The contractor wanted to get as much as he could out of the workers, even though the sky was getting darker by the minute. At first Alex felt a light sprinkle, but soon clouds drew closer, and he saw more lightning and heard more claps of thunder. Alex and the other workers braced themselves for what was sure to come. Yet nobody dared leave without the OK of the field boss. The wind picked up and a wave of rain hit them. Now, nobody had to tell them it was time to leave.

The workers dropped their hoes and ran toward the trucks, but before they'd reached the end of the field, the heavy rain had turned the dry soil into a sea of mud, and Alex had trouble keeping his footing. As the workers piled into the trucks, the bed became ankle deep in mud, much like the field from which they had come. The driver, once he was sure all his crew was aboard, started out in low gear. The truck was a good half-mile from the dirt road; two other trucks were ahead of the one carrying Alex and Olivia. The first truck drove off without any problem, but the next one got bogged down. Max did not want to stop, and he tried going around the one stuck in the mud, but he got only a few yards ahead of that truck, lost his traction, and could not go any further. The mud had not reached the rear axle, so Max tried going in reverse and then in forward to rock back and forth, but he could not get unstuck and he did not want to stay where he was while the rain was coming down so hard. Much as he hated to do it, Max asked his crew to get down and push. He wanted to get his truck out and his crew home, but it was every trucker for himself. One by one, the workers climbed down without so much as a murmur. Max looked at the women and children and thought: "God, what a damn shame when a man will put the almighty dollar before the welfare of his workers."

The crew from the other truck just looked on as Max's crew lined up on three sides of his truck. "You stay," Alex urged Olivia. "The rest of us can push."

"No, we'll all push," she insisted.

"OK," Max yelled as he revved up the Chevy motor. "Start pushing."

Inch by inch the truck started to move, fishtailing from side to side as the dual wheels spun and the engine whined. The spinning wheels flung mud on the crew pushing directly behind. Alex saw a woman and the girl next to her fall and get up covered with mud from head to toe. Finally, the truck was able to go under its own power. Max did not stop so his crew could jump on more easily. He did not want to risk getting bogged down again. He drove the quarter-mile to the country lane and then waited for the rest of his crew. Some of the older boys hung on to the racks, but most had to walk out. Alex never left Olivia's side. All were soaked to the skin, and those who had fallen in the mud had been washed clean by the heavy downpour long before they reached the truck. Once on the road, they started on the twenty-mile trip home. Alex looked to see if the truck behind them had made it out, but the rain clouded his view. He sat huddled with the other workers in the driest spot they could find in the bed of the truck. The wind whipped the tarpaulin and sprayed them with the water that had collected on the top. He thought they must have looked like a herd of cattle in a stock car.

They finally arrived in town. They climbed down from the truck, and he heard Max swear to his wife, "That's the last time I'll ever put my crew through that kind of hell. I don't care what them damn contractors say."

"Yes, we could have left at noon and avoided all of this nonsense," she replied.

Their comments made Alex ask himself if anyone cared about the cold and discomfort the crew had just gone through. As God knew, there would be plenty more rainy days ahead. He looked at the soaked, cold, and hungry women and children around him and wondered who would answer for their pain and anguish. He saw that two of the women were pregnant and were being comforted by other women. Some of the younger children were crying from the cold. Even after the rain had stopped, the breeze blowing in through the racks on their wet clothes felt worse than the rain itself. The ride home had been hell, but Alex could sense that the crew was like one big family, caring for each other.

On Wednesday, he and the others were back working in the field, sweating and straining for a few pennies. The day before was just like a bad dream. He did not dwell on the past, and he guarded the hope that the next day would be better, although he knew more difficult days lay ahead. He remembered the words of some of the workers, who remarked bitterly that conditions were beyond human cruelty.

Olivia had obtained permission from her field boss for her and Alex to take the Fourth of July off so they could visit their grandparents at the *rancho*. There they would stay until it was time to return for the wedding on Saturday. Alex thought that he and Olivia were lucky because they did not have to work in the fields until Monday. He knew some members of their crew were planning to go back to work on Friday because they could not afford to take any time off. He also remembered the carnival was setting up in town.

Thursday, Tomás was up before the sun. Nena had already packed for their fifty-mile trip. She had taken a month to prepare for the journey, and she still could get only half of what she needed. She and Tomás saved ration stamps to buy enough gasoline, and Tomás found a badly needed spare tire and someone to lend him a car jack and tire pump. Money was scarce, but rationed items were even harder to find.

By sunup they had loaded their old car and were anxious to leave. Tomás, Nena, and Lupe sat in the front seat, and Alex and the rest of the children climbed into the rear. Tomás turned the crank, and the Chevy came to life. He backed up into the alley, shifted into low gear, and headed onto Main Street. Alex looked out the car window to see who was up and about that early in the morning. He spotted the carnival trucks parked in the big vacant lot and saw men busily setting up the tents. The carnival crew had placed a big generator near the spot where the Ferris wheel would sit. He saw the merry-go-round and the other rides taking shape and could hear the rhythmic click, click of the heavy sledgehammers as men drove metal stakes into the ground to hold up the tents. He knew the carnival would still be there when he returned. He saw James standing in front of the Cumbres Café, watching the tents go up. James waved at the car, and Alex pretended not to see him. He felt bad for not waving back, but he feared a scolding from his parents, especially his mother. He saw Milo further on down the street, carrying his gunnysack and disappearing as he rounded a corner. He wondered if his two friends ever slept. Ahead were the old flour mill and grain elevator, where the old Chevy turned east onto the road that would take them the fifty miles to his grandparents' *rancho* across the valley.

For the first seven miles, they drove along green fields on both sides of the road. Some were planted in peas, potatoes, and grain, and others were big meadows used to pasture sheep and cattle. They passed a thick grove of willows and cottonwoods, where Alex had never seen so many magpies; they were perched by the tens of hundreds.

"Look at all the birds!" marveled Tommy. "There must be thousands and millions and maybe even hundreds!"

Alex watched the green fields give way to the sagebrush of the prairie, which unfolded for miles and extended up the sides of the hills. Alex recognized the rock formation that looked like a petrified prehistoric beast at the base of the hills to the north. He remembered the old man who had told him about seeing balls of fire during Lent and told him about the sacred Indian burial grounds.

Tomás slowed down a little further on, and Alex asked, "Why are we stopping? Is something wrong with the car?"

"No. Lupe is driving from here on."

Tomás got out, and Lupe took over, jerking the car every time he changed gears. Alex did not make any smart remarks about Lupe's driving even when he noticed the jackrabbits speeding ahead of their car. Soon Lupe's driving became steadier, and the purr of the motor lulled Alex's younger brother and sister to sleep. Alex still kept an eye on the sacred rock until it was out of sight. Nobody said much; Olivia read a comic book. Lupe was weaving as he drove, but Alex did not worry because he could see that theirs was the only car for miles around. They reached the Rio Grande and drove over the bridge. The rattling of the loose boards made him wonder if the bridge would give way and their car would plunge into the river thirty feet below. Tomás told Lupe to stop and get a bucket of water for the overheated radiator while he checked the air in the tires. Two coyotes sitting on a knoll watched Lupe head down to the river as Tomás stepped out of the car and opened the side panel of the hood.

After filling the radiator, they continued their journey and Lupe asked, "How am I driving?"

"Fine, just fine," said Tomás. Alex kept his remarks to himself.

Dirt and dust kicked up by the tires came in through Lupe's open window and settled right where Alex sat in the backseat. He looked over at Olivia and saw that her head was back and her eyes were closed. The comic book she was reading was open on her lap. He also fell asleep a little further on, and the next thing he knew, they were driving into the lane that led to his grandparents' old farmhouse. It seemed like ages to him since he had seen his grandparents' home, but it was just as he remembered it: peaceful, quiet, and sitting against the background of the apple orchard and the green meadow that stretched to the foot of the Sangre de Cristo Mountains. His gaze extended several miles to the east and fell on the church steeple in the little village of El Rito. His eyes followed the creek west to the one-room schoolhouse, and then he heard a dog barking.

"It's Rex!" Olivia yelled. "It's Rex!"

Tommy and Linda were too young to remember Rex. He was the dog they had left when they moved from the ranch to the town on the other side of the valley. The old dog recognized the car and came out, along with Grandpa and Grandma and aunts and uncles and cousins, to greet them. They had come for the family reunion, and Rex ran himself ragged as everybody tried to talk at once.

"Where has time gone?" Grandma declared. "Just look at how these kids have grown. Look at my Lupe! Why, he's a man already." Grandma fussed over Olivia, Tommy, and Linda, and then went to Alex. "And you, my Alejandro, there's no mistake in your looks. You're the image of your father!"

Bridge over the Rio Grande.

They took a while to get settled. There was no room for everyone to sleep inside the house, and so some of the aunts, uncles, and cousins went to stay with relatives, and some of the older children slept in tents. The grandparents had set up tables under the cottonwood trees near the apple orchard in their yard, where the families would gather to eat watermelons, cakes, pies, and every kind of meat, including sausages, roasts, and hams. Alex met relatives he did not know he had during the two-day family reunion, which he would never forget. Still, the hardships of travel had kept some in his family from being there.

In the evening, the families gathered in a one-room schoolhouse to dance to music played by anyone who had an instrument. Some neighbors joined in, filling the pasture next to the school with their cars. Alex's relatives gathered again at his grandparents' home on Friday and made up for what they had missed during the time they had been away from each other. Different groups gathered to take pictures, and everyone helped cook outside as well as inside the house and spread out a picnic that was like a king's banquet. Alex did not think once about his friends back home. He spent most of his time with his grandmother, whom he had missed since moving across the valley. He tagged along, following her wherever she went. He could see that everybody demanded some of her time and she could not be partial by denying attention to any of her children.

The children and grandchildren gathered near the house and knelt to say a prayer of thanks as the day ended. The heartbreaking moment came when they had to go, and Alex felt just as bad leaving Rex as he did leaving his grandparents. As dusk set in, they started the fifty-mile trip back and talked of their experiences during the two wonderful days. Linda and Tommy quickly fell asleep, and Lupe was at the wheel again. Alex heard his parents talk about the wedding and the war. He had reached the age of reason and awareness and realized how lucky he was to have his parents, sisters, and brothers. He looked out the window into the dark and could see the moon, which seemed to be moving right along with the car, and he fell asleep wondering why.

He awoke to the gentle, soft voice of his mother. "Wake up. We're getting close to town."

Roused out of his slumber, he felt groggy and struggled to stay awake.

"Wake your sisters and brother," she said.

He woke Olivia, Linda, and Tommy. Then he rolled down his window to let in some fresh air as Olivia tugged at Tommy and Linda to keep them awake. Lupe stopped the car to let his father take over. Alex caught the scent of clover that drifted in with the fresh air and heard water rippling in the ditch by the side of the road. He heard an owl hooting somewhere far off in the night. When the car reached Main Street, he saw crowds of people walking to and from the carnival. He could easily make out the lights circling around the Ferris wheel, and he could hear the tune of the merry-go-round filling the air. He heard screams of excitement carrying through the night from the carnival, and he spotted seats rocking on the big wheel when it came to a stop. He noticed lights flickering on the marquee in front of the movie house and saw that all the bars and dance halls, on both sides of the street, were in full swing. He could hear firecrackers exploding and saw a rowdy bunch shoving and pushing each other down a side street. "Another fight," he thought, "and James will surely be waiting to reap his reward."

"What a mess," his mother commented.

"If you think this is bad," Tomás added, "wait until tomorrow night at the wedding dance."

"Can we go to the carnival for a while?" Olivia asked.

"Not tonight," her father replied. "It will still be there tomorrow and the day after."

"Besides," Nena added, "you had your fun for one day, and I'll need you to help me unpack. Your father and I have to get up early tomorrow."

"Well, I'm going out for a while," Lupe said in a defiant tone. "I have some money to collect from my boss."

"Can't it wait?" Nena asked.

"It can!" Tomás said with authority. "Like I said, and I don't like to repeat myself, what's out there will still be there for the next two days."

Bright and early the following morning, Tomás and Nena started getting ready for the wedding.

"Olivia," her mother called, "make sure you feed the children and let them sleep late, and be sure to have them ready by eleven."

"Don't worry, Mamá, I'll have them ready by then."

"Be sure they're dressed neatly. We'll be having dinner at the Romeros'."

"All of us?"

"*Sí, hija*, we're all invited to the wedding feast after the ceremony."

Alex was not used to sleeping late and decided to get up. He was in a good mood and helped his sister with breakfast and the kids. He figured that Lupe would sleep all day, given the chance, and yet he envied his brother for having freedoms that none of the rest of them had. He knew Lupe would not help, because there was a limit to what he did and housework was not part of it. After helping his sister, Alex went out the back door to the alley and circled the block to get onto Main Street. His mind was a hundred miles away, in one of his daydreams. The morning was peaceful, birds chirped in the bushes, and the air smelled fresh and clean. He passed a house where he picked up the aroma of frying bacon and headed onto Main Street across from the carnival in the vacant lot. The big Ferris wheel was still, and the carnival area was silent. The flaps were down on all of the tents, but he knew they would not stay that way for long. Most of the stores were open, but they did not have any people in them. The druggist was lowering the large canopy to shade his storefront window. Alex thought of the town as a sleeping monster soon to awaken as he saw his parents join a procession of cars on their way to church. The bride rode with Tomás and Nena, and streamers of crepe paper flew from several of the decorated cars. Alex waved at his parents, but they did not see him standing on the street. Then he saw Gilbert coming toward him. Gilbert was his third-best friend. He was a gossip, and he knew everything that happened in the school, the town, and the county, for that matter. He knew about the fight Alex had seen the weekend before, but he had the story all wrong. Even so, the boy coming his way was just the person who could fill Alex in on what he had missed while he'd been away. When Gilbert had news, he didn't waste time finding someone to tell it to, and the way he was burning up the sidewalk made Alex think he had something to tell him.

"Did you hear about James?" Gil burst out.

The first thing that came to Alex's mind was that James had been caught with the town marshal's gun and had been put in jail. "No," he replied. "We were gone for two days. What happened to him?"

"He's dead. He got himself killed in a car accident."

Gilbert's news jolted and stunned him. He could not register the word "dead" in his mind. He knew people died all the time, but never anybody he knew or anyone as young as his friend James. Just two days ago he had seen him alive, standing not two doors down the street from where Alex now stood listening to Gilbert tell him James was dead. Gil rattled off the details of how it happened, but Alex's mind went numb and his body froze in shock. Then, as if a movie projector was in his head, he shifted from the image of James's death back to Gilbert telling him about what happened, and he felt sick to his stomach. He wanted to think he was having a bad dream, and he wanted to cry out, but he could not release his anguish.

"Alex! Alex!" Gilbert shook him. "What's wrong with you?"

By then he knew he had tears in his eyes, and he felt something in his throat choking and gagging him.

"I'm sorry," Gilbert said apologetically, nearly crying. "I know he was your friend, and I thought you knew about it."

Alex came out of his state of shock, but he could not stop shaking.

"Want me to walk you home?" Gilbert asked.

"N-no, I'm OK."

"Are you sure?"

"Yeah. Yeah."

As he walked back home in a daze, he did not remember anything else Gilbert had said. Outside his house and alone, he finally broke down and sobbed bitterly. Later, when the shock had worn off, he returned to Main Street and learned that his friend's funeral would take place after the Romeros' wedding, on the same day. After a month of planning, the Romeros could not put their wedding off for a funeral. "But how can they?" he thought. "How can they have a wedding and a funeral on the same day? How could anybody possibly attend both?"

He had learned his friend's body lay in his mother's home and would remain there until the funeral, only a few hours away. He was confused about what he should do. He wanted to attend James's funeral to show his loyalty, but he could not ask his parents for permission because he figured they would want to know how James had become his friend. He wondered if his parents could understand his wish to pay James his last respects, but he was also tormented by the thought of seeing his friend's dead body. He felt he could only confide in his sister Olivia, and he was glad he did, because she encouraged him to go to the funeral: "The worst they can do is give you a whipping. And you get one all the time anyway."

"If I do go, then this time it's worth it," he decided.

He took the ten-minute walk to where James had lived and found a large crowd of people of all ages. He recognized some from school and town, but he did not know the others. They packed the house and stood outside the front door. He pushed his way through the mourners and went into the house, where he could see the coffin. He had never been to a viewing and, scared as he was, he advanced toward James's dead body. He did not know if he was being disrespectful, and he figured the only way to find out was to walk right up to the coffin. His body shook with fear. The closer he got to the coffin, the clearer the body became. He looked right at it and was relieved to find that James seemed to be asleep. He knew he was in the eternal sleep everyone enters at one time or another. He softly spoke. "I'm gonna miss you, James. I hope that somewhere, somehow, you can hear me. I'll never forget you. I have to go now. Good-bye, James. Good-bye."

He jumped when he felt a hand on his shoulder.

"I'm his mother," he heard a gentle but shaky voice whisper. "I loved my son. He was all I had and now he's gone."

A force inside him made him hug the woman, and soon they were both crying as they held each other. He did not feel ashamed and did not care if he seemed weak. James was his friend, and he had come to say good-bye and he did not care who knew it. He stood next to James's mother until they were both cried out. Then she walked him to the door, and he saw that there was not a dry eye in the crowd.

"Thank you for coming, Alex," she sobbed.

There was so much he could tell her, and he wanted her to know James was his real friend, but he knew there was no time. As he walked away, the hearse drove up and he heard James's mother sob in a loud voice, "They're here for my son. They're going to take him away from me."

He was looking back at her and thinking he would pay her another visit, when he ran into his parents. He felt he had to confess, but he did not know where to start. He wanted to reveal his feelings, tell them he was sorry for disobeying them, and explain how he and James had become friends. He did not have to say a thing. His mother put her arms around him and gently stroked his hair, and his father placed his arm on his shoulder. They obviously knew about his friendship and seemed to understand his pain. He could see that his parents loved him and knew more about him than he thought. Above all, he saw that they knew how to respect his feelings and forgive him for being disobedient. They appeared to understand the pain of losing a loved one and seemed sad to see a young boy dead. He could tell that his parents sympathized with James's mother and were glad it was not their son inside the coffin. He watched his parents walk over, pay their respects to the grieving mother, and apologize for not accompanying her in her time of grief. He heard them explain that they were committed to carrying out another responsibility. Then his father turned to him and said, "Alex, if you want to accompany your friend, you can go."

"You can ride with us," Gilbert offered.

"Is that OK?" he asked.

"Yes," his father replied, adding, "Meet us at the wedding dinner."

His parents had never mentioned a word about James, although they had cautioned him to be very careful when picking his friends. He understood that silence sometimes speaks louder than words, and the silences of his parents sent him a message that was loud and clear even for a boy of his age. He later learned from those who saw the accident how his friend had died. On that same morning when he had seen James in front of the café, a man had parked his car and left the motor running while he went into the drugstore. Alex knew that James had a wild streak and, although he was not a mean boy, he acted on impulse. Someone saw him jump into the car and drive off at a high rate of speed, though he knew only the very basics of driving. He was driving too fast when he got to a curve at the end of town, and he lost control of the car. It rolled over several times. James was thrown out on one of the flips and was crushed when the car rolled on top of him. Alex remembered the words of the know-it-alls who had predicted that sooner or later James would kill himself. To him, James was a friend with a wild streak whose death held a hard lesson: some mistakes are final.

Death was on many minds. Nearly everyone Alex knew had a family member in some branch of the armed services. The husbands of two of the women he worked with were in the war. Every week or so, he heard of a soldier from a town nearby getting killed in action. He knew about Pearl Harbor, but he did not know much about the other fields of battle.

He heard some say this was the time the story of La Llorona started up again. He thought of the story as the mystery of the Crying Woman. Gilbert was at Alex's house just before it got dark and he asked, "Did you hear La Llorona last night?"

"Yes, Gil. It was about nine o'clock when we heard it."

"I wonder who she is?" Olivia asked.

"I don't know, but I'd hate to meet up with her," Olivia's friend Helen answered.

"She's a woman who lost her son in the war and she cries every night for him," offered Gilbert, the know-it-all.

"How do you know that?" asked Helen, with a tone of doubt in her voice.

"My mother told me," replied Gilbert.

"What mother lost her son?" wondered Olivia.

"I don't know. But that's what she said."

Many people had heard her cry, but nobody seemed to know why she cried and no one had seen her. Alex had heard some say that her story had started in the time of Coronado and that it was true, although much about her was a mystery. One thing was for sure, the story of La Llorona kept children closer to home. Like Helen, no one wanted to meet her face to face.

Work in the fields continued for Alex in August, although the type of work changed when the time came to pick thousands of acres of peas. Each worker filled a bushel basket and carried it to an area where another worker put a lid on it and loaded it onto a truck. It was then taken out of the fields and into the big sheds by the railroad tracks, and finally shipped out of the valley. The average picker could do eight or nine bushels a day, and the better pickers averaged ten. Workers earned twenty-five cents a bushel. Alex considered a quarter a lot of money.

Migrant workers drifted in to help with the harvest, and they did not face any competition for jobs. The migrants worked hard in the fields, and some had a lot of fun at night and little respect for the law. They did not wait for Saturday to hang out in their favorite bars and taverns. Sometimes the local gangs invaded their turf, causing big fights that ended up with one or two deaths and many stabbings each year.

Alex continued working in the fields and saw the day finally come when Milo kept his promise and asked him to go fishing the following

Sunday. When he asked his parents for permission, he saw that his request started a big family argument. His mother flatly refused, saying, "Why do you have to hang around such filth?"

"He's not filthy, Mamá. He's always clean."

His father had the last word. He stood up for Alex, saying, "He's a harmless man. When have you heard of him being in trouble?"

Olivia also sided with her brother, and after a heated discussion, his mother gave in. He and Milo were constant companions by then, except on Saturdays when Milo paid his visits to the lady China. Alex accepted that part of his friend's life. Milo had rigged a fishing pole for him. They walked along the railroad track to the river, about a mile away, and got to the bridge, where Milo found out Alex was new at fishing. The river was low for this time of the year, and they sat near a big hole that was perfect for beginners. Milo showed him how to bait his hook, and, as they waited for the fish to bite, Milo gave him a few pointers. With plenty of time on their hands, they talked idly, and he asked Milo questions about his past life.

"Where did you live before you came here?"

"Before I came here, I'd just arrived in New York City, a place called Ellis Island."

"Is New York far?"

"Yes, it is. But I came from Austria."

"Where is Austria?"

Milo tried his best to explain and gave him a lesson on geography.

"Well," Alex asked, "why are you here in America?"

"Because of the war. I was afraid Germany would soon conquer all of Europe, and I didn't want to live under Nazi law."

Milo told him what the Nazis would do if they won the war. Alex didn't know much about Europe, the war, or what Nazi Germany stood for. He asked, "Is that why you became a hobo?"

Milo chuckled and asked, "Where did you hear that? Do you think I'm a hobo?"

"I don't know. I don't know what a hobo is." Then he turned to look at Milo and asked, "What is a hobo?"

"Well, Alex, a hobo is a vagrant, a man without a home."

"Do you have a home?"

"No. I don't even have a country now."

"Is it bad not to have a home or a country?"

"*Ja*, it's bad, especially when you come to a new country. Dey might think I'm even a deserter."

"Oh, I see," replied Alex, who had thought the world was one big place where people could come and go as they pleased.

"Do you have money?" he asked Milo, who was talking now more about himself than before and seemed willing to answer questions.

"Money? What do you know about money?"

"We don't make enough is all I know. My mother says we work and work and never have enough."

"Vell, for now we'll just let that subject drop, but I will show you a place I found."

They left the fishing hole and walked upstream while Alex kept on questioning him.

"They say you're not dumb."

Milo just shook his head in amazement, but he was willing to answer him. "In Austria, I vas a schoolteacher. I taught English. I studied in London before the war, but when the war came, I used my passport to leave my country. If I show you my secret place," Milo asked, changing the subject, "will you promise not to tell anybody where it is?"

"I will. I promise," Alex answered as he crossed his heart.

"Vell, I think I can trust you, Alex."

Milo took him at his word, and soon they came to an old mine entrance — a shaft someone had dug many years before that was now the hobo's secret hideout. Milo had placed an oil lamp, clothes, and a mattress inside the shaft. They left after Milo re-covered the entrance.

"You vill promise to never come here?"

"I promise. I will never tell."

As the end of August loomed, and Alex continued to work in the fields, he thought about the Labor Day celebrations that would be held in several valley towns. On Labor Day were horse races and ball games. It was the biggest event of the year. Another carnival was due, and then school would start up again. He went with Olivia to the fields that morning and came back at noon. He would not be going away for this holiday. He watched the town buzzing with activities. The carnival and the dances attracted big crowds. He felt excitement in the air and sensed harmony as he listened to the laughter, which expressed the town's mood. It was harvest time, and vendors from New Mexico came selling green chiles, apples, and Indian melons. Crates of peaches were imported from Grand Junction, and truckloads of melons arrived from Rocky Ford.

He knew that Labor Day honored the workingmen and -women of the nation, and that included him because he and other children had worked alongside grown-ups in the field. He had a mind to dig up his jar of money, but then he thought about the death of his friend and how they had obtained it together. He figured it would be bad luck if he spent it, and so he did not even check to see if it was still there. Maybe his brother Lupe had found it. He had become very close to Olivia during the summer. They sometimes fought like cats and dogs, but they shared their childhood secrets, dreams, and ambitions. Still, Olivia stuck to her two girlfriends when she went to the carnival, leaving him to be with Gilbert. He went to the Ferris wheel first, and Gilbert rocked the seat to scare him, but without success. They rose high into the air as the Ferris wheel turned, and they could see for miles when they reached the top. The top of the wheel was higher than most buildings, and the crowd below looked small. On one of the turns, he happened to spot the house of the lady China, and he wondered if his friend Milo was with her. He made up his mind to peek in through the window again, but he would first have to find a way to get rid of Gilbert. He decided to wait until it got darker, and when Gilbert was pitching pennies at a game board, he found his chance and darted off behind the tents and into the dark street leading to China's house. He headed for the lilac bushes nearest to her window, where he figured no one could see him. As he crawled toward the window, he heard loud voices coming from inside the house. It seemed there was an argument, and he heard China crying and yelling at the same time, but he could not make out her words. Then her screams were muffled, and he thought he heard the sounds of a fight. He could not see if she was fighting with Milo, and he could not tell what they were fighting about. He heard dishes break and furniture crash, and then everything went quiet. He saw the light go out and a man come through the door. He thought the man was either hurt or drunk, by the way he staggered. He was sure the man he saw was not Milo. He was shorter than Milo and wore big glasses. From Alex's hiding place, he saw the man head toward him and then stagger past the lilac bush without seeing him. In seconds, the man appeared and disappeared. He disappeared through the alley. Alex was terrified, and for a short time he could not move. He wanted to cry out, but a lump formed in his throat. He knew that something terrible had happened to China, but he did not want to find out. He finally got the strength to move and was up and running like a scared rabbit. He could not feel his feet touching the ground and seemed to be gliding. The next thing he knew, he was back at the carnival listening to the music of the merry-go-round. He stopped in the first tent he came to and felt scared but safe. He breathed hard and felt sweat running down his face. He was more composed now, but he felt his heart beating hard in his chest, and his legs seemed rubbery. He leaned against a tent pole, his mind reeling with questions about what he had heard and had seen. He stayed put until he felt more calm. Just as he was ready to move on, Gilbert suddenly screamed in his ear and jabbed him in the ribs. Alex jumped a foot into the air and landed with a chilling scream. He felt his eyes coming out of their sockets and then saw Gilbert rolling on the ground with laughter. Gilbert's big white teeth made him look like a horse. At first Alex felt angry and wanted to kick his friend as he rolled on the ground. Then he noticed the wet spot.

"I made you pee," Gilbert laughed, pointing to his pants. "I made you pee."

For a moment, Alex forgot he was scared, but then he remembered what he had seen and heard and he felt guilty because once again he had disobeyed his parents. He wondered how many times he had committed that sin, and he asked himself why he had gone to China's house in the first place. What business did he have peeking into a stranger's house? What was he going to do now? He saw that Gilbert was still laughing when Olivia and her two friends came up to them.

"Alex," she said scornfully, "look at your pants."

"It's pop," Gilbert said. "We were running, and I tripped. I spilled my pop on him."

"Yeah," Alex agreed.

Olivia did not act like she believed them, but she did not want to make a scene.

"We have to go, Alex. Lupe said Mamá wants us to be home before ten."

Normally he would argue or make a nasty remark, but he just said, "See you later, Gil."

"OK, guy," Gilbert replied, and then added with a smirk, "Maybe after you use the toilet." Then he let out another burst of laughter.

That night Alex had the first of several nightmares. He dreamt he was inside the house watching Milo fight with China, beating her over and over again. He was helpless to stop him. China's dead body lay on the floor, and then Milo turned on him, his face distorted, his eyes wild, and his lips curled in a sneer like a mad animal.

"No! No!" he cried out, as Milo came at him in his dream. "Please don't hurt me!"

Milo reached down and grabbed him by the neck and shook him vigorously, and then he heard, "Wake up, wake up!" and felt his mother shaking him. He awoke crying, and his mother asked, "What's the matter?" She held him close to her bosom and comforted him. In between sobs, he told her he was only having a bad dream.

"Don't be afraid," she gently whispered. "I'm here. Now lie back and go to sleep. I'll stay here until you do."

He could feel her stroke his hair until he fell off to sleep. He did not wake until morning. He sat up feeling groggy and started to get out of bed. He knew it was Sunday; he heard his mother getting the rest of the family ready for church. She came over to him and said, "No, *hijo*. You had a very bad night. You stay and rest."

"But I'll commit a mortal sin if I don't go to Mass, Mamá."

"No, you won't. The Lord understands and will make an exception this time."

"Are you sure?"

"I'm sure, Alex. Now get some rest."

The family left him alone in the house, except for Lupe, who slept in another room. Not used to sleeping late, Alex thought of the saying he had learned in school: "Early to bed and early to rise makes a man healthy, wealthy, and wise." He dressed in his bibbed coveralls rather than his Sunday clothes and went outside to the backyard. The scene of the night before was vivid in his mind, and he knew something terrible had happened at China's house. He was curious and was anxious to know what it was, although he knew he would find out sooner or later. He did not want to risk disobeying his parents by leaving the house that day because too many bad things happened when he went out alone. He knew there were no secrets in his small town, and many were aware that Milo spent a night or two a month at China's house. It was no secret that several other men, many of whom were married, visited her frequently, and he had heard that she was a woman of loose morals, or a *vagabunda*. He had also heard she did not go bar hopping like some women did.

Tomás and Nena and Tommy, Linda, and Olivia returned from Mass talking about the murder. Alex learned what happened when he heard his father telling his mother that China's friend and neighbor, Didi, had heard an argument and thought of going over to find out what the quarrel was about. Didi thought all was well after she saw the lights go out and the arguing had stopped. The next morning, she knew she could go over without seeming nosy, because she often had Sunday coffee with China. When she found the door ajar, she knew right away that something was wrong. She noticed the kitchen table was up against a wall and the chairs were scattered on the floor. She called out to China as she made her way inside and was horrified to find her friend in the bedroom. There she saw China's partially nude body lying on the floor with a horrible expression on her face. Didi rushed to her side, knelt beside her, and screamed out in horror as she realized that her friend was dead. Didi became hysterical and ran out of the house, yelling to spread the word of China's tragic death. Her shouts of alarm brought a parade of onlookers to see what was going on. Then she ran out to find the marshal so she could tell him. Didi rattled on to anyone she met what she had found when she went into China's house. "It was horrible! Horrible what they did to China!" she wailed. "She was my best friend. Why her? Why?"

The marshal arrived and ran everybody out of the house. He posted a man at the door and told him not to let anybody in until he got back. Then he got into his car and drove off to notify the sheriff. The marshal thought the sheriff was more qualified to do an investigation. As Alex's father told the story of China's murder to his mother, the boy realized how close he had come to getting hurt or even killed if the man who had run out of China's house had seen him hiding in the lilac bush.

"Just imagine," he heard his mother say, "you wouldn't think a thing like that could happen here. What's this world coming to, anyway?"

"Did you know her?" Olivia asked.

"No, not personally. I knew who she was. Mrs. Aragón pointed her out to me at the church bazaar. You remember her, don't you, Tomás?"

Alex did not feel like leaving the yard, so he spent some time with Tommy and Linda, a rare treat for them. His mother appeared after a few minutes and asked him if he wanted to go to the carnival. Alex, still shaky from his nightmare, told his mother he would catch up with her in a while. As usual, Lupe had already left the house and was with his friends, and so Alex found himself alone in the backyard. Not even Gilbert came around, something unusual for him. Alex later realized that Gilbert was at the scene of the crime carrying out his own investigation and would not leave until he had all the "facts."

Alex's house was the back part of his father's barbershop, and in the yard next to the south wall, the landlord had put up an eight-foot wooden fence. Next to the fence was a tavern, and the gap between the tavern wall and the fence served as a shortcut and the site of many bar fights. He had punched a spy hole in the boards so that he could look out into the alley and beyond to Main Street. He walked over to his spy hole and looked out. He could see that the carnival had started, but the street was nearly empty of people except for the marshal and a man walking with him. Alex was shocked. The marshal was walking with the same man who had run out of China's house on the night of her murder! The man was short and slim, in his fifties. He had a full head of hair combed straight back, and wore dress pants and a white, short-sleeved shirt with a bow tie. Alex knew he did some bookkeeping for City Hall; later he learned that the man ran an insurance office. He noticed that the man wasn't wearing his big glasses. The marshal was much broader at the shoulders and taller, towering at least six inches above the other man, and the two were arguing. The marshal seemed angry and suddenly pushed the smaller man against the wall, just inches from where Alex stood watching through the hole in the fence.

From what the marshal said, Alex got the impression that the man drank too much and was a gambler and a womanizer. His wife knew of his cheating, but she was a strong Catholic woman who did not believe in divorce. She stayed out of his affairs and devoted her life to raising their four children. Three of the four were with her in town, and the fourth was in a boarding school in Canyon City. Alex had heard that the insurance man, the marshal, and the judge had been friends since their school days. He listened as the two men argued.

"Look, Greg," the marshal asserted, "I know it was you, so don't try and lie to me. I found your glasses there." The smaller man protested, but the marshal continued, "No, Greg, you had a thing for her. Now, what went wrong? Did she turn you down? Is that it? Couldn't you take her rejecting you?"

"OK, OK," Greg confessed. "But I was drunk. I didn't know what I was doing. You have to believe me, Sam. I swear it. You have to help me out of this."

"I've got a job to do. I've got a wife and kids to consider. I've got my reputation to think of."

Greg pleaded like a child until the marshal relented.

"It's not up to me alone. I won't do it if the judge doesn't go along."

"Well, let's go over and talk to him. Besides, that hobo was at that woman's house many times. Blame him. Who is he, anyway? He doesn't even belong in this town. He's just a damn hobo tramp. Who's going to think any different?"

"I don't know, Greg. He's never harmed anybody, and you know it."

"Well, it's him or me, Sam. Doesn't our friendship mean anything to you? I'll make it up to you, Sam. I swear I will."

"We'll try, damn you, Greg. But if the judge doesn't go along, I'll turn you in."

"That's all I'm asking. Give me that chance."

"Let's get out of here, Greg. And stand up like a man."

Alex saw them walk across the street to avoid two couples headed their way. He did not know what to do and wondered if his word would hold up against the marshal's. Wasn't the marshal the law? He had heard his father speak very highly of Sam. What would his parents say if he told them what he knew? What would happen to his family if he got them involved? He could warn Milo, but would Milo believe him? He thought about his dilemma; he knew that time would soon run out. He decided he would let the law handle the matter, figuring the authorities knew best what to do. After all, he had to consider his family first. Maybe the judge would not go along with the marshal and Greg. He saw that the day was coming to an end and the crowds were arriving at the carnival. Tomorrow would be Labor Day: a small parade, and then school would start.

His thoughts turned from Milo to the work in the fields. Alex and the other workers had picked tons of the produce shipped out of the valley and he wondered if anyone knew where it came from. Did they know what he and Olivia and the others went through to pick it? He thought of the heat, the cold, and the rain and asked himself if anyone cared.

The sound of someone running through the alley pulled him out of his thoughts. He was not surprised to see Gilbert coming like a race-horse down the home stretch. He could see puffs of dust lifting from Gilbert's feet when they hit the ground, and he was sure that Gilbert had something to tell him. Gilbert was wearing bibbed overalls like the other kids, and he noticed that one of his straps was flying in the air. Watching Gilbert run reminded him of a barnyard hen after a fight, with its feathers all ruffled and its head bobbing. Gilbert reached the yard and puffed out, "You know that hobo? He killed China, and the marshal is bringing him in!"

Alex jumped to his feet and ran to meet Gilbert, asking, "How do you know?"

"I saw them. There must be at least twenty guys with him. They're dragging him and beating him up."

"Where?!" Alex yelled.

"Over by the jail. They're gonna kill that tramp. Let's go over if you don't believe me."

The two ran side by side down the alley, around the J. C. Penney building and out onto Main Street. They saw the mob, and he could see his friend being dragged through the street. He heard the mob yelling and saw people pushing and kicking at Milo, who tried to ward off their blows. He could see that Milo was no match for that many men. The mob passed right in front of the two boys, and Alex stared at Milo's bloody face and his clothes, which had been torn to shreds. He did not think Milo could see him, and he tried to call out to him, but he could not form the words in his mouth. His heart ached from seeing the beating his friend was getting. He saw that Milo's hands were tied with a rope. The marshal tried his best to keep the mob from beating the hobo as Greg ran alongside, yelling and shouting nasty remarks. Alex felt angry and thought Greg was like a little weasel. The scene reminded him of the Stations of the Cross in church when the Innocent Christ was dragged to His Crucifixion. He thought of the Virgin Mary, who watched helplessly as they took her son away from her.

He and Gilbert followed the mob until it disappeared into the jailhouse. For once, Gilbert was silent, and Alex thought he was just as scared as he was. He could not imagine humans acting with such cruelty.

"He's not guilty," he whispered to himself. "He's not the man that killed her."

"What?!" Gilbert asked.

"Nothing. I didn't say anything. What will they do him, Gil?"

"I don't know. But I think they're gonna hang him."

Alex did not know for sure what was done to criminals, but he thought Gilbert must be wrong. The two boys walked to the carnival, and he watched Gilbert spread the word about what had happened to Milo. Alex ran into his parents and his younger brother and sister and joined them on their way home.

"What do they do with people who kill other people?" he asked his father.

"Why the sudden interest?" Tomás asked.

He told him about seeing Milo being dragged by the mob and what Gilbert had said about hanging Milo, but he concealed what he had seen on the night of the murder.

"Myself," his father replied, "I don't believe for one minute that hobo did it. He doesn't look like that kind of a man to me."

"I don't know," his mother said. "If it wasn't him, then who else could have done it? And to think, Alex, you made a friend out of him!"

"Wait, wait," Tomás countered. "Let's not put the carriage before the horse. Nobody saw him do it. Now it's up to the court to decide."

"Who's the court, Papá?" Alex asked.

As best he could, Tomás explained to him what he knew, while Nena raved on about Milo's character and asked, "Now what are people going to say about us? Everybody knows you followed him around like a puppy dog!"

Alex did not say anything because he did not want his family to get into a quarrel. If he uttered one word about his involvement, his mother would *really* wonder what the town would think of them. His father did not press it and let the matter drop. Alex figured he would have to wait to see what happened to Milo, however long that would be. That night he had another bad dream in which an angry mob was taking Milo to the stockyards to hang him. Alex could see his friend's lifeless and broken body dangling from a rope while the little weasel, Greg, cheered the mob on. Alex woke up, but this time his mother was not there to comfort him. He lay in his bed and cried, drifting in and out of sleep as his dream continued with the mob dragging Milo down the street and Greg egging them on with mad laughter.

On Labor Day morning, the town awoke early, and the Martínez family made plans to watch the parade and then drive to the county seat of Conejos, where they would watch ball games and horse races. Conejos was only one mile away, but they needed to take the car because Nena and Olivia had spent hours preparing a big picnic lunch for their long outing. Alex watched his father and Lupe get the car ready. Lupe was already good with cars and a big help to the family. Alex felt a mixture of pride and envy toward his older brother. Whatever Lupe did earned him praise from his parents, and he could come and go as he pleased. Within reason, that is. Their father had the last word and carried a lot of authority when it came to discipline. Alex knew his father had the respect of children, relatives, and friends. If kids got out of hand, it was up to his father to keep them in line. Fathers were expected to dish out discipline.

When Alex and his family arrived in Conejos, his father found the plaza full of cars and had to park some distance away. Conejos was already crowded, and he heard his parents tell him, Olivia, and Lupe to keep track of each other. Little Tommy and Linda were not old enough to be on their own and had to go with their parents.

Nothing excited the crowd more than a good, competitive game of baseball. The teams that came to the Labor Day tournament were from all over the valley and from northern New Mexico. The horse races also attracted a lot of interest, and they went on at the same time. People made heavy bets on both events.

Alex saw Lupe and Olivia go with their friends, and so he was left on his own. He was sure Gilbert would show up, and as he passed a pickup truck, he heard a familiar voice call his name. He looked to see who it was and heard the same voice ask, "Have you forgotten me so soon?"

He recognized the old man from the ranch where he had gone with his father to pick up the ewe.

"Buenos días, Señor Sánchez," he responded. "No, I haven't forgotten you. How are you?"

They chatted for quite some time, and Alex learned that the S.P.M.D.T.U. had sponsored the events at the Labor Day celebration. Some friends of Señor Sánchez came by to chat, and Alex was about to leave when he heard someone mention China's murder. He learned that Milo had been transferred from the city jail to the county jail, just a short distance away from where he stood. He heard that Milo was as good as convicted. There did not seem to be a way for Milo to get a fair trial. Alex concluded that the community had already convicted an innocent man. He did not think they had much liking for an outsider, especially a tramp, and they wanted to hang him for his crime.

He heard enough, and now that he knew where his friend was, he headed toward the courthouse, where he came upon a parade of onlookers trying to peek in through the jail bars and get a glimpse of the "dangerous, caged killer." He could hear his father's words: "It's up to the court to find him either guilty or innocent." Still, after overhearing Greg appeal to the marshal and learning that the two were friends with the judge, he wondered how the court could be fair. He waited a long time for the spectators to move on, and when the way was clear, he went over to the jail and stood next to the window. He looked in through the iron bars and saw Milo. Tears came to his eyes when he saw how badly he had been beaten. Milo came over to him and said, "I don't know what they accuse me of. I don't know why they did this to me."

"Are you alone?" Alex asked.

"*Ja,* but I've never been in jail before. I don't like to be here caged like a wild animal."

Alex could not think of what to say as Milo talked to him as if he were the only friend he had in the world and the only person he trusted. Then he said, "I'll get you out. I'll bust you out."

"But how can you? You are but a child, what can you possibly do?"

"I don't know, but I do know you didn't kill China."

"No, Alex. Don't get yourself involved. Promise me you won't. Don't be a foolish boy." Alex only shook his head as Milo went on. "I came to this country looking to help. I'm responsible for my own actions. Maybe there is a way out, but you can't help me, Alex. Promise me you won't try."

Alex, moved by the sight of his brutally beaten friend, whom he knew was innocent, suddenly knew that his loyalty to Milo had to mean something if he were to be a man.

"I promise," he replied, but he could see the pleading expression in Milo's eyes. He had a hard time thinking of the right thing to say. "But I'll be back to see you," he added.

"No, Alex, just stay away. Now go before they see you here."

Alex was sad to see his friend unjustly accused of a crime he had not committed, and he resolved to help him even though he had promised Milo he would not return. He spent the rest of the day with Olivia, Lupe, and their friends. He heard Olivia talk about boys and Lupe go on about girls. He saw the crowd start to leave for home; they would be getting ready for the last night of the carnival during the last holiday of the summer. He knew school would start right away, and he felt this year would be not be the same as others because of what had happened to his friend James and now to Milo. Although Milo was not dead, he might as well be, and Alex did not think he would ever see him again.

On their way home, they drove in front of the courthouse and the jail. Alex strained to see if Milo was at the barred window, but the sun was in his eyes and he could not see him. As they drove past the church and headed for home, the whole family talked about going to the carnival; his parents would only stay for a short time to let Tommy and Linda go on a few rides. Lupe and Olivia were thinking of heading to the carnival as soon as they arrived home, and Alex thought of looking for Gilbert. However, before he left home, his mother remembered that the Romeros wanted to borrow their meat grinder.

"Alex," she called, "will you run over to the Romeros' for me? I promised them they could use our meat grinder."

"Sure, Mamá. From there I can go to the carnival."

She put the meat grinder in a paper sack and handed it to him, and he left through the back door and went down the alley. He thought about Milo as he walked, in no particular hurry. There was still plenty of daylight, although the sun was already down. As he neared the large incinerator at the back of the J. C. Penney building, he noticed that it was full of empty boxes and paper. He heard several men arguing, and his first impulse was to run back down the alley and take another route to the Romeros'. He did not want to run smack into a bunch of drunks or stumble into the middle of a fight. He saw that the men were walking toward the back of the J. C. Penney building and were closing in on him. So without thinking, he crawled into the incinerator and hid beneath the piles of boxes and paper. Scared of giving himself away, he remained perfectly still. The men stopped right next to where he was hiding, and he could see their feet. He hoped they would leave and feared they might set fire to the boxes. He was sure they were drinking, but then he heard a voice he recognized as belonging to that weasel Greg. He could not tell who the other men were and guessed they were a couple of migrants.

"Now you get it straight," said Greg.

"Yeah," replied one of the migrants. "You'll pay us half now and the rest later, after we burn down the jail."

"That's right. We'll wait until two or three in the morning. I want that bastard dead for what he did to China. Just set fire to the jail and head out of town."

"When do we get the rest of the money?"

"I'll find you in Alamosa and pay you, but only if he's dead."

"Don't worry, that tramp'll fry."

"Good. Here's your money. Use plenty of gas."

Alex was shocked to hear that Greg wanted Milo dead even if it meant that the whole courthouse would go up in flames. He heard the migrants leave in a car and saw Greg head back to the bar. He was frightened and waited, making sure he was not seen before leaving his hiding place, because he feared they might try to kill him. He felt he was in a difficult situation. He had learned of the plot to kill Milo, and he felt something had to be done, but he did not want to involve his family because he feared what might happen to them, since Greg was in league with the marshal and the judge.

After delivering the meat grinder, he ran to meet his parents at the carnival. He knew he had to act alone to help Milo break out of jail, and time was running out. He came up with the only solution he could think of, and the first step was finding a way no one would miss him for a while.

"Mamá," he asked, "can I go to the movies?"

"But it is a double feature, Alex, and you have to get up early for school tomorrow."

"Oh, let him go, Nena. What can it hurt?" said his father, whose word was law.

"Well, I guess. I guess you deserve it. Do you have your own money?"

"Yes," he lied. He was tired of lying, but this time he felt he had a good reason.

"OK, but you come straight home."

"I will, I promise."

He remembered seeing a big padlock on a chain holding the door of Milo's cell. In the movies, he'd seen crowbars used to force locks open. He knew his father had a crowbar in the shed near his house. Making sure Gilbert was not around, he headed into the alley, where he found the crowbar in the shed. He wrapped it in a gunnysack and headed down the alley and onto a dark street, where he would not be seen. He did not want to follow the main road to Conejos, and so he cut across a field, feeling scared as he left the lights of the town behind and headed into the darkness. He could tell he was walking through a field of waist-high sagebrush. The night was quiet, and he could see the big orange harvest moon beginning to rise. He knew he was walking where people had heard the Crying Woman. He recalled Mr. Sánchez's story of balls of fire and felt himself choking on a scream that would have put the Crying Woman to shame. Then he felt something move and heard a noise near his feet. He managed to control his fear and noticed he had stumbled over a jackrabbit. Shaking and regretting that he was there alone, he looked toward town and wondered if he should go back. He could see the lights of the Ferris wheel turning far away, and he knew he would be safe and secure at the carnival, if he wanted. But he also knew that he was on a mission. He figured he was at least halfway to the Conejos jail, although he could not tell for sure. The bright moon gave him courage to go on. He took the crowbar out of the sack and held it like a club over his shoulder. He came to a willow-lined fence, crossed over it, and was startled to find himself face to face with a big white cross. He realized he was in the middle of the Conejos cemetery. "James is buried here," he thought. He remembered the stories of the walking dead he had heard a million times before, but he had gone so far—he decided to forge ahead. He had never felt this scared before. He started running and stumbled over a headstone, which sent him sprawling onto the ground, but he did not drop his crowbar. He thought he felt a hundred arms stretching out of the graves to get him, but he kept on until he ran into a fence he could not see in the darkness. He did not know how he got over it and onto the road. He found himself fleeing for his life. He recognized the church and saw the jail. Feeling safer, he stopped to catch his breath and then threw up, gagging until there was nothing left in his stomach. He realized he was covered with sweat. He got his bearings and saw that the houses in Conejos were dark, probably because the people who lived in them were at the carnival. He was relieved; he wouldn't attract attention. With the crowbar still in his hand, he went ahead with his knees shaking and a cold sweat running down his back. He saw the lonely light in front of the courthouse and walked over to the iron fence surrounding the yard in back. He walked down the cement sidewalk and along the cottonwoods and lilac bushes that lined the fence, coming to the steps that descended to the jailhouse door. There were no lights, but the moon enabled him to see. When he reached the door he called, "Milo, Milo." He did not hear an answer. He felt for the lock, put the crowbar into the loop, and pried hard. He was small, but he had some leverage. He could not open the lock on his first try, and so he continued prying until he took the slack out of the big chain. He pried again until the padlock finally snapped and the big heavy door swung open. He was startled when he heard the rusty hinges squeak and found himself in the first chamber of the jail. He could see, with the dim light from the ceiling, two cells on the south wall. He saw Milo, braced to put up a fight, inside one of the cells, and he realized Milo was expecting the lynch mob. Now Alex understood why Milo had not answered when he called his name—because he did not know who had called out to him. He could see Milo's expression change when he realized who it was.

"Alex!" he blurted out. "For God's sake, what are you doing here?!"

"I came to let you out," he cried. "They want to kill you. They want to burn down the jail."

"What? Who? Why?"

"That man who killed China. Him and the marshal blamed you. Now that man, Greg, wants to make sure they kill you."

"What man? How do you know?"

"I just know. Now you have to get outta here before they come."

He handed Milo the crowbar, and from inside his cell, the hobo pried the lock open easily with his greater strength. Milo dropped the bar and pushed the door open.

"Let's go."

"Wait, Milo, I think it's better if we take my crowbar."

Milo picked up the crowbar and followed Alex out of the jail and up the steps; then Milo led the way. As they headed toward town through the field, they heard a rowdy commotion from a bar, almost drowning out the jukebox playing in another tavern some hundred yards to the east. They passed the cemetery, but this time Alex was not scared because Milo was with him, and he explained how he had found out about that plot to kill him. When they reached the edge of town, Milo stopped.

"Vell, Alex, my friend, this is where we part company."

"Where are you going?"

"I have to get out of here. Someday I will write you. Right now I can't tell you where I'm going. I will never forget you, my friend. Maybe someday we'll meet again."

He felt sad to see his friend go, but he knew that Milo had to leave. "How will I know where you are?"

"Right now I can't tell you. Someday, some way, I'll let you know."

He watched Milo disappear into the darkness, and then he returned home.

The news of Milo's escape spread like wildfire the following day. At school, Gilbert told him that Greg was the one who murdered China and had been found dead himself. He recounted the story of how the men Greg hired drove up to the jail just as the marshal was locking up a drunk at about two in the morning. They discovered that Milo had escaped and wanted the rest of the money Greg had promised them. They caught up with Greg, who was drunk and on his way home, and demanded the money. Greg tried to run, but they caught him and dragged him into their car. His body was found in a ditch with his throat slashed from ear to ear. The migrants, like Milo, left the county without a trace. Alex figured the marshal had become fed up with Greg and had spread the word about the plot to burn down the jail and kill Milo.

When Alex was thirteen, he, Olivia, and Tommy returned from the fields and walked into the house, where their mother told him a package had come for him in the mail. She gave it to Alex, who could not find a return address but noticed that it had an Austrian postmark. He opened it and found a smaller package and a letter that he read to his family as they listened, full of curiosity.

Dear Alex,

I hope you have not forgotten me. Now that the time is right, I will tell you who I am. During the war, I was a spy for the United States Intelligence Corps and was waiting in your town under cover until I was needed. The postmaster was an agent of the United States government and was my contact. I have only you to thank for my escape and my safe return to Washington, D.C. The U.S. sent me to spy on Germany because I know the country and can speak the language. For my services, I received several medals, including the medal of valor. But I'm giving it to you because you deserve it. My mission and identity are still a secret, and that is all I can say for now. So, I say good-bye, my friend, and I hope we'll meet again, but if we don't, I will never forget you.

Your friend forever,
Milo

Alex had some explaining to do to his family. He later learned that Milo had had one last mission in town, and he had not wanted to involve Alex. At the risk of being caught, he had gone to his shack and picked up his shortwave transmitter and his red codebook from their hiding place and then removed an envelope from under his mattress. On his way out of town, he shoved the envelope under the post office door. The End

PART II   THE LIFE

CHAPTER **3**

 **THE VALLEY**

Joe Taylor set *Alex and the Hobo* in the San Luis Valley, a high alpine basin in southern Colorado extending north and south between ranges of the Rocky Mountains. Alex moved across the valley floor between the Sangre de Cristo Mountains to the east and the San Juans to the west. In this he replicated Joe Taylor's experience of moving from a *rancho* near San Luis in the valley's southeastern corner to Antonito in the southwest. Joe Taylor modeled the *rancho* after the *plaza* (small settlement) of El Rito, where he spent his early childhood. He was five years old when his family made the move to Antonito in 1943. He set *Alex and the Hobo* in 1942, when Alex was nine years old, basing the story on his recollection of his later childhood during the war years.

Tracing Alex's Steps with Joe Taylor

To gain a sense of the story's setting, Carole Counihan and I had many conversations with Joe Taylor about his memories and experiences in the valley from the early 1940's, as well as his thoughts and observations about the valley in its present state. As an adult, he spends a great deal of time in the llano, the vast space between El Rito and Antonito. He defines himself as a *llanero,* a man who is more comfortable on the plains than in the mountains, and we discovered that his llano is filled with memories, mystery, and magic. With Joe Taylor, we retraced Alex's steps as he made the trip across the llano to his grandmother's home on the other side of the valley.

On that trip, Alex headed east out of Antonito on Eighth Street, passing irrigated alfalfa fields owned by an Anglo who had been in the area long before Joe Taylor and his family moved there in 1943.

San Luis Valley

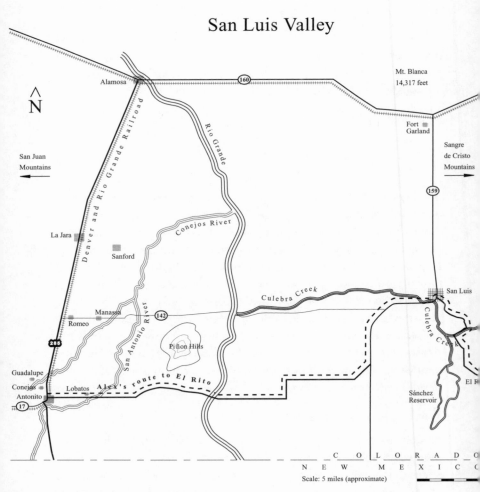

The San Luis Valley. Map by Beatrice Taggart.

As we continued on that road a few miles, Joe Taylor pointed to a small Catholic church in the tiny hamlet of Lobatos, also called "La China." He explained that the hamlets on the valley floor **all had their little groups of people.** During the war, they used to **all pile into one vehicle and . . . go to town as a gang. When you went as a gang in town, you more or less watched over each other. They used to call these guys "La China" because they'd just go to town and they'd fight each other like the Chinese.** The similarity between the nickname for Lobatos and the murder victim in *Alex and the Hobo* is purely coincidental. "China" is a Spanish nickname for a woman who has curly hair.

As Alex passed through Lobatos, he could see the rock formation that looked like a prehistoric animal at the foot of the Piñon Hills. He had spotted it earlier from the ranch, where he had gone with his family to fetch the ewe. The old man Alex met at the ranch told about seeing balls of fire above the rocks during Lent and Holy Week. Joe Taylor explained that **those balls of fire were seen over here until somebody dug out a treasure and then they quit seeing them. These spirits of greed, they stay around a treasure. And when the treasure is gone, the balls of fire are gone. But they're there to protect that treasure. They're there to scare people away, to intimidate people.** He took us to the rocks and showed us how they could provide shelter and a view of the valley from a crevice large enough for a person to stand in. The roof of the crevice was black with soot. This is where they say **the Spanish used to melt gold** and where witches from Antonito continue to practice devil worship.

Alex continued down a dirt road between two rivers flowing out of the San Juans: the Conejos to the north and the San Antonio to the south. Willows lined both sides of the lane, and Joe Taylor recalled that in his youth they **were full of magpies' nests. You'd have to see it to believe it, and then there were a million jackrabbits around here. All of the fields over here have wild irises. I've seen people come over here and take the seed pods away by the gunnysack full.**

Alex crossed the San Antonio River, which was dry on the Fourth of July because farmers diverted all of the water into a system of irrigation canals or *acequias.*[1] The riverbed marked the point where the irrigated fields ended and the llano began. The llano, filled with gray sagebrush, or *chamiso pardo,* extended for miles in all directions. *Chamiso pardo* and *chamizo pardo* are San Luis Valley and northern New Mexican Spanish terms for sagebrush (artemisia).[2] Joe Taylor continues to drive out into the llano whenever he has the chance, and he seemed at peace with himself when in fields of sagebrush, referring to this place with great affection as **my valley.**

Chamiso pardo has a subtle and very agreeable aroma, particularly after a rainstorm. I discovered by accident that it may also have the power to clean away the effects of witchcraft practiced by those who gather in the soot-blackened crevice in the rock formation seen by Alex. This revelation emerged in a conversation between Joe Taylor and a woman I shall call Juana, who had formerly lived in Antonito and who believed she had been bewitched. Joe Taylor listened sympathetically to her testimony and suggested, as a cure, that she burn *chamiso pardo* inside of her house.

Chamiso pardo was only one reason Joe Taylor seemed serene when out in the llano. Another was his belief that he acquired energy from certain rocks. One example is *el cerro de las brujas,* which he translated as "witches' mountain" or "magic mountain." The *cerro de las brujas* is a rock formation in the middle of the llano on a gravel road that travels up the middle of the valley just west of the Rio Grande. About the llano and its magical places, he said: **This is my place to come to regenerate myself.**

Alex continued on his journey past the Piñon Hills. There, as we continued to follow Alex's path to the other side, Joe Taylor found a brass marker. On one side it said "The United States," and the other side said "Mexico." The marker was one more physical reminder of the valley as the meeting place for Mexicano settlers from the south and Anglos from the east in the last half of the nineteenth century. He pointed out the Ute burial ground, a reminder of the Native Americans who were here long before other settlers arrived in the valley. The burial ground was off the main road and was marked by a path of carefully placed stones that a casual observer could easily overlook. The events in *Alex and the Hobo,* of course, took place long after Mexicano and Anglo-Saxon settlers had displaced the Utes and taken the land and water for their commercial farms and ranches.

Joe Taylor explained that when he was Alex's age **these llanos over here were full of sheep. You had sheepherders on both sides of the road. They used to do a lot of grazing here. They used to graze a lot of cattle. They still do a little bit of cattle but not as many as they used to. And sheep, you don't see them anymore. But this was sheep and cattle country at one time.** To the north of the magic mountain, the Conejos and the San Antonio Rivers converge and empty into the Rio Grande. Joe recalled an incident that took place when he was about Alex's age and was fishing with his father, Anastacio Taylor. As Joe Taylor will explain in a later chapter, his father had a very important influence on the formation of the masculine moral vision incorporated into *Alex and the Hobo.*

We went fishing because my dad was a big fisherman. And we went to where the San Antonio River and the Conejos River meet, and they'd go into the Rio Grande. And there was a little island and a lot of rocks. I must have been under twelve years old. And we went in there to fish, and I saw this little cub, this mountain lion cub. And I went to go get it, and I saw my dad screaming at me. . . . And I couldn't hear him because the river was sort of high. He went over there to where I was, crossed the river, and got me and took me across the river and put me in the car. And when I turned around, this mountain lion mama had the little cub in her mouth and she was going away with it. . . . If my dad hadn't have been there, I'd be fertilizer in some cave up there.

We continued tracing Alex's steps, past Kiowa Hill. Joe Taylor recalled that the Kiowas came out of the plains, crossed the Sangre de Cristos, and fought with the Utes. He reported hearing about struggles between Spanish-speaking settlers and Native Americans in different parts of the valley. He said he knew of other Native American burials and Spanish altars in the Piñon Hills.

Halfway to El Rito, Alex made the gradual descent across the llano to the Rio Grande, which flows south to New Mexico, into Texas, and finally into the Gulf of Mexico. Following Alex's route, we saw the dra-

Joe Taylor and James Taggart on Kiowa Hill. Photo by Carole M. Counihan.

matic path that the river has cut through the llano: the moist green grass growing at the water's edge contrasted sharply with the gray fields of sagebrush. As Alex crossed the bridge, he could see through the wooden planks to the river flowing beneath him. Joe Taylor remarked that the bridge is much better now than when Alex made the trip in 1942.

The soil on the other side was less rocky. Joe Taylor motioned to the trailers that dotted the landscape and the patchwork of roads scarring the llano and marking off a subdivision that did not exist when he was Alex's age. He observed: **They're buying all these properties over here. They used to call this "Top of the World Ranches."**

No subdivision existed on the western side of the Rio Grande, though, where the llano is under the jurisdiction of the Bureau of Land Management (BLM). The BLM leases grazing rights to cattle and sheep ranchers but does not permit subdivisions. The buyers on the eastern side of the river were mostly Anglos, living in widely scattered trailers. Joe Taylor explained that Anglos and Mexicanos preferred different settlement patterns: **A lot of the Spanish families settled in**

communities. They stayed mostly in groups, while the Anglo would come over and settle twenty, thirty miles from his nearest neighbor. The Anglo-Saxons in this conversation are relatively recent arrivals to the valley who prefer to live out in the llano rather than in settled communities. The valley also has a number of earlier Anglo-Saxon settlements, the most important of which for understanding Joe Taylor's story are Manassa and Sanford, north of Antonito on the western side of the valley. Manassa was settled when a group of Mormons from the southeast, under the leadership of John Morgan, petitioned to lease state lands in the spring of 1879. A branch of these settlers, together with other Mormon families from Utah, established Sanford, which had become a very prosperous town by 1888.[3]

As Alex continued on his way to El Rito, he passed a low bluff that once rose six hundred to one thousand feet above the llano. Joe Taylor explained: **There used to be a little mountain right there . . . it was a little volcano, and they finally shipped it all out. Trucks used to have roads up to the top.** The mountain consisted of red volcanic rock used for landscaping. **They took it and crushed it and it came out in different grades. Different sizes. Some they ship in big rocks.** All that was left was a butte twenty feet high. To the south we saw Ute Mountain, a volcanic cone just across the border in New Mexico, rising two thousand feet above the valley floor. **That's where they claim to hear La Llorona.** Alex, it may be remembered, heard stories of La Llorona (the Crying Woman), and Joe Taylor thought he actually saw a woman like her near the cemetery that Alex crossed on his way to free Milo.

Joe Taylor noted that wild horses used to run through this part of the llano, which **was full of prairie dogs too at one time.** Alex passed through the tiny town of Mesita, formerly an Anglo community on a now abandoned railroad line once used to ship produce out of the valley. The Mesita schoolhouse, constructed out of red volcanic rock, eventually became a Mormon church. The San Luis Valley Southern Railroad line reached Mesita sometime after 1910 with the intention of going all the way to Taos, but the idea was abandoned because of the lack of commerce.[4] The differing railroad histories on the western and eastern sides of the valley are one indication of the contrasting patterns of Anglo settlement around Antonito. Far more Anglos

Train headed north out of Antonito.

settled on the Antonito side, where the railroad operated continuously from 1880 through the entire twentieth century.

Joe Taylor recalled that when he lived in El Rito, he could hear the train's whistle all the way from Mesita, and he thought the whistle was the *abuelo* (grandfather or boogeyman). The *abuelo* appeared on Christmas Eve, when the community made a bonfire (*luminaria*). The *abuelo* carried a big whip and came out of hiding to chase the children. Joe Taylor said: **The abuelo and the bonfires were to scare away the evil spirits.** He recalled, **We were playing out there and we called that train part of the abuelo, part of the Llorona. We'd hear it come and it sort of echoed, and we'd head for home, boy!**

Rising a few hundred feet, the San Pedro Mesa separates Mesita from El Rito to the east. On his way around the mesa, Alex passed through San Luis, which lies right below the chapel on the hill where later there would appear a beautiful bronze sculpture of the Stations of the Cross, commemorating the last stages of Christ's life, from the Last Supper to his crucifixion.[5] That sculpture did not exist when Alex made the trip to visit his grandparents. The sculpture of the stations is a legacy from the Penitentes, who were among the first settlers along the banks of Culebra Creek and the Conejos River. The Penitentes are actually several brotherhoods, or *cofradías,* dedicated to observing Christianity by identifying with the life and the suffering of Christ. Religious brotherhoods (*cofradías*) are common in the Spanish-speaking world, and those of the Penitentes hold beliefs about Jesus that originated with the Franciscan friars, who introduced Christianity to what is now the state of New Mexico. The brotherhoods of Penitentes formed to carry on Catholicism at a time when there were few priests in the Southwest.[6] Joe Taylor paid his own tribute to the Penitentes in *Alex and the Hobo* by alluding to the stations in the episode where Alex watches a crowd, egged on by Greg, drag Milo through the streets of Antonito.

Alex continued another ten miles south to a small, beautiful valley—called "La Valley"—nestled at the foot of the towering Sangre de Cristo Mountains. He passed the Church of San Pablo and the school building, where, when Joe Taylor was a young child, families held dances and performed songs and plays. Up the road we came to the Church of San Francisco and the *morada* (chapel), where the Penitentes hold their meetings. Joe Taylor pointed out the apple orchard where he spent the first years of his early childhood and where Alex celebrated the Fourth of July reunion.

El Rito and Antonito

Nearly all of the stories Joe Taylor has written take place in the vast space on the llano between El Rito and Antonito. The valley means much more to him than a physical location, as he expressed in several short essays such as the following, which he called "Goodbye to My Beautiful San Luis Valley."[7]

I was born brown. The only language I knew was Spanish. I knew only the heritage of my Catholic religion, mestizo culture, and Hispanic last names. My Valley. Majestic are the mountains that embrace it: the Sangre de Cristos, Crestones, and San Juans. Mountains named by the Spanish conquistadors that discovered them. I say "My Valley" because it gave birth to me and fed me. Then my family

moved—only fifty miles and, I thank God, not out of the San Luis Valley. But we left behind my closest relatives: my beloved grandmother, Tonita, and many of my aunts and uncles on both my parents' sides of the family. I was taken from them and transplanted to a little town called Antonito. I was five years old then and this country was at war. I did not know much about the war in Europe and the Pacific, but I did know many of my relatives fought and some died in that war. My Valley was once young and healthy, like a big wild animal. It stood solid and firm like a big oak tree and survived the wrath of nature and time. My Valley was rich beyond human imagination. My mestizo grandparents, who were pioneers, knew that the wind, sun, and rain were the basic elements for the soil to produce their food. They knew if they took from the land, they'd also have to give something back. Then came the Anglos, who raped the land, bled its precious supply of water, and broke its spirit. They branded me as Mexican, Chicano, Hispanic, brown, and everything but white. Without a conscience and in their greed, they left My Valley for dead and they called what they did progress. So I say goodbye to all that is beautiful, pure, and good, because I am also slowly dying with My Valley.

The mention of the Anglos who raped the land, bleeding its precious supply of water and breaking its spirit, alludes to the history of the San Luis Valley, which Joe Taylor also refers to in *Alex and the Hobo,* as well as in his oral commentary about how he created his story out of his experience. He often converted the history of the valley into a spatial contrast between the pastoral El Rito of his early childhood and the commercial center of Antonito, where he came of age and lives as an adult.[8] To give us a clearer picture of El Rito, he took us to visit his cousin, who currently lives in the house of his maternal grandmother, which is across the street and down the road from the site of the Fourth of July reunion in *Alex and the Hobo.* Sister Concetta explained: **Well, I think we were all like one family. There were a lot of neighbors around. And there used to be a school just across the road there. And you could stay from first to eighth. And so we all went to school over here. And it was just like one family. And they used to have parties. There was a teacher one time, he was, I** don't know if you, Joe, remember. Hipólito Martínez was his name. And he used to have a party every month for the whole community. And so everybody would go. The schoolchildren and their parents and brothers and sisters and everyone would have a party and they'd have dancing and play games. There's a dance where you dance for a little while, and they'd stop the music, and you'd have to tell whomever you're dancing with a little verse.

El Rito and Antonito are and were both agricultural communities, but they have different methods of food production. Joe Taylor recalled the self-sufficient food producers in the El Rito of his childhood: **What little a man would have, he'd raise in his own garden. Everybody had a garden here at one time, where they raised cauliflower, they raised cabbages, they raised turnips, they raised carrots, potatoes, and horse beans . . . They call them** *habas.* **And they used to have their little apple orchard and maybe an apricot tree. And the string beans, you could make them two ways. You could either dry them and thresh them and make your cooking beans. Or you could make your string beans. You could take them and thread a needle through them and hang them up. Everybody had what you call a** *dispensa.* **It was separate from the house. And you could also put your** *carnes secas* **there, your dried meats. There were a lot of people that made their home brew out of hops. And then they used to make the wine, chokecherry wine. But everybody would prepare for a winter. If you were lazy, you didn't make it. You didn't survive. But everybody in those days had to work. Everybody had to work. And that's why we used to go out to work the fields when we were five and six years old. We used to have to go work. It wasn't that they were being cruel or anything else with us. It was a matter of survival.**

Neighborhood ties reinforced by kinship formed the basis of work groups in El Rito, as Joe Taylor's older sister, Cordi, recalled. She told how planting took place as neighbors, many of whom were also kin, assembled to prepare the fields and put the crops into the ground. The contrast between the kin-based neighborhood work groups in El Rito and the work crews Joe Taylor described in *Alex and the Hobo* is dramatic. The work crews on the Antonito side of the valley had to endure an uncomfortable and sometimes cold and wet trip in the back of a truck, they lacked toilets, they drank bad water, and they worked long hours in the hot sun. Some field bosses were abusive and attempted to fondle young women.

The contrast between the pastoral economy of El Rito and the harsh commercial farms north of Antonito has a basis in history. The first Mexicanos came into the valley and formed comparatively egalitarian hamlets with herding and farming economies, but Anglo-Saxons eventually brought many changes, particularly on the western side of the valley. El Rito and the other hamlets in the San Luis area were part of the Sangre de Cristo land grant, created by the Mexican government in 1844. Mexicanos colonized the San Luis area first in 1850, when they settled along Culebra Creek. The Utes drove them out, but they returned the following spring and have remained ever since. The Mexican government also encouraged Mexicanos to settle the southwest corner of the valley by creating the Conejos land grant in 1833. Mexicanos soon thereafter attempted to settle on the banks of the Conejos River, but also met stiff opposition from the Utes and left. In 1842, Cornelio Vigil, a *juez de paz* (justice of the peace) from Taos, journeyed to the Conejos River and declared that eighty-four families, most of whom were descendants of the original Mexicanos named in the 1833 grant, had a right to settle the area. As a condition for being a grantee, a settler had to build a house and farm the land. Settlers enjoyed the right to graze cattle on the open range and unlimited access to water as long as they did not infringe on the use-rights of other settlers. However, as grantees, they could not sell their land as private property. The first permanent settlement did not materialize until 1854, when José María Jaquez brought a group of settlers from New Mexico to establish a hamlet (*plaza*) near the present-day county seat of Conejos.[9]

The economic and social organization of the valley changed with the arrival of the Anglos, who came in large numbers after the railroad reached Alamosa in 1876. As the railroad extended to Antonito in 1880, Anglos poured into the western side of the valley, settling in the towns of Montevista, Del Norte, Alamosa, and further south into the northern part of what is now Conejos County in the communities of Manassa, La Jara, and Sanford. Land speculators rapidly converted the Conejos land grant into private property and established aggressive commercial agricultural ventures based on irrigation projects. One of the most ambitious was T. C. Henry's project around Del Norte and Montevista, north of Antonito, which used water from the Rio Grande.[10] Frances León Swadesh reports that the project used so much water from the Rio Grande that "between 1880 and 1896, 65,000 acres out of 125,000 farmed downstream had to be abandoned for want of water." She reports: "Hand-in-hand with vast expropriation of lands went a wave of violence and terrorism which caused many Hispanos to leave the San Luis Valley."[11]

By 1942, the time of Joe Taylor's story, Anglos owned many of the commercial farms along the railroad lines that went west and south from Alamosa. Mexicanos still outnumbered the Anglos in Antonito and the outlying hamlets, and they supplied much of the labor on the Anglo-owned commercial farms to the north. A number of Anglos had established businesses in Antonito, which had become an important commercial center because of its location on a main railroad line from Alamosa to Santa Fe and Durango. Working conditions for Mexicanos were harsh on the Anglo commercial farms north of Antonito because owners and contractors seemed to care very little about their workers. Joe Taylor described the callous attitude of Anglo employers in the following way:

You'd work for your own people over here, and they went by the same regulations as the white people did. So they weren't exploiting. They were just going by the rules that were already laid down but they did one more thing. When you went to work for your own people over here, they took you into their house and they fed you. They took you water out into the field. They treated you like the next-door neighbor. They treated you with sympathy because you were little kids out there. And they were moms that went out there to see how you were doing and blow your nose if they had to because they were caring people. The Chicano people, the Chicano people that we worked for, like the De Herreras and the other De Herreras and the Luceros and the Garcías or the Durans, whomever you worked for, there was that care. There was that feeling. But there wasn't that feeling when you worked over there for the Anglo. If you

got sick, if you had to go to the bathroom, where would you go? You
had to go there in the field. They didn't have facilities for you to go
to and they didn't care. Whether you were a man or a woman, there
were no facilities. All they wanted you to do is go ahead and get as
much work out of you as they could for as little as they would pay.

The Mexicanos in El Rito and other hamlets on the San Luis side
of the valley maintained a greater degree of independence from the
Anglo-Saxon incursion in the valley, although much of the Sangre de
Cristo land grant had fallen into the hands of Anglo speculators by the
end of the 1870's. William Gilpin and the English lawyer William
Blackmore carved up the land in various moneymaking schemes.[12]
The Mexicanos in the southeast corner of the valley nevertheless
maintained their right to graze their animals, cut their firewood and
lumber, and fish and hunt in the towering Sangre de Cristos above
their communities by virtue of a clause in a deed drawn up by Charles
Beaubien in 1863. Charles Beaubien was a French Canadian who
acquired Mexican citizenship and acquired sole possession of the
Sangre de Cristo grant in 1848.[13] Access to the mountains helped
the Mexicanos in the Culebra Creek area to continue living in their
kinship- and neighborhood-based egalitarian hamlets, which had a
mixed farming and herding economy until 1960, when Jack Taylor
purchased a 77,524-acre tract that included the 14,069-foot Culebra
Peak. Jack Taylor (no relation to Joe Taylor) is a descendent of
Zachary Taylor, the Anglo-American "hero" of the Mexican-American
War and former U.S. president; he restricted the Mexicanos' access to
the mountains above their community.[14] **When they took that moun-**
tain away from the people—that land grant that they had—they
took part of the livelihood away from these people. Because they
used to take their cattle up there and graze them in the summer.
They used to get their firewood and they used to get their game.
When they sold that place, which had no title to it—I don't know
how they sold it—they took those people's livelihood away.

Jack Taylor sold the tract to former Enron executive Lou Pai, who
continued to restrict the Mexicanos' access to the mountain. However, on June 24, 2002, the Colorado Supreme Court decided in the
case of *Eugene Lobato et al. v. Zachary Taylor et al.* to allow the resi-

dents of the San Luis area to graze their animals and gather wood on the former Taylor ranch.[15]

Greed in *Alex and the Hobo*

Joe Taylor attributed the Culebra watershed dispute to greed, an important component of the masculine moral vision that led to his writing *Alex and the Hobo*. His description of the llano between Antonito and El Rito contains other clues for interpreting the significance of greed in his story. He alluded to greed when he mentioned the balls of fire appearing above the rock formation out in the llano. The balls of fire came up in the conversation with Mr. Sánchez when Alex and his family went to the ranch on the edge of the llano to fetch the ewe. Joe Taylor explained that the balls of fire are the spirits of greed that sometimes appear in sacred places and at sacred moments. He elaborated by saying, **Those balls of fire were seen over here until somebody dug out a treasure and then they quit seeing them. These spirits of greed, they stay around a treasure. And when the treasure is gone, the balls of fire are gone. But they're there to protect that treasure. They're there to scare people away, to intimidate people.** He explained why the balls of fire appear in certain places in the llano and at certain moments in the religious calendar. He began by noting, **The rocks were sacred to the Indians, and Mr. Sánchez had respect for Indian beliefs because of his relationship with the Indians.** I think Mr. Sánchez had a relationship with the Indians because he and other Mexicanos in the valley are mestizos and thus have mixed Native American and Spanish ancestry. In response to why the balls of fire appeared during Lent, Joe Taylor explained: **Lent is a time of making sacrifices,** which is the opposite of being greedy. Evil spirits appear at sacred moments like Lent because **they are from the devil and they mock holy celebrations.** His allusion to greed early in the story is a portentous omen because it anticipates corruption, which Joe Taylor associates with greed. It also is part of his conception of the valley as a place with which he strongly identifies. As he wrote in his essay, he has seen his valley violated by greedy miners and farmers who have scarred the landscape, used the land, and taken the water without giving anything in return. They are capitalists and **capitalism is an**

economic system that is based on greed and the spirits of evil. The greedy, who have taken so much from the valley without giving anything in return, have carved up his llano into "Top of the World" ranches, created aggressive land-grabbing schemes and ambitious irrigation projects, provoked violence and intimidation against Mexicanos, and produced the factory food system in which Alex and Olivia toiled and suffered. They threatened the livelihood of the members of Joe Taylor's extended family, who continue to live in El Rito. Many bad things in *Alex and the Hobo*—James's death, China's murder, and the near murder of the innocent Milo—have some connection to greed for money, which in turn is connected to the economic system brought to the area by the Anglos. James dies after he and Alex pick up the coins, the knife, and the marshal's gun after the drunken brawl at the tavern. China dies at the hands of the town's Anglo bookkeeper and insurance broker, whose business was money. Milo nearly dies when China's murderer pays migrants to burn down the Conejos County jail. Attributing so much evil and human suffering to greed is understandable, particularly if one considers that Joe Taylor has been a worker all of his life. In his view as a union man and as a Chicano, he sees greed as the source of all forms of corruption.

One important theme that emerged in our conversations is that greed drove the Anglo-Saxon penetration into his valley and posed a threat to his culture. Joe Taylor equated the state of his culture with the health of his valley. He imbued his valley with a great deal of meaning, some of which he acquired as a member of a Spanish-speaking family. He recalled how he learned from his parents to be generous rather than greedy and to have a big heart. Greed drives corruption, which he defines as sin, a concept he learned from his churchgoing mother. This concept of sin was the foundation of the masculine moral vision he developed over his years as a union man, a Chicano, a young farmworker, and the son of Spanish-speaking parents. In the following chapters, Joe Taylor describes how he developed his moral vision out of his culture and his experience. He reveals precisely how the Anglo-Saxon penetration has posed a threat to his culture by placing in peril Spanish-speaking women like his mother, who taught him the concept of sin.

 **AWARENESS**

Joe Taylor believes that the Mexicanos need to band together under a leader to protect themselves from the greedy, who have exploited them and taken much from their valley without giving anything in return. His ethnic awareness and class consciousness developed and reinforced each other in different ways, particularly after he got out of the army and returned to Antonito in 1961.[1] He acquired the most recent layer of his ethnic awareness when he joined the Chicano movement in the late 1970's. That layer came after he had developed some degree of class consciousness while working for the perlite processing plant south of town. His ethnic awareness and class consciousness also have deep roots, which he traced all the way to his early childhood in the bosom of his family. To explain the perspective that he brought to writing *Alex and the Hobo,* he laid out his ideas by way of interpreting "The Three Little Pigs":

Well, look at "The Three Little Pigs." Right? The Three Little Pigs lived with their mom till their mom couldn't take care of them anymore. So she sets out the Three Little Pigs, but they didn't stay together. OK, in any community you have a Big Bad Wolf. You have that guy that's always instigating, making trouble. So the Big Bad Wolf, he finds the Three Little Pigs in different places and he can terrorize them [*atemorizarlos*]. That first little pig is like someone in every community. He isn't going to make the best house for when the wind comes up. He's a little bit on the lazy side. But he did have his house, the one made out of stakes. And the other one made his out of straw. But it looked like there was one thinker in the community. Like we say, we're all brothers in there. So the one thinker of the community built himself a nice house. And then when his brothers were in need,

he fought back to get his brothers back. He got his brothers back out of the wolf, and he impressed the wolf by showing a little bit more power and a little intelligence. They won out over the wolf at the end because the wolf was coming in with just one power: the fear that they had. But when they utilized other forces against the wolf, they conquered it. Or at least they subdued it to a point where that wolf was gonna think before he came back. Sometimes a community might come together because of a tornado, sometimes a flood, but whatever brings it together, if it wasn't together before, a tragedy might bring them together. And a lot of times they're not thinking together. They might be against each other. But when they see the real needs, the real force, the real danger that is there, they do band together.

Becoming a Chicano

Joe Taylor refers to becoming a Chicano as his period of *awareness.* He described how he learned about the movement from his cousin, who came down from Denver in the late 1970's. The two of them hit it off, and she encouraged him to organize a chapter of the Raza Unida Party in Conejos County. In 1977, he took a Chicano studies course at Adam State College, where he read Rudolfo Anaya's *Bless Me, Última,* the book that inspired his own story. He discussed Anaya's book many times, noting that it struck a deep chord because it described beliefs he had heard as a boy in El Rito and Antonito. Última is a curer who befriends Antonio, a seven-year-old boy who becomes her apprentice and learns about her supernatural power. She personifies goodness and, in the form of her *tecolote* (owl) protective spirit, she battles the evil Trementina sisters, who turn into *coyotes.* Joe Taylor experienced an important moment of awareness when he read Anaya's book, which was very different from the popular fiction about the "pioneers" and the films about Anglo-Saxon cowboys that he had read and seen as a boy. Anaya was the first author he read who wrote from the perspective of a New Mexican Mexicano. Moreover, the two men were of the same generation; both were born in 1937[2] and grew up when stories about humans with the supernatural power to turn into *tecolotes* and *coyotes* were circulating in northern New Mexico and southern Colorado.[3]

Crabs in a Bucket

Joe Taylor's Chicano awareness is unusual in his community and is not shared by some members of his own family. He uses the word "Chicano" to mean Mexicano, even though some members of his family and his community prefer to use a different term for themselves. **Chicano is the word that the Raza Unida fought for to identify ourselves. When I was growing up, there was no such word as Latino, Hispanic, or Hispano. An Anglo would call you a Mexican if he meant to be derogatory. If not, then he would use Spanish American. Yet after the Chicano battle, there were many who were not involved in the struggle and who objected to the word Chicano because they classified a Chicano as a political activist or a radical. They did not want to identify themselves with the name. Yet the same people could not find a word for identifying themselves.** He ran into considerable opposition within Antonito when he attempted to organize Mexicanos to defend their ethnic and class interests. He described that opposition with the metaphor of crabs in a bucket, which he learned from others in the Chicano movement. **If a crab is trying to get out of the bucket, the other ones reach out and pull him back in instead of helping him to get out.** He believed that the source of the opposition to his organizing efforts was *envidia* (envy), which made others suspect his motives.[4] Envy made revolution "hard to think"[5] among those who experienced class and ethnic oppression.

Perhaps one should expect resistance to any effort to organize others to defend their class and ethnic interests. Class and ethnic consciousness does not automatically follow from the experience of being dominated or exploited by another class or group.[6] Antonio Gramsci explained resistance to revolution with the concept of hegemony, which refers to how a dominant class can affect the consciousness of a subordinate one; relations of domination and subordination affect consciousness to such a degree that they "saturate the whole process of living" and become "common sense."[7]

The Antonito School Strike

Joe Taylor's awareness came at a time when he faced several difficult moral challenges, each of which he alluded to in *Alex and the Hobo.* One was the bitter Antonito school strike of 1979–1980, just after his cousin encouraged him to join the Chicano movement. The strike was a particularly severe moral challenge because it pitted members of the Mexicano community against each other. Joe Taylor recalled the same kind of moral complexity he described in *Alex and the Hobo;* like Alex, he recognized corruption when he saw it, but found revolution "hard to think."[8]

The events leading up to the strike were widely reported in the *Valley Courier,* a newspaper published in Alamosa that circulates throughout the valley. According to the *Courier,* the first indication that all was not right in the Antonito schools surfaced in late August of 1978, when Lionel Ruybal and Pete De Herrera registered several complaints against the South Conejos school superintendent, a Mexicano from a large and prosperous family in town. One complaint was that the superintendent sold his own property to the school and hired his relatives to work in the school system.[9]

At the time the complaints surfaced, the Antonito teachers were organized into the Antonito Classroom Teachers Association (ACTA), an affiliate of the Colorado Education Association (CEA). However, ACTA had not succeeded in negotiating a master agreement or contract with the South Conejos County Board of Education. On December 18, 1979, just before Christmas vacation, Antonito teachers staged a "sick out" to protest their treatment by the board, and high school students walked out in support of the teachers. Teachers complained about their "demoralizing treatment including the practice of patronage, threats of firing and non-renewal, and pitting faculty members against each other."[10] School reopened the Monday following Christmas vacation, but the contract dispute continued. The board voted some pay raises for faculty and staff, but the ACTA president, also a Mexicano, declared that the contract was still not forthcoming. The superintendent was quoted in the paper as saying he could not accept the terms of the contract, registering his strong objections to a

clause that allowed "teachers complete freedom to teach any controversial, religious or political material they desire in the classroom."[11]
The strike lasted for fifty-nine days in the spring of 1980 and divided the Mexicano community sharply, because some aligned themselves with the striking teachers, others sided with the school superintendent, and several worked as strikebreakers. **Up to today this
town is divided because of that strike. Up to today people will
not talk to each other. Up to today people will not unite with each
other because of the strike that they had here, which hurt every
family, every child, every parent and relative. It was a big struggle.**
One alarming development was the use of armed guards walking
around the school. Joe Taylor voiced his opinion against some of the
board members. **I was not going to send my kids to a school where
there is a guard with a gun. Guns should not be involved in a strike
of that size.**

Lionel Ruybal, better known as "Liono," was one of the men who
registered the first complaints against the superintendent; he was a
Chicano, and he encouraged Joe Taylor to get involved. **He was one
of those Corkey González, he was one of those Reies López Tijerina,
he was one of those César Chávez people. He had that kind of spirit
in him. Like I say, he was great. He's one man I'll always remember.
Anytime they needed something, they'd come for Liono. He was one
of the people that helped me out the best.**

The school strike, however, presented complicated moral dilemmas for Joe Taylor, dilemmas similar to those Alex faced when he befriended the hobo. **Liono kept asking me to go [to the meetings]. He
kept asking me to go. And I said, "No. Some of my friends are on that
school board. I've known them all my life." I said, "I don't want to in-
terfere." I said, "I've known teachers there all my life. Really," I said,
"it ought to be between the principal and the teachers."** Moreover,
he did not consider the school strike a Chicano issue at all. **It's corruption. I've never been in any job as long as I've been alive, and I've
worked in a lot of places, where there isn't a form of corruption,
where there isn't a form of favoritism, where there isn't a form of
greed. I dare challenge any man that in his lifetime he has not seen
corruption or injustice done to his community or to himself.**

He recalled how Liono persuaded him to get involved by saying: "The teachers don't have any home, and the state has all the power. We're all one people. We got to stand up for our rights. We got to fight these people. We've got to fight corruption. We've got to fight this power. They need support. They need help." I didn't like what was going on. I was still a union man at heart. I always will be. And we went in there, and I started to support the teachers. Finally it turned out to be war. They had big motorcades right in the front of the teachers' homes that were crossing the picket lines, and in front of the principal. They had an election and they won. They got out the old school board and had to vote in a new school board.[12]

Opponents of the former school superintendent convinced Joe Taylor to run for the South Conejos County School Board, and so he ran on the Raza Unida party ticket, won, and was elected president of the board. During his term in office, he drew on his experience of working for the union to rectify the unfair labor practices of the old regime.

Acquiring Class Consciousness

Joe Taylor said that his Chicano awareness came after he developed class consciousness, which he attributed to becoming a union man when he went to work for the perlite plant after serving six years in the army. Perlite is volcanic stone that bursts like popcorn when heated and is used for insulating material. The mine is twenty miles south of Antonito, and the two processing plants are one mile south of town. The mine and the plants are the main sources of steady jobs for Mexicanos lucky enough to work year-round in the Antonito area. When Joe Taylor returned from the army in 1961, Great Lakes Carbon (GrefCo) owned one plant, and John Mansfield owned the other. He described his early years working for GrefCo:

Well, basically I got started in the union back in 1961 when I started working for the perlite outfit over here. Then it was Great Lakes Carbon. And I didn't know too much about the union there. I wasn't too interested in the union there. I heard too much about the union and union corruption and all that. So I was hesitant to even join them, but they had a meeting one time. Because I started work-

Great Lakes Carbon (GrefCo) perlite processing plant.

ing, I was just happy to be in the plant. I was just thankful that I had a job at a dollar seventy-five an hour. So that's what the wages were here then. Back in the sixties they were anywhere from a dollar to a dollar seventy-five. And that was the highest you were getting paid. A dollar seventy-five over here an hour plus the forty-hour work week. It would give you time and time-and-a-half. You were getting what professors were getting at colleges.

Anyway, I didn't feel that I wanted to join the union. I didn't feel that I had the authority to go up against management because in the military you were taught that you follow the chain of command. If you're a private that's like being nothing. And about the only people that begin to carry authority in the military are from your sergeant on up. Everybody else is just a workhorse. So I didn't think that I could go and voice my opinion against an outfit like Great Lakes Carbon. A big organization. So they asked me to go to a meeting anyway. And United Mine Workers was over here representing the perlite plant, but they had a representative that came on over when the dues were supposed to be collected and that was about it. You had a grievance or something like that, and you were put off. "Whenever I can get down there." And before long you'd forget.

Anyway there was the Teamsters Local 146, run by Bob and Michael.[13] And they wanted to see if we wanted to go Teamsters. So they were competing. They came on over here to see if we wanted to go union. And finally they bought more beer for us. So we figured that was the union to go with. So when they had the election, the Teamsters won, oh by a big margin. About eighty-five percent of the votes went to the Teamsters. And still I went to the meeting and sat down at the meeting, and they read the agreement to us. What we were going to have and that we might have to go on strike. And that didn't hit me too well. Going on strike, and we had just started working. But they took the other agreement that they had and they basically whipped the same language that they had in the other one into this one. We had guys like the job shop steward. That guy really wanted to push the union. He really had it in for corporations and he was a good union representative. And so I'd go to the meetings. And I started getting the hang of the meetings.

The mine consisted of two separate places. One was in New Mexico and the other was in Colorado. The agreement was the same and the payment was the same. But you had to have a job steward over there and one down here. I was pretty vocal when it came to a lot of things. And before long I got the job as an assistant job steward, and [the job steward], this guy Carlos,[14] quit and he went with the law enforcement. And I became the job steward for them then. And I was still pretty vocal and I still helped the guys out pretty good. I still understood the agreement. Anyway we went from a dollar seventy-five to ten cents an hour raise plus you work differential shifts. You know if you worked the swing, you'd get three cents more. If you worked the graveyard shift, you got a little more. Anyway we started to get better wages. And the fact that they came out of New Mexico wasn't too bad. It wasn't too prejudiced. But they brought their own people. Yet they brought a lot of Chicanos with them and a lot of Anglos. And there was not too much discrimination. And we started to get good wages with the union.

John Mansfield perlite processing plant.

Ethnicity and Class in the Union

Joe Taylor recalled how it was impossible to separate ethnicity and class in his confrontations with management while working for the union. He recounted what happened when he faced the "Miner" brothers, a pseudonym for the managers of the John Mansfield processing plant, right next to the one owned by Great Lakes Carbon. The Miner brothers were Anglos who belonged to a community north of Antonito.

John Mansfield was the competitor to Great Lakes Carbon, and they wanted our wages. They wanted better wages. And I don't mind saying there were the Miner brothers. They were the prospectors who found the perlite for John Mansfield, which gave them a choice. They'd give them so much per ton for the rest of their lives or they'd give them one lump sum to buy their claim from them. And they figured, everybody figured that nothing ever lasted here. So the perlite wasn't going to last. And they were a fly-by-night outfit. So

these Miner brothers decided that they wanted one lump sum. But then John Mansfield offered them a job supervising the mining over here. Anyway I was working with Great Lakes Carbon, and this Michael had a lot of confidence in me because he liked the way that I used to voice my opinion. That I understood the agreement. That if you had a grievance, you had a grievance on that one specific deal, not the whole agreement, you didn't sit there and argue the whole thing. So these guys from John Mansfield wanted to join the union. There were a lot of them. We finally got enough of them to sign up so they could have an election.

But then these Miner brothers, they were very prejudiced. Because the whites had the better jobs. I don't mind saying it. And I don't care what anybody says. The whites had the better jobs, and the Chicano people were the labor part. And so we started negotiating wages for the people, and the union was beginning to be pretty good. We had pretty good wages. And one thing that a person never had over here was good credit. You couldn't buy anything because you didn't have a good secure job. And once you started with GrefCo (or John Mansfield) you'd go on over there to the bank and you could borrow money. Only if you were working for the union, you could get money. But there was still a lot of discrimination going on over here. There was still that separation between the white, the Anglo, the gringo we used to call them, and the Chicano, the Mexicano.

And anyway, Michael sent me over to this John Mansfield to do a couple of things for him. Our main office was in Colorado Springs, and the only communication that we had real quick was by telephone. And then there was a time limit when you felt that you had to file a grievance. There were only so many hours before you filed a grievance. So that was the job of the job steward. And if Michael wasn't down here, he made me a part-time business agent for him over here. So when I went to file a grievance, settle a grievance one time at John Mansfield, the guy said, "Hey, you got no business in here. To begin with you work for Great Lakes Carbon. You don't work over here. You can't come over here and tell me what to do."

And I said, "Well, I'm here. I've got this grievance. And I'd like to sit down and discuss it."

He said, "Nah. I'm tired of you Mexicans coming over here and trying to tell us what to do. We've been organized over here for a long time."

I said, "Well, I have this grievance over here."

And he took the grievance and he read it and he says, "Oh," he said, "didn't I tell you?"

And I said, "No, you didn't tell me."

He said, "We brought that out in church the other day and we settled it in church."

And I said, "Hey, let's get one thing straight," I told him. "We don't go to your church and tell you how to run your church." I said, "But your church isn't going to come on over here and tell us how to run the union, how to run our agreement."

"Well," he said, "that's done. That's the way it is. Besides, I don't even want you in my office. Get out!"

So I got out and I called my boss and I told him what went on. The main office was in Denver then. The John Mansfield office was in Denver. And boy he got word to the Miners over here that if I wanted to go over there, that if I was sent by Local 146, that Miner better listen to me. And he said, "Well," he said, "maybe he might listen to me."

And when I went in there, Bud Miner usually avoided me and had one of the other guys, one of his other workers, a supervisor of whatever it was, handle the grievance. He didn't even want to face me. Because he didn't like me. Because I was stepping on his toes, and he didn't like that. They'd never done that to him. He was an elder in his church or whatever it was. And then he was a supervisor over here. He thought he was above God and the law. Anyway we went and negotiated an agreement with them, and what you call your demands of the employees. One is the language and the other one is money. You separate the two. You propose your demands, and then that's what negotiations are all about. But they didn't want to give us anything. And so we had to go on strike against John Mansfield to get the money. And those people were really mad then. The Miner brothers were very, very mad because we were disrupting their little kingdom. His little world that he had there. He was no longer in control of his workers and he didn't run them the way he wanted to. And so we went on strike. And he was very bitter. And after so many days of crossing the picket lines and fighting and people that were crossing the picket lines, John Mansfield decided that they wanted to settle. Give them so much money. And the Miner brothers were pretty snobbish about the first leg of the agreement. They still wanted to do it their way.

I went to fight a grievance for one guy that was there. His name was Hernández, Juan Hernández.[15] They didn't want to give him a raise. They figured the only thing he was good for was for sweeping. They didn't want to give him a raise on the dump truck or whatever it was because they felt he was illiterate. They had my *raza* down on the lower paying jobs sweeping and doing the cleaning and doing all the hard labor. The white boys were up above. And the white boys didn't like the union because they were being pushed out of their little cozy nests. And they were against the union. But there was still a majority of the workers there that wanted the union. That they wanted to advance, and the only way to advance was get to a better paying job. And then they could go like everybody else, go to the bank and get a loan if they went from one of the outfits. They'd lend you the money for a car.

And anyway, those four years of that agreement passed pretty rough. We had a lot of difficulties with management. And we had a lot of grievances with management. And we had a lot of grievances that reached the third level, which was to arbitrate them with the federal mediator. And it was costing John Mansfield too much money to come down over here. And the union didn't care because that was what they were supposed to do. And by the time the other agreement came up, there were more demands giving the workers a lot freer hand. A lot more rights to fight back. And the Miner brothers didn't like that. One did whatever his older brother said. His older brother would go tell him, "Tell those two guys over there, put them to work regardless of what the seniority was. The seniority status." And he'd put his favorite ones, pets, favoritism, on the easier jobs, and he'd give the guys with more seniority the other jobs. And when they complained against him, he said, "Oh that's what Bud told me." He said, "Go settle with Bud."

So they filed a grievance, and we'd have to come. And Bud used to just hate to see me go on in there. He just hated to confront me. So it came pretty close to the end of the four-year agreement for that contract. And we had to renew the contract. And we had to go on strike again. And we had the same problems with the Miner brothers. And finally they [John Mansfield] told the Miner brothers, "You're going to have to do this. You're going to have to give in to their demands. They're going to have to have this many rights. And you're going to have to just go by it."

And Bud Miner says, "I don't think that I have to take that."

And I wasn't there, but I heard that they told him, "Well, the choice is yours."

And Bud Miner said, "Well, I don't know that I want to go on over there and be told what to do by a bunch of Mexicans."

"Hey," they told him, "make up your mind."

And he said, "Well, I don't think I want to go."

And they told him, "All right, if you don't want to go, you just pick up your paycheck and pick up your brother, and both of you get out of here."

Because they thought they had a lifetime job here. But they didn't have a lifetime job, and both of them were fired. And I tell you that Bud Miner, I saw him a couple of times, one time in a drugstore here in town, and boy, if looks could kill, I'd have been dead then.

Opposition to the Union

One evening we watched *Salt of the Earth,* a film about the zinc miners' strike in Bayard, New Mexico.[16] The striking miners were Mexicanos like the ones who worked for John Mansfield and Great Lakes Carbon. I asked if the film reminded him of the early union years in Antonito. **Well, it reminds me more or less of the first strike we had over here because it was very primitive compared to other places that had been union already for years. You're [not] in a big town over here. You're sort of in the boonies. Pueblo, for example, was all union** at one time. Practically everything was union. Sometimes even the people that worked in the bars were union, and you got a lot of support from the people. But you take the rural areas over here, and nobody is supporting your strike over here, except you. People over here were strictly against unions to begin with because they never had a union before.[17] I've heard it said time and again: "You don't even have a pot to pee in or window to throw it out of and here you are sticking your nose into that other person's business. Why don't you just do for yourself and let them do for themselves." There's no unity. Instead of banding together, you just separate yourselves.

Joe Taylor described how resistance to the union was particularly acute during one strike and told about the complications he faced when he set up a picket line at the perlite plants south of town. People thought they could just cross our picket line, and there were people that crossed our picket line, although we stood and we shouted in front of them. We didn't touch them. We just told them, "Don't cross our picket line." And we made some other statements we shouldn't have like, "You've got to sleep tonight and your house might be set on fire." And stuff like that because that's the only defense we thought we had. Bad feelings continued between those who walked the picket lines and those who crossed them for years afterward.

The second and more serious problem occurred when some of the strikers turned against their own people. It is not bad to see a guy here from town going over and crossing your picket line and going to work for the company to replace you. But it is bad when one of the people that was on strike with you decides that he doesn't want to go on strike anymore. He thinks he made a mistake by going on strike and he's being pressed for the payment for his pickup and his house and everything else and he crosses the picket line. Those are the people that hurt. Your own members crossing the picket line. Those are the people that hurt us the worst. And then after you settle the strike, they're branded. They might as well be brownnoses [lambes]. During all this time you do have to represent them and you have to accept them and you have to work with them, but you've lost that respect for them. And that respect you're never going to give them back.

Complicating matters is the strength of kinship ties, which make the problem of one the problem of many. **In a small community like this one, one member over here affects ten people around him. You have influence over ten people around you. Through relatives, through your mom and your dad and your sisters and your brothers and your in-laws. It's the same thing in politics. If you're a politician over here, and let's say you have the last name of Ruybal, you sure know that you're going to get a lot of votes because you're a Ruybal and they say that blood is thicker than water.**

In mentioning the importance of family ties, Joe Taylor introduced the topic of his place in Antonito's social structure. In the next chapter, he will present his recollection of the complicated intersection of family, class, and race in the valley's hierarchical world.

CHAPTER 5

➤ SOCIAL STRUCTURE

The roots of Joe Taylor's moral vision extend deep into his past and include the years when he came of age, from about 1943 to 1955. This twelve-year period began when he and his family moved across the valley from El Rito and ended when he graduated from Antonito's high school and went into the army. In Antonito, a relatively rigid hierarchical social structure was firmly in place by 1943; by 1955 there were signs that this structure was beginning to crumble. Joe Taylor recalls that structure as a pyramid with Anglos at the top, wealthy Mexicano ranchers below them, and Mexicano workers at the bottom.

The development of ethnic and class divisions on the western side of the valley was like that for the region as a whole, judging from Sarah Deutsch's historical study of the Upper Rio Grande basin.[1] From the Treaty of Guadalupe Hidalgo in 1848 to the outbreak of World War II, increased ethnic tension between Anglos and Mexicanos appeared together with intensified social stratification. In 1900 the Mexicanos of Antonito organized the first of eight Colorado branches of the Sociedad Protección Mutua de Trabajadores Unidos (S.P.M.D.T.U.) to fight Anglo discrimination.[2] Anglo racism and nativism increased in the 1920's during the post–World War I depression in agricultural prices. The Ku Klux Klan operated in southern Colorado in the 1920's, and Anglos referred to Mexicanos as "Mexican greasers" and "foreigners." During the Great Depression, the tension between the two groups only increased in many places, including the San Luis Valley.[3]

Meanwhile, a new class of *ricos,* wealthy Mexicanos who readily adapted to the Anglo-Saxon–dominated economy, appeared after the Treaty of Guadalupe Hidalgo in 1848.[4] A Mexicana woman in Antonito, who with her late husband was a prosperous sheep rancher during much of the twentieth century, defined a *rico* as someone with "money and ranches and animals and cows and water."[5] Deutsch noted that the appearance of *ricos* meant "increasing stratification" that threatened the egalitarian values of former village life.[6] These two trends—Anglo racism and the appearance of *ricos*—occurred at about the same time on the Antonito side of the valley.

Ethnic Relations

Joe Taylor and his friend Manuel Ortiz recalled the racial climate in the valley during the 1940's and 1950's.

Joe Taylor: **Well, a *huero* [white man][7] used to come over here and have a lot of authority, right? They used to look up to a *huero* at one time.**

Manuel: **People were stupid as hell. Years ago they were mean with the Hispanic people in Monte Vista. And then the kids after World War number two, they really beat the shit out of the Anglos over in Monte Vista. They straightened 'em out. You couldn't go to a restaurant there in Monte Vista. "No Mexicans are allowed." They were mean. Man, those kids after World War number two, they weren't going to take no shit from nobody. They had a free-for-all in Monte Vista. They raised Cain with all the Anglos, boy! Then they settled down. That's when I was in Center. That was the last time they had to be settled down. In Monte Vista they were rude. Well, even over here they rude. They were bad over here.**

Joe Taylor: **I know Alamosa was. Because in Alamosa, there was that theater over there, not the Rialto, the other one. The Globe. The Globe theater in Alamosa. They had a sign up, "No Mexicans allowed."**

Manuel: **I went to a restaurant. They didn't tell me anything but they wouldn't serve me a meal. They would serve everybody else. That's why I went to Center. "Shit, I won't stay over here if they won't serve me." Well those kids after World War number two, they straightened everything out. You know, what is right is right. But there was a lot of discrimination. Even over here in Antonito.**

Joe Taylor: **When the lumber mills were over here, that was in fifty, or however early they came, there was the Cumbres Café. They wouldn't allow black people in the Cumbres Café. Right here in our own hometown they would not allow black people in the Cumbres Café.**

The Big Fight

In the years after the war, ethnic tensions broke out at football games, and many in Joe Taylor's generation remembered the big fight in 1952 when the team from Del Norte came south to play Antonito on their home field. Joe Taylor played fullback and linebacker for several years on the Antonito team, and he and Manuel recalled how the fight started.

Joe Taylor: **Do you remember the big football fight they had on the football field here with Del Norte?**

Manuel: **Yeah. I remember that. I was there. Was it Monte Vista?**

Joe Taylor: **Del Norte. Well, I was in that game. And we were playing the game and we'd fall over on their side, and they'd kick us and they'd shout at us that we were Mexicans and catlickers. That was what they called a Catholic. A catlicker and Mexicans and everything. And we fought through the game. And I remember running on their side and then getting tackled and falling right pretty close to the sidelines, and the spectators would go on over there and kick you. They would actually kick you. And then, after the game was over, this guy by the name of Abraham Lobato, he used to play end. He went and told the other players, "Hey, good game."**

And the guy told him, "Ah, get out of here, you Mexican." And he pushed him. I remember.

And Abraham said, "Did you see what that guy did?"

And I said, "I saw what he did."

I went over to the guy, man, and I punched him right in the face. I didn't even move him. I remember the guy's name. And the other players went at it, buddy! And then the spectators came in. And then everybody was fightin', man!

Manuel: **I was there.**

Joe Taylor: **Yeah.**

Manuel: **Even old man Curtis and his son, he was for Antonito. He was for Antonito.**

Joe Taylor: **Yeah, they were knocking people down left and right. And then the coach, a big old redheaded coach, went over there and he said, "You guys get over here."**

And my dad didn't understand English good. He thought he was cussing us. And man, he went and laid him out, man. He hit him. Even the women were fighting on that one.

Manuel: **Oh, it was big brawl. That was a fight. No?**

Joe Taylor: **That was a fight.**

Manuel: **It was a racial thing.**

The Antonito Pyramid

The social structure of Antonito was divided along class as well as ethnic lines during the forties and fifties. Joe Taylor remembered how the racial and class divisions were manifest in the town's geographical layout in the 1940's. Antonito was a grid bisected by the railroad track, running north and south, and by Eighth Street, going east and west. Immediately after the town's founding in 1880,[8] most of the stores and commercial buildings were on Front Street, which was adjacent to the railroad track on the east. Businesses moved to Main Street, the highway that runs just west of the tracks, as cars and trucks became more important.

In Joe Taylor's memory, workers, *ricos,* and wealthy Anglos lived in different sections of the town.[9] Many wealthy Anglos and a few of the *ricos* lived on River and Pine Streets from Eighth to the southern edge of town. River Street, which runs parallel to Main Street and one block to the west, was called *la calle de los ricos* (the street of the rich). Pine is one block west of River. The northern half of town beginning with Eighth Street was known as México (or in English as "Mexican Town") and included the homes of a few wealthy Mexicano ranchers and many Spanish-speaking families of workers who labored on the ranches and farms of the *ricos* and wealthy Anglos.

From Joe Taylor's perspective, the wealthy Anglos were at the top of the class hierarchy. He used the example of marriage to illustrate how the class system worked. A Mexicano seeking to move up in the

Main Street in Antonito looking south.

social structure might marry an Anglo: **A well-educated Chicano man would not come back and marry a Chicana woman. He'd marry an Anglo woman. A very well educated Chicana woman would not come back and marry a Chicano man. She'd marry an Anglo. That was sort of "class" in those days.** The judge in *Alex and the Hobo* is modeled after Mexicano men who married Anglo women. Although a remote figure in the story, he is nevertheless a key person in the corrupt conspiracy that enabled Greg to blame the hobo for China's murder. Although reluctant to identify the judge by name, Joe Taylor included him in his story to represent how some Mexicanos abused their positions of power in Antonito's hierarchical social structure. Joe Taylor also explained that in the early forties, few Spanish-speaking men married Anglo women. Instead, wealthy Mexicano ranchers tried to promote marriages between their children. **I know a lot of ranchers over here who were well-to-do. Their kids married other well-to-do ranchers' daughters or sons. They didn't come and marry the commoner here in town. A lady I knew was the most miserable**

lady that ever lived because she didn't marry whom she wanted to marry. She married whom her parents wanted her to marry.

As in Spain,[10] class divisions were maintained by controlling the behavior of women. The courtship practices, coupled with notions of family honor, supported marriage within the same social class and ethnic group. Joe reported that in the early 1940's, a woman's conduct affected her family's moral reputation. **Well, everybody was strict with their daughters. In those days, a woman had to keep up the morals. She couldn't be of loose morals because it offended the whole family. They judged the whole family by one character, by one member of the family. Well, actually [my father] wouldn't let my sisters do anything. Because if they went to the movies, they had to go as a group, and one of them had to be in charge of the other one. My parents wanted them to stay together. If they went to carnival, it was the same thing. And about the only time that they didn't care where you went, if you went by yourself or not, was when you went to church.**

A neighbor who fits the definition of a *rica* described her courtship and marriage in the early forties. She said her courtship period began when her father took her and her friends to dances held at the S.P.M.D.T.U. hall. He told her: **"You have to dance with all who ask you"** [Tienes que bailar con todos que te inviten]. A man who wanted to dance with a woman paid ten cents to escort his partner into the dance circle on the hardwood floor of the hall. Her suitor proposed to her on the dance floor after repeatedly paying a dime to enter the circle. This woman was reluctant to become engaged at first, but she recalled that the young man told his parents he was interested in her, and they spoke to her parents. A little later, he asked her parents for permission to come by on Sunday afternoons. She remembered that her mother and his mother spoke to her and convinced her to marry the man who became her husband. She told Carole Counihan she agreed to the marriage because her husband was a good worker.[11] Kinship and friendship played a role in her marriage, as it did in those of other men and women we have interviewed in our oral history project in Antonito. This *rica* was very good friends with her fiancé's sister, and they went together to the dances at the S.P.M.D.T.U. In many of the cases that came to our attention, the sibling tie was an important avenue to marriage: many married their friends' siblings.

Corruption

In the hierarchical social structure of Antonito during the 1940's and 1950's, there was a great deal of corruption, which Joe Taylor characterized as abuse of power. He recalled that Anglos and *ricos* who owned businesses in town—store, cafes, and service stations— sometimes harassed and exploited their workers, many of whom were Mexicanos. Joe Taylor recalled instances of employers pulling the blouses of women workers and dropping money into their bodices. The Mexicanas who were the victims still burst into tears when they recall these experiences. As Joe Taylor explained, the same women were expected by their parents to maintain their moral reputations by following the strict courtship practices described earlier. Many Mexicanas were afraid to tell their parents about what happened at work and thus had to keep their harassment to themselves. Some parents were quick to accuse their daughters of bringing on the advances of their *rico* or Anglo employers. Joe Taylor explained that Mexicano workers rarely took action against their corrupt employers, particularly in town, because they could not afford to lose their jobs.

In his story, Joe Taylor decided to represent the corrupt Mexicanos in town with Greg, the marshal, and the judge. Although he identified only Greg as the owner of a business—he sold insurance— all three stand for a hierarchical power structure that enabled *ricos* and Anglos to mistreat and sexually harass their workers. The judge and the marshal represent the law of the hierarchical social structure of the town, in which employers had a great deal of power. Greg sells insurance, which has the ostensible purpose of protecting those who are vulnerable, but he murders China. I think Joe Taylor made China's murder the central crime in his story because it is a dramatic metaphor for the sexual harassment of Mexicana workers that took place in the 1940's and 1950's—harassment that he recalls with anger to this day. He used imagery strongly suggesting she was the victim of a sexual assault. When describing what Didi found when she went into China's house, he wrote: **There she saw China's partially nude body lying on the floor with an expression on her face indicating she had died a horrible death.**

Mexicano workers were sometimes victims of other Mexicanos, those who held intermediary positions in the organization of labor in the fields on the western side of the valley north of Antonito. Two important examples of those in intermediary positions were the field boss and the truck driver. Both were part of an economic organization that included the contractor, who purchased the crop from the landowner. The commercial crops grown in the southwestern corner of the valley were usually peas, potatoes, sugar beets, cauliflower, and string beans. Joe Taylor explained that around Antonito itself **there were few people that really went into the pea business and the potato business. There were some but they were very few. But we moved a little north around La Jara and Sanford, and those people were Anglos who did go into the pea and potato business.**

Contractors were usually Anglos and they typically hired Mexicano field bosses. Joe Taylor explained that **a *huero* field boss would not last. They'd probably kick his butt and send him out. It was sort of insulting to have a *huero* field boss there. And besides, he didn't know the people. He didn't know the language. Well, to tell you the truth, we just didn't get along with the whites.** A field boss was called a *mayordomo* or *caporal*. He supervised the workers, who were generally Mexicanos. During World War II, they included children, women, and men too old for military service. There were two categories of workers—those who actually picked the crops in the field and those who worked in the sheds packing and loading the crops into railroad cars for shipment out of the valley. The pickers tended to be younger children (some only seven or eight years old), women, and older men. Older boys, like Alex's older brother Lupe, usually worked in the loading sheds, where they made wooden crates, filled them with produce, and loaded them into refrigerated box cars.

The truck driver operated independently, charging a quarter to transport workers to and from the field. He also used his truck to transport crops to the sheds, and his wife often went to the fields in a separate car carrying soda pop to sell to the workers. Truck drivers from Antonito were typically Mexicanos, whereas those from towns to the north were sometimes Anglos.

In Joe Taylor's memory, field bosses and truck drivers had quite of bit of power and sometimes took advantage of workers. Field bosses had the power to fire workers, making them stand at the edge of the field until the workday was over. Some field bosses took advantage of their power by pushing independent-minded workers around and even sexually harassing the women working under their authority. The truck driver expected fired workers to pay the quarter for transport back to the home community. Truck drivers sometimes exploited workers by asking them to load and unload their trucks without pay. Workers did not earn an hourly salary and were only paid for crops they picked by the row, the bushel (peas), or the half-sack (potatoes). The contractors provided thirty-gallon milk cans filled with water that was often unfit to drink and that made the workers sick. In Joe Taylor's view, some truck drivers' wives took advantage of workers by selling them soda pop when they knew that they did not have access to clean water in the field.

Some field bosses and truck drivers empathized with the plight of workers and did not try to abuse their power. One example is the truck driver Max in *Alex and the Hobo,* who cared about what happened to the workers he transported to the field, expressed sympathy for their hardships, and criticized the contractor for sending them out to work in the rain and the mud. Joe Taylor identified some of the conditions that encouraged a Mexicano truck driver like Max to sympathize with the plight of the workers. **Well, the truck drivers (like Max) were the people you lived with every day. They were people that lived in your community. They were people that sent their kids to your school. They were people who went to the same church that you did. You were from this community and you were very small and everybody knew everybody else. So he was sympathetic with his employees because they made his livelihood. They paid twenty-five cents every time, every day, per employee. That's what you paid for him to take you to the field and back. You were part of his livelihood.**

However, these social pressures were not enough to keep other Mexicanos in intermediate positions from abusing their power. The field boss who fondled Olivia in *Alex and the Hobo* is an example. Joe Taylor based this episode on an actual experience of seeing his older sister, Tonita, fondled when they were working in a field north of Antonito. **They would send me and her to go pick peas. Up to today, we're very, very close. We were like two peas in a pod. They would send us out to do most of the work when the other ones got a little older and left. There wasn't a woman that went out in the fields that wasn't sexually harassed. I saw it happening over there. But a lot of them would keep their mouth shut in order to keep peace in the family. The field bosses were out there and were going over and talking to the girls and looking down their blouses or trying to. And they had the authority, and the poor girls, some of them liked it but the majority of them didn't. And there was very little that they could do about it because if they fired you, you'd have to come in and explain to your dad why you were fired from the field.**

I asked: In the story, you have Alex jumping the guy. Literally jumping on top of him. And you did that?

I did that for my sister. And this guy went and slapped me all over the field. But then that was the biggest mistake he ever made. But at the time he didn't know. I grew up fast and every time I saw him, I'd plow him into the ground. And I'd kick his butt and if he was drinking a bottle of wine, I'd go just take the bottle of wine deliberately away from him and keep it myself. And there was nothing he could do. I'd defy him to do something about it. These guys, they were over there thinking they were all big and macho. Their day came and they got their butt kicked. They got their butt kicked for a long time because of a couple of little gestures that they did.

I said: "In the story, you have Olivia also getting hit because she resisted."

Well, when she jumped in for her brother, then she got pushed, and they said, "If you guys want to keep your job, you just go back on over there." And everybody was there, but nobody told my dad. Because if my dad would have got a hold of that guy, he'd have killed him. And then he'd have wanted to know why my sister got fondled. Did she provoke it? Because that was a man's world then. It was strictly a man's world.

I asked: Now when your sister, Tonita, saw that you were being slapped around when you jumped on this guy to defend her, did she jump to your rescue and did get she hurt?

She didn't get hurt because she used to get a whipping every day. It hurt a heck of a lot more when we'd get a whipping from our parents. But she did jump in for me and [she] wasn't the only one. There was a bunch of other little kids. And hooting and hollering and everything else like when you're trying to scare off a big bear. Eventually he gets intimidated. He just walks away. But it did happen. It happened that way. It happened to a million girls that were out there.

The *Lambe*

In the hierarchical social structure that Joe Taylor described for Antonito in the 1940's and 1950's, Mexicano workers directed a great deal of hostility toward those among them who appeared oriented toward the top of the class pyramid. A Mexicano who seemed to curry favor with those in positions of wealth and power or who aspired to obtain such a position was liable to be considered a *lambe* (brownnose). The word comes from the Spanish verb *lamer* (to lick) and noun *lamedor* (licker) and carries a very negative connotation. Joe Taylor considered a *lambe* to be a particularly odious person who was corrupted by greed. He applied the term to a Mexicano who acted big and sold out his own people for personal advantage.[12]

He explained his feelings toward a Mexicano who tried to change his class position and acted big while remaining in Antonito. **If that guy went and picked peas with you, and later on he wanted to better himself, and he bettered himself, and he came back, you never placed him in that other bracket. You always placed him where you knew him. And if he did come on over here, you'd probably take him out to a back alley and kick his butt because he was acting . . . *lambe* is what you'd call him. Greed is what creates all these things. Greed for maybe power, greed for money. To me, the key word in this whole thing is greed.**

The *lambe* might be a rich man's field boss—a *mayordomo*, *caporal*—or a foreman, particularly if he did not maintain his loyalties to Mexicanos who were workers. Speaking in Spanish, Joe Taylor explained. **If he were a rich man's foreman and he had thirteen men working under him and he had the job of putting them to work, it would be hard for this foreman to go into town to a dance or another place without being hassled. The rich man would tell him, "You have to do this, you have to do the other thing." He'd do what they told him to and in that way he'd hurt a lot of feelings. And when he went into town, as they say, they'd hunt him out.**

Joe Taylor recalled the time he was picking potatoes north of Antonito when he was about the same age as Alex. **There was this forty-acre field, and it took us a long time to finish that field. They were paying by the half-sack. They'd give you twenty-five half-sacks, and they'd give you a little stub to keep track. We finished that field, and then they moved us to another field, and in that field there were potatoes that you wouldn't believe. We were whooping and hollering and saying we were going to get rich on that field. But we suddenly stopped when we were told they were going to pay us by the row. And it would take us practically a whole day to take one row.** He mentioned this experience more than any other anecdote when critiquing the class system on the western side of the valley.

Street Fights

One effect of the class system was to increase tension and anger among Mexicanos, which erupted in fights at dances, in bars, and on the streets of Antonito during the 1940's and 1950's. In Joe Taylor's opinion, Mexicanos fought with each other because they could not direct their anger toward those who oppressed them. He spoke in Spanish and I translated. **There was a lot of anger among the people here just because they discriminated so much. But the fights weren't against those who discriminated against you.** Gang violence, like that which James Diego Vigil reported for Los Angeles,[13] sometimes broke out on the streets of Antonito. Joe Taylor recalled the time when a gang of *pachucos* from Alamosa came into Antonito. He remembered the *pachucos* in the valley during the 1940's and 1950's as Mexicano adolescents who wore a distinctive style of dress, the zoot suit, and who spoke a dialect of Spanish called "caló." The zoot suit usually consisted of pants worn low and pegged at the bottom, a long sport jacket, a wide-brimmed fedora, often with a white band, shoes with wide soles painted white around the edges. A chain connected to the belt was attached to a knife or hard object that would come in handy in a fight. Caló, Joe Taylor recalled, included unusual grammatical constructions such as the greeting, "¿Qué húbole ése?" for "What's happening, man?" and "¡Chále ése!" for "No way, man!" Joe Taylor remembered *pachucos* bobbing as they walked down the streets of Alamosa, Monte Vista, and Antonito. He noted that they smoked marijuana, which they called *yerba* (weed),[14] something Joe Taylor's parents strongly discouraged. James Olmos immortalized their distinctive style of dress, speech, and gait in the film *Zoot Suit*.[15]

The *pachuco* gang that came to Antonito was looking for "El Chile," a rival gang member, but they attacked "Liono" Ruybal in a case of mistaken identity. (Joe Taylor's friend, Liono later became a Chicano and, together with Pete De Herrera, filed a complaint against the school board superintendent, which led to the bitter school strike in 1980.) Joe Taylor recalled that **it was about fifty-two. There were two boys here called Lionel. One of them lived in Mogote, and the other lived here in Antonito and they called him "El Chile." And Liono (from Mogote) wasn't a troublemaker, he wasn't a fighter, and El Chile went with another group that liked to fight. I'm not signaling him out as bad. He was in with this gang and he had been with them for a long time. And some boys from Alamosa came, and this guy Liono from Mogote was coming out of the pool hall, and they shouted, "Lionel!" That was his name. And one of them shouted, "Are you Lionel?" And he said, "Yes." Then they jumped out of the car and attacked him. They beat him up. And when they beat him up, then the whole town came together. Because this boy played football. It seems to me it was football season. I don't remember if it was. But the whole town got together. I'd bet there were fifty people. They put those kids—the *pachucos* from Alamosa—in City Hall because they hunted them down. They dragged them to the City Hall. And one of them tried to run away. And the entire town went after him and they found him there by the incinerator. When they found him there, it would have been better if that kid hadn't fled because** when they found him, they beat him up completely. They kicked him and everything.

Respect

Anger erupting in violence among Mexicanos was related to prevailing notions of manhood, according to which a man had to show his willingness to defend himself in a fight. A man had to maintain his respect, and this required, among other things, that he not be a coward lest other men **eat him alive.** Joe Taylor explained, speaking in Spanish, and I translated. **Those who were looking for a fight, the drunks and the ones looking for trouble, they knew who they could mess with and who they couldn't. A docile man, well it would be better if he didn't go to a dance because when I was a boy like in forty-five, when I was still very young, very small, if there weren't any deaths, if there had been a dance and there weren't any fights. . . . Not once [did that happen]. I can't remember, nor do I think that anyone else would remember, a dance where there wasn't a fight, because it was part of the grand finale.**[16]

However, he explained that respect also involved other qualities that were part of a man's moral reputation. **If you were a good person, and you go out, there would be a lot of respect. Yes, there was a lot of respect among men.** A good man was brave, he was not a *lambe.* He maintained his loyalties to other Mexicanos, particularly workers, stood up for other men and women, was a man of his word, and hated corruption. To provide a fuller picture of a good man who maintained his respect among other men, I turn in the next chapter to Joe Taylor's description of his father, Anastacio Taylor.

 **ANASTACIO TAYLOR**

Joe Taylor's father, Anastacio, and the protagonist of *Alex and the Hobo,* Alex Martínez, have a lot in common: they both recognized and stood up to corruption. Joe's father was a central force in defining his moral vision. When Joe Taylor was the same age as Alex, he learned a great deal about his father while spending time in Anastacio's *zapatería* (cobbler shop). The shop was a little community center where many paid a visit to "old man Taylor" and talked about what was taking place in Antonito. Joe heard stories of corruption and of his father standing up to town officials who abused their positions of power. Anastacio was a model of the masculinity toward which Joe Taylor and his protagonist, Alex, aspired. Alex stood up to corrupt authority when he foiled the plot to blame the hobo for a crime he did not commit.

Joe Taylor spent hours in his father's *zapatería* when not working in the fields or going to school. **When we were kids, the first thing we would do, we'd rush home. Right? And we'd change clothes. Nobody used the same clothes. You had your school clothes and shoes and everything, and you'd change and then you'd run back to the shoe shop. And you'd stay in the shoe shop until the end, until four, five o'clock. Six o'clock. And Saturday was a very, very busy day so you'd stay in there sometimes until eight or nine o'clock at night. But as long as that shop was open, we stayed there. He knew where we were and he didn't want us going into the pool halls. Later on we'd sneak into a pool hall, but later on. If they'd told us not to go to church, we'd have snuck in the church just to defy them.**

My dad's shop was a community center because people would go on in there and they would talk to my dad. Whenever a guy would

Anastacio Taylor's *zapatería*.

come into town and he's from out in the country, the guy says, "Hey, I'm going to see Taylor, viejo Taylor, old man Taylor." So they'd go on over there and they'd talk to my dad until the women finished shopping. Or they'd say, "I'm going to take a pair of shoes to old man Taylor." It only takes five minutes to bring a pair of shoes, but they would stay there for quite a while. They would catch him up on what was going on. But that's the kind of a shop my dad had. It was like a little community center. Everybody would go sit in there. I used to know a guy who worked as a butcher. And he liked his drink. And he used to buy a bottle of wine and take it to my dad's shop, where we had a couple of little compartments in back of the shop, where we kept our coal and a bathroom. And he'd sneak out of the grocery and go on over there and take a nip of his whisky, and [my dad] covered up for him because he was a good man. He was raising a family. But there is always that person that has a weakness for alcohol. So all kinds of people used to go down and see my dad for one reason or another.

Learning about Corruption

Joe recalled learning about corruption through his dad in the *zapatería*. **People who had problems with the law, they thought the law had done them an injustice, would go to my dad. And my dad knew that some of the cops were corrupt. And he wasn't afraid of the cops—he'd go face them—because they knew better. They couldn't jail my dad. They wouldn't jail my dad. That's one thing you just didn't do. They accepted him. They accepted him when he criticized them, and they wouldn't take him to jail. The cops that were over here, they respected my dad. They respected my dad immensely. And they wouldn't put him in jail.**

One reason Anastacio Taylor garnered so much respect was that **he was a good man and he was very big. My father was six feet one or two inches in height. And he was a very strong man. And there were bad people here, but the bad people didn't mess with him. Perhaps with others, yes, with others who were more docile, other men who'd take more punishment, they'd get it. With my dad, no. He wasn't a bad man, he was a good one. But the bad ones didn't bother him. The bad people didn't bother him because, as he would say, "I'd straighten them out"** [*los compongo*].

Joe Taylor recalled his father standing up to corrupt cops who took advantage of sheepherders and merchants who came into town. **The sheepherders saw the law as somebody to look up to and they'd come in with big amounts of money and they'd give it to this certain cop. And then they'd go out and get drunk with every intention or hope that that cop was going to have their money taken care of. The following day when they'd go pick up their money when they'd sober up, this cop would tell them, "Hey, when you were drunk last night, you don't remember, you come in here and you begged me for the money and I gave it to you."**

And the guy says, "Hey," he says, "there's a lot of things that I can do when I'm drunk but I think I would've remembered that."

People used to come in from New Mexico with their produce, to come and sell it over here. And [a cop would] say: "If you want to sell

in my town, you give me so much fruit, so many watermelons, so much this and so much that."

That was corrupt. That was corrupt. And he used his authority to steal. That's what it was. Then a lot of these people used to come to my dad and complain. And my dad said: "We know it's true. We know what kind of a man he is."

He got a petition to get this man fired. One time he went around and got a petition because he saw the corruption of this man. Yet when he submitted his petition to the town board members, they rejected it. And they kept that cop on because they said he was a good man and this and that, but they were in cahoots like [in] *Alex and the Hobo.* The judges and the town board and all of that, there was corruption. They had their little clique and that is a fact. And most of these guys are dead, and I knew most of 'em. And I believe in life after death and I know some of these guys are being punished right today.

Anastacio Taylor's Independence

Joe Taylor mentioned Anastacio Taylor's independence as one of the reasons he stood up to the corrupt officials in his community. For one thing, Anastacio did not have close kin in Antonito, his adopted town, who might have drawn him into corrupt schemes to promote their special interests. Also, as a cobbler with his own shop, he had a comparatively independent economic position in his community. He did not work for wages on the farms and ranches of the wealthy Anglos and Mexicano *ricos.* He performed a valuable service by repairing the shoes and the boots of the workers and landowners alike. Historically, such artisans have been relatively independent. E. P. Thompson noted that cobblers and other artisans were very independent politically during the early stages of the Industrial Revolution in England. Cobblers were among the original members of the "London Corresponding Society" (LCS), which was the first manifestation of working-class consciousness in England. The first meeting of the LCS took place in 1792, soon after the French Revolution of 1789, and was influenced by the Jacobin ideas of equality and democracy. Thompson also noted

that cobblers were among the artisans in Paris who "took the doc-
trines of Paine to their extreme—absolute political democracy; root-
and-branch opposition to monarchy and the aristocracy, to the
State and to taxation."[1] E. P. Thompson's description of English
cobblers as "radical," "independent," and "insubordinate"[2] could
apply to Anastacio Taylor, even though Anastacio lived during a different time and in a different place.

The move from El Rito to Antonito, occasioned by a business
difficulty that Joe Taylor's father experienced in San Luis, where his
former cobbler shop was located, was a dramatic transition that left
a strong impression on Joe Taylor's historical imagination. Living
through the move must have seemed like entering the world of modern capitalism for the first time.

To be sure, not everyone got along in El Rito, and there was corruption when some took advantage of their positions of power to
feather their own nests. Joe Taylor recalled that his grandfather, José
Inez Mondragón, got into a fight with his neighbors over water rights.
Joe Taylor's uncles had a parting of the ways, and one took his large
family to live with Joe Taylor's parents, Anastacio Taylor and Beatri z
Mondragón. Anastacio Taylor himself ran into problems that caused
him to move his family to Antonito in 1943. **One of the reasons that
we left El Rito was because another shoemaker turned my dad in because the other guy had a license. So my dad left and he came here.
I don't even know if he was fined or not. He settled over here for a
couple of reasons. It's because there was no shoemaker in this town.
There was a good school for his kids. It was pretty important to him
to give his kids as good of an education as he could.**

Anastacio Taylor's background in a small egalitarian *plaza* contributed to his unusual perspective on his adopted community of
Antonito. He probably witnessed corruption on a larger scale than
in El Rito. Corruption, as Joe Taylor explained, is the abuse of power
driven by greed, and Anastacio Taylor, who came from a kin-based
hamlet, was a generous man. Speaking in Spanish, Joe Taylor described his father's generosity. **My father was a very good man. I
think that is the reason he never had any money. He gave a lot to
people. They'd go to him to have their shoes fixed, and he would not**

charge them or he charged them and gave them credit, and they never paid him, and he didn't go after them. And they wouldn't pay him and they wouldn't pay him and he was fine about it and he didn't care what he had. He'd give it away. You'd go to his house when he was retired, and he'd give you dinner. He'd take trout to the nuns, to the priests, to everyone.

On another occasion, Joe Taylor elaborated in English on his father giving away the fish he caught in the streams and rivers around Antonito. He would give some to every businessman, he'd give some to the priest, he'd give some to the nuns. There were twenty-one nuns here at one time. Because I remember he used to count two fish for each nun. He'd put them in a big box with wax paper and, boy, he'd send us over there to take fish to the sisters, take fish to the priest, take fish to the doctor. He was a *granjeador, granjeaba*. He wasn't what you call a *cuzco*. A *cuzco* is a guy that hoards everything. He won't give anybody anything. He won't share. But my dad, no. If you came to his house, you ate, and if he had something, he'd give it to you.

Rubén Cobos defined *granjeador* as someone "who brings or works himself into another's favor."[3] From a historical and comparative perspective, a *granjeador* is someone who carries out what Marcel Mauss called "gift exchange," according to which the act of giving creates or maintains moral bonds with another person.[4] Being a *granjeador* fits being the member of a kin-based society, where family loyalties are very important. Joe Taylor's cousin remembered Anastacio as a *granjeador* when she knew him in El Rito. She said: We heard that he used to take candy with him. So everywhere he went, the kids would just [come], and he would give them candy. When Anastacio moved to Antonito, he had no close kinship ties and he continued to be a *granjeador* in order to create ties where none had existed before.

The opposite of a *granjeador* is a *cuzco*, someone who is greedy, hoggish, selfish, and stingy.[5] He is the employer who tries to get the most out of his work crews for as little pay as possible. He is the contractor who subjects his workers to the inhumane conditions that Joe described in *Alex and the Hobo*. The contrast between the *granjeador*

123

and the *cuzco* fits Joe Taylor's earlier comparison between the kin-based farming community of El Rito and the commercial center of Antonito. Agribusiness in general and the commercial enterprises around Antonito in particular generally operated on the *cuzco* rather than the *granjeador* principle at the time *Alex and the Hobo* was set.

"Juan Chililí Pícaro"

Joe Taylor recalled hearing his father tell a popular folktale that conveyed the limits of acting on the *granjeador* principle in the class system of Antonito. The story warned against being a *lambe* by currying favor with those in positions of power and stressed the importance of being a man of one's word (*palabra*). Joe Taylor considered the tale an allegory for Antonito's social structure and told the tale to me in 1998 in his secondhand shop, which at that time was on Main Street. The story is pretty well known among Spanish speakers in northern New Mexico and southern Colorado,[6] and Joe Taylor's particular version and interpretation of the story's meaning reveal how he and perhaps his father defined their social position in accord with their masculine moral vision.

The story is about a trickster named Juan Chililí Pícaro, who lives in a kingdom terrorized by a giant. A troublemaker tells the king that Juan Chililí bragged that he could steal the giant's mare, parrot, and eventually the giant himself. The king summons Juan Chililí Pícaro and orders him to make good on his boast. To Joe Taylor, the "kingdom" represented Antonito, and he expressed his perspective on that kingdom in the particular way that he told and interpreted this story. This is an English translation of the story he told me in Spanish in 1998:

This is the story of Juan Chililí Pícaro. And this happened a long time ago. There was a kingdom, and there lived the king. And the people of the kingdom were terrified of a giant who lived nearby. The giant had all of the people so terrified that no one went outside the walls of the kingdom out of fear of the giant. And there was a man in the kingdom whom they called Juan Chililí Pícaro. And for one reason or another, there was also this other man who did not like Juan Chililí Pícaro. And one day that man went and told the king,

"Listen, Your Highness," he said, "do you know that Juan Chililí Pícaro said he would dare to steal the giant's mare?"

The giant had a mare that no one could catch. It was the fastest mare in the kingdom. And the king replied, "Are you sure Juan Chililí Pícaro said that?"

"Yes," the man said.

"Well, run along. Tell Juan Chililí Pícaro to come see me."

The man went to where Juan Chililí Pícaro was working and announced, "The king wants to see you."

"What does the king want with me?" asked Juan Chililí Pícaro.

"I don't know. There is nothing for you to do but go, so he can tell you."

So Juan Chililí Pícaro went and said to the king, "Your Highness, you wanted to see me."

"Yes," said the king. "Someone told me you would dare to steal the giant's mare."

"No, Your Highness," replied Juan Chililí Pícaro. "I didn't say anything of the kind."

"Well, you're going to do it or suffer the pain of death," ordered the king.

Well, what else could Juan Chililí Pícaro do but heed this? And so he said, "Well, if I go, you'll have to give me some oats."

"Fine," agreed the king.

"I'm going to see if I can steal the giant's mare tonight," said Juan Chililí Pícaro.

And that night Juan Chililí Pícaro went into the giant's stable. He took a sack of oats and went to see if he could steal the giant's mare. Well, when he got there, he went into the stable where the giant's mare was and said, "Come on, little mare, eat some oats. Eat some oats."

And the mare started to take notice and whinny, and while she was taking notice and whinnying, making noise, she woke up the giant's wife. And the giant's wife said to her husband, "Someone is in the stable. Someone is in the stable."

So then the giant got up out of bed, and Juan Chililí Pícaro heard him coming. He heard the giant coming. And he went into a pile of straw. The giant had some straw for the mare to eat. So then Juan went under the pile of straw. There he hid. And the giant appeared and looked around and grabbed a pitchfork and stuck it into the pile of straw. He only wounded Juan Chililí Pícaro, who was hiding there. When the giant was satisfied there was no one there, he went back to bed. After the giant went away, Juan Chililí Pícaro came out of the pile of straw. He said again to the mare, "Come on, little mare, eat some oats. Eat some oats."

He tried to see if he could make the little mare come a little closer. And she started to eat the oats. Once the mare began eating the oats, Juan Chililí Pícaro put on her saddle, he put on her bridle, and he opened the stable door and left, fleeing on the mare. Well, no one could catch her because she was the fastest horse in the kingdom. And he took her to the king.

Well, that troublemaker wasn't satisfied. He was not satisfied. He went and told the king, "Listen, Your Highness, do you know what Juan Chililí Pícaro said?"

"What did Juan Chililí Pícaro say?" replied the king.

"Juan Chililí Pícaro said that he would dare to steal the giant's parrot."

"Are you sure Juan Chililí Pícaro said that?"

"Yes, I heard him today."

"Well, then, tell Juan Chililí Pícaro to come and see me."

Then the troublemaker went looking for Juan Chililí Pícaro. "The king wants to see you."

"Why does he want to see me *this* time?"

"I don't know. He just told me to tell you to go. He's coming to find you and he wants to see you."

So then Juan Chililí Pícaro went to see the king, and when he went to see the king, he spoke to him as he had done the first time. He said, "Here I am, Your Highness. You wanted to see me?"

"Yes," replied the king. "They told me you would dare to steal the giant's parrot."

"No, Your Highness," replied Juan Chililí Pícaro. "I haven't said any such thing."

"You do it or suffer the pain of death," said the king.

Well, Juan Chililí Pícaro told the king he would need a little bit of cheese. That night Juan Chililí Pícaro went to steal the giant's parrot. He went into the giant's house when the giant and his wife were asleep. And he went to where the parrot was and said, "Come on, little parrot, eat some cheese. Eat some cheese."

And the parrot started shouting, "Giant! Giant! Juan Chililí Pícaro is here and wants to steal me!"

So then the giant got up out of bed and chased after Juan Chililí Pícaro. He took him outside and tied him up. "You've already stolen my mare," he said. "Now you want to steal my parrot. As for what I'm going to do, I'm going to throw you into a kettle of water. We're going to cook you and eat you."

And Juan Chililí Pícaro couldn't say much. The next day, they had Juan Chililí Pícaro tied up. They put on the kettle of water, but they did not have enough firewood to heat the kettle. The giant said to his sister (or wife), "I'm going to the forest to bring some firewood. You watch this man. Don't let him get away because we're going to eat him. He is our dinner."

"Fine," said the giantess.

The giant went to look for and bring back some firewood to throw on the fire. And after he left, the giantess, who was nearly blind and couldn't see very well, had to bend over to see if the water was boiling. And Juan Chililí Pícaro, since he was a trickster and had his means, said to her, "Listen well, Mrs. Giant, you can't see. Why don't you untie me? I'll throw on the firewood and heat the kettle so you can cook me, so you may eat me."

"I shouldn't trust you," replied the giantess.

"Why not? Where am I going to go? I can't run away."

Well, the giantess trusted him. And Juan Chililí Pícaro went and threw more firewood onto the fire. Well, he got the kettle very hot. The water was boiling. And he said, "Giant sister, come here. Look and see if the water is hot enough."

And since the sister giant was blind, she stood on her tiptoes to see into the kettle. And Juan Chililí Pícaro came up behind her, he grabbed her, and pushed her, throwing her into the kettle. He cooked her and dashed into the house. He grabbed the parrot and put it into a sack and went to the plaza. He gave the parrot to the king. He brought it to the king and still the troublemaker was not satisfied. He went and spoke to the king. After Juan Chililí Pícaro had stolen the mare and stolen the parrot and killed the giantess, the troublemaker went and told the king, "Your Highness, do you know what Juan Chililí Pícaro said?"

"What did Juan Chililí Pícaro say?"

"Juan Chililí Pícaro said he would dare to steal the giant himself."

"Is it certain Juan Chililí Pícaro said that?"

"It's certain he said that."

"Run, bring Juan Chililí Pícaro here."

And the troublemaker went to Juan Chililí Pícaro and told him, "The king wants to see you now."

"And now what does the king want this time?" asked Juan Chililí Pícaro. "I'm getting tired of him making an ass out me."[7]

"I don't know why he wants you," replied the troublemaker. "But there is nothing else to do except go."

Juan Chililí Pícaro went for the third time. He said to the king, "Now, Your Highness, why did you call me again?"

"They've told me you would dare to steal the giant himself. If you steal the giant himself, we'll have a huge bonfire," said the king, "and burn him and we'll be rid of him. We'll be free to leave the kingdom and go to other lands. Now we're terrified of the giant. We can't go anywhere," declared the king.

"I said no such thing, Your Highness," replied Juan Chililí Pícaro.

"Well, now, Juan Chililí Pícaro, you go or face the pain of death. Now, what are you going to need?"

"I'm going to need a box, a cart with a team of draft animals, a hammer, and a handsaw."

"Fine."

Well, Juan Chililí Pícaro went to where the giant roamed during the day. And he put on a disguise. He put on a beard and a mustache and a wig of long hair so the giant wouldn't recognize him, since the giant had seen him before, the time he stole the parrot. That way the giant would not recognize him. The giant saw him and spotted him cutting wood, shaping it, making a big box. He attracted the giant's attention. The giant wondered what this man was doing on his, the giant's, turf. He went to where he was. Juan Chililí Pícaro was cutting and measuring. He had the box all made.

"Listen, who are you?" asked the giant.

"Oh, I'm just a man who lives in the kingdom and I'm very afraid of . . . I don't like Juan Chililí Pícaro. I'm making a box. I'm making a box to capture Juan Chililí Pícaro and put him inside and take him away. I have a stack of firewood over there, and we're going to burn him. He is a man who does nothing for me. I don't like him."

"Is this true?" asked the giant.

"Yes."

"Well if that's the case—he stole my mare, he stole my parrot, he killed my wife—I'll help you."

Well, they finished the box and everything, and the giant asked Juan Chililí Pícaro, "Now what do you want me to do?"

"I want you to get into the box, put the top on, and let me close it, because I don't want Juan Chililí Pícaro to see anything."

"Well, right away," agreed the giant.

The giant got into the box, and Juan Chililí Pícaro came and put the top on and nailed it shut. "This is just a strip of wood I'm nailing down," he told the giant. When he had nailed the box shut, he fetched a huge chain and wrapped it around frontward and backward. Now the giant could not get out. And he took him to the king. And that's the end of the story.

"Juan Chililí Pícaro" as Social Allegory

Anastacio Taylor did not explain the meaning of the story when he told it to Joe Taylor sometime around 1948. Joe Taylor explained (in Spanish) that storyteller commentary was not part of his father's culture. In those days, there wasn't much time to talk about a particular story. You came home really tired. After supper, there was conversation, but there wasn't time to discuss the moral of a story. Nevertheless, Joe Taylor came up with his own interpretation of the story as a social allegory. Well, what it means is that there always has been a meddler in whatever town one lives in. There always has been what they call a trickster, but the trickster is a person who is a pretty good shyster. And they say the king is the one who upholds the law. And then, as for the giant, there always has been a person or persons who make others afraid because of their size or for the power they have, be it with money or one thing or another.

Joe Taylor expanded on the meaning of each of the four characters he mentioned in his interpretation: the *metemal*, the *pícaro*, the king, and the giant. The *metemal*, or *metóte*, in San Luis Valley Spanish, is a gossip who creates trouble by telling others what a third party allegedly may have said about them. Antonito is now a small town of nine hundred, among whom remarks, even very casual ones, get around very quickly. Joe Taylor provided an example from his own recent experience. Since you know a lot of people, a meddler brings you, he brings you gossip, and to avoid offending one or the other, you listen to it and you say, "Yes, yes." One time there was an accident here. And they told me . . . that there was this accident and it was very bad and this person was to blame. . . . That is what I heard. A little while later, the mother of the boy . . . who caused the accident . . . comes and tells me, "Listen! Why are you going around saying that my son is to blame for the accident?"

He added that a *pícaro*, whom he also called a *pelegartero*, or cheat,[8] is a person who has no shame, a *sinvergüenza*. He lacks honor because his word cannot be trusted. A *pícaro* has troubled relations with those in his own community, where a man's moral reputation rests on his word and is vital for avoiding political trouble, particularly when one is caught in a web of crosscutting loyalties. He is vulnerable to the actions of a *metemal* (meddler or gossip), who could challenge his word (*palabra*). Even after Juan Chililí Pícaro got rid of the giant, he still did not have good relations with his peers because they did not trust him. Joe Taylor put it this way: Juan Chililí Pícaro had honor with the king, he was respected by the king. But I don't think that he was respected much by the citizens of the town. The kingdom, as they put it.

He equated the king with the law, by which he meant the Anglo-Saxon law that came in with the Treaty of Guadalupe Hidalgo. He remembered he omitted a key phrase linking the king to the rule of law, explaining that every time the king ordered Juan to perform a difficult theft, he said,

> Yo soy el rey
> Y lo que digo es ley
> Vas por esta yegua [ese perico, el gigante]
> O penas de la vida.
>
> I am the king,
> And what I say is the law
> Go get this mare [this parrot, the giant]
> Or you'll suffer the pain of death.

He expanded on the meaning of the "king's" law in the Antonito region, saying: **The gringos came here with a lot of power. Since they brought their law, and we could not understand their law because the law . . . that was here, the law that prevailed here no longer existed because you were no longer a Mexican, you were no longer a Spaniard, now . . . you were an American. But you were an American who was third class.** The fruits of this legal system were that speculators gained control of the Spanish and Mexican land grants, ethnic stratification developed in the valley, Anglo employers exploited their Mexicano workers, and Jim Crow laws were put into effect.

In the symbolic language of a folktale, Joe Taylor described, in his story and his commentary, the social structure of the "kingdom of Antonito." Using what he told me in our dialogue, it is possible to elaborate further on the meaning of the main characters in "Juan Chililí Pícaro." Juan represents the Mexicano worker, who by 1943 was among the many Spanish-speaking men and women toiling in the fields outside of Antonito or herding sheep on the llano and in the mountains. The king was the worker's *patrón* (employer), who might be a Mexicano *rico* or a wealthy Anglo who owned a lot of land or a big herd of sheep. In either case, the *patrón* operated according to Anglo laws governing the ownership of land and water rights and access to credit. Anglo law laid the foundation for the hierarchical social structure of Antonito, which Joe Taylor contrasted with the more egalitarian community of El Rito in his historical memory. The giant is a more remote figure, outside the kingdom, that poses a threat to those who live within it. His great size is likely a metaphor for social power. Spanish speakers in the San Luis Valley, in fact, have used the words *los grandes* (the big ones) and *los altos* (the tall ones) to refer to "the bosses, people in high positions."[9] Without stretching Joe Taylor's meaning too much, it is possible to see the giant as representing Anglos like the "Miner brothers," who lived in communities north of Antonito. The giant could also represent the Anglo contractors and owners who have the power to make workers endure the hardships of fieldwork, as in *Alex and the Hobo,* who pay workers by the half-sack or the row, as in Joe Taylor's commentary.

El Rito and Antonito

The story of Juan Chililí Pícaro contains some useful information for placing Joe Taylor's contrast between El Rito and Antonito in historical perspective. As noted earlier, he made many allusions to that contrast in *Alex and the Hobo.* He compared the family atmosphere of the work groups in El Rito to the harsh, uncomfortable, and dangerous conditions of the work crews on the Antonito side of the valley. A comparison of different versions of the Juan Chililí story by narrators living on the two sides of the valley lends support to this contrast. Juan B. Rael collected two variants of this story in 1930. One was from Felix Esquivel, who lived in the community of San Pablo, an egalitarian hamlet a stone's throw from El Rito, and the other was from Cecilia Lobato, who lived in Antonito.[10] Felix Esquivel and Cecilia Lobato expressed their different experiences in their particular ways of recounting this story.

One obvious difference between the two versions was the characterization of the giant and his relative threat to the kingdom. Although Rael did not record any storyteller commentary, and so there is no way to know for sure what Felix Esquivel and Cecilia Lobato had in mind when they depicted the giant, it is probable that their respective descriptions reflect their contrasting experiences with people who have social, economic, and political power.

In Felix Esquivel's version, the giant is big, but his power is relatively circumscribed, and the challenges to him are vital and strong. He described a continual war with the giant, possibly alluding to the Mexicanos' protracted struggle to hold on to their land in the San Luis area.[11] His giant is strong, but not as powerful, for example, as Joe Taylor's giant, who nearly annihilates the hero by cooking and eating him. Notably, Joe Taylor often used the word *comerse* (to eat [another]) when describing what men did to a man who did not know how to stand up for himself. Felix Esquivel's giant did not threaten to dominate the hero so completely, and in fact he cooperated more fully in his own demise by cutting down a poplar tree (*álamo*) and making his own coffin. In most versions of the story, the hero tricks the giant into trying on the coffin for size; only in Felix Esquivel's version does the hero wound the giant by pounding a nail through the wood and into the giant's rib cage. In allegorical terms, Felix Esquivel presented a picture of considerable Mexicano power relative to the Anglos, who by 1930 had gained control much of the rest of the valley but had not invaded the Culebra Creek area, which included Felix Esquivel's community of San Pablo.

Cecilia Lobato, who lived in Antonito in 1930, described the giant as a more ominous threat. Her giant killed all of the king's soldiers and he almost ate the hero *twice,* a poetic reference to Juan Chililí's vulnerability to complete annihilation.

Joe Taylor's version more closely resembled that of Cecilia Lobato by also including the detail about the hero nearly losing his life when he is almost eaten by the giant. Similarly, he told how the giant wounded the hero when Juan Chililí attempted to steal the giant's mare. One would expect similarities between their two versions because they both lived in Antonito. However, Joe Taylor expressed the novel element of independence in several details of his story.

First, he converted Juan Chililí into a *pícaro* and blamed him for failing to get along with his meddling peers (the *metemal* or *metóte*). As a *pícaro,* Juan was not a man of his word and was vulnerable to the actions of an envious meddler who wished to make trouble for him with the king. His description of the *pícaro* lacks the playful and even heroic qualities found in other descriptions of this character in

Chicano expressive culture. For example, Yolanda Broyles-González described the *pícaro* and the related character of the *relajo* (trouble-maker) in El Teatro Campesino, a dramatic ensemble organized to recruit workers into César Chávez's farmworkers' union in California, as using their verbal skill and cunning to outsmart powerful adversaries.[12] Joe Taylor has, however, described the *pícaro* in playful terms in other narratives. The key is the context. In his commentary on the meaning of "Juan Chililí Pícaro," he is drawing attention to how a lack of honesty affects one's reputation within the Mexicano community in a very small town where *palabra* (word) is taken very seriously.

Second, Joe Taylor eliminated the hero's reward for ridding the kingdom of the giant. When I brought this to his attention, he said that was the way he learned the story from his father. I think the lack of a reward is meaningful and fits with his father's independent position in his community. By eliminating the reward, Anastacio may have made the point that if one does the king's (read *rico* or wealthy Anglo's) bidding, one will not get much for his efforts. As Joe Taylor put it in his commentary: **Juan Chililí Pícaro had honor with the king, he was respected by the king. But I don't think that he was respected much by the citizens of the town.** The English equivalent of the moral to Joe Taylor's story is: "Be true to your word (*palabra*) and don't play the rich man's game." He may have picked up such a moral in his father's *zapatería*.

In summary, Joe Taylor's version of "Juan Chililí Pícaro" incorporates a conception of masculinity that he learned from his father in accord with his position in the hierarchical social structure of Antonito. His version of the tale expresses the envy among workers (Juan's relations with the *metóte*) but also makes the point that a man must earn the respect of his peers by being a man of his word and by not seeking favor with those in positions of power (being a *lambe*). The story takes on greater meaning in light of what Joe Taylor learned about his father standing up to corruption by coming to the aid of sheepherders and merchants who found themselves at the mercy of corrupt cops. According to Joe Taylor, his father had the respect of his peers because he acted on principle and did not play the rich man's game. To be sure, he was a *granjeador,* but he was by no means a *lambe.* In this sense, Anastacio Taylor was the model for Alex Martínez, who similarly demonstrated independence and courage when he acted against the corrupt officials in his community by breaking the hobo out of the Conejos County jail.

Joe Taylor's father and the world of the *zapatería* thus figured largely in the young man's transition to manhood. Beneath and behind the father's world, however, is the world of women. Joe Taylor's mother, his older sisters, and his grandmother all cared for him and the other younger children in the family, providing not only love and nurturance but also early lessons about morality and religion. Accordingly, the next chapter delves into Joe Taylor's memory of his mother and her influence on his life and his story.

CHAPTER 7

▰▰▰➤ BEATRIZ MONDRAGÓN

In recalling his early childhood, Joe Taylor revealed how his mother as well as his father laid the foundation of the strong moral vision that appears in *Alex and the Hobo*. However, he remembered his mother as being very different from his father: she showed her children more affection; she taught her children strong religious beliefs; she saved Joe Taylor from beatings by his father; and she tried to protect all of her children from the chaos of the streets. Perhaps like many boys, Joe Taylor had to acquire his masculinity by moving from the world of his mother to that of his father. Recent studies of masculinity have paid particular attention to the different ways that boys make this transition.[1] Joe Taylor recalled how he made the transition from his mother to his father. He began by explaining how his mother and other women in his life, particularly his grandmother, exerted a strong influence on his early moral development.

He described his mother, Beatriz Mondragón, **as the typical Chicana woman who stayed at home and raised kids. And when you raise seven kids and some were animals like me, there is a lot of work she had to do.** Women were the ones who primarily cared for young children in Joe Taylor's family and, therefore, probably influenced the early formation of his conscience. He explained that his mother was the one who **raised the kids,** and he did not come under Anastacio's care until he started spending time in the *zapatería*. The important exception to this rule is grandfathers, who frequently care for their infant grandchildren, changing their diapers, feeding them, and holding them. **Men mellow out when they become grandfathers,** Joe Taylor said on many different occasions. However, he barely remembers his paternal grandfather, who died before the family moved from El Rito to Antonito, and he never knew his maternal grandfather. Needing help in raising a large family, Beatriz Mondragón turned to her daughters. Joe Taylor explained that he, his brother Bobby, and his sister Tonita **were the youngest in the family. And each of my sisters used to take care of one of us. I belonged to my sister Martha. She was the one who took care of me. My sister Marvina took care of my brother Bobby. And my sister Cordi helped take care of probably my sister Tony. And my brother Felix was one of the older ones. He was the "Lupe" in the family. So they were the ones who took care of you. The ones who saw you combed your hair, you had a halfway clean shirt, and everything else.** His only living grandmother, Antonia Segura, was also an important person during his first five years, when the family was still living in El Rito.

He recalled how his mother was like Alex's mother, Nena, in **setting the examples and finding the qualities in her kids. She'd say, "You have qualities that other people don't see, but I see them."** He mentioned another parallel: **I'll tell you one thing, if you were sick in the family—most of the time they had you working, but—when you were sick, you were pampered. When you were sick you were** *pampered!* **I remember sitting in her lap and her comforting me.**

Talking about food over the kitchen table was one of the ways that Joe Taylor was able to remember his mother's love. He saw feeding others as an expression of love and recalled some of the ways that his mother fed him when he was about Alex's age. He recalled how his mother could convert mud suckers—fish shunned by many because they have a lot of bones and taste like mud—into a delicious meal through a great deal of hard work.

He began by noting that his father caught two kinds of fish: **one was the mud sucker and the other one was a trout. Trout he gave to businesspeople, the church, and the school. Anybody else in town that had families could go in and get the mud suckers, including his own family. Because that's what he used to give us. That's what we ate. But the trout was for the higher class, and the mud suckers were for anybody else who wanted them. The mud suckers, you'd take them and you'd skin them and you'd cut the head off, the little wings, and fins and everything off, and you'd fry them. My mom** used to skin them, cut their heads off, cut the fins off, and then take boiling water, and that water was boiling, boiling, and she'd take that fish by the tail, and she'd dip it into that boiling water. And all the meat would just come out and she'd take a fork and she'd take all that meat off and leave the bone of the fish and throw that one and do the next one. And then when it was all done, she used to sort of let it boil a little bit. And then after that, she used to take one of those *coladeras* [colanders], she'd take it and she'd dump the fish in there. She'd take what was left of the fish in the colander, and she'd pick out the bones that happened to go on in there, which weren't that many, and then she'd take the crackers and she'd grind them in there with pepper and then she'd make patties out of them. And then she'd fry the little patties, and to me they were delicious. A master of the understatement, he is giving his mother very high praise; he does not usually like to eat fish.

Love and Sin

As our conversations continued, Joe Taylor made it clear that his mother and other women, particularly his grandmother, mixed love with a strong sense of sin. Beatriz Mondragón taught him that greed and envy were the source of corruption. He recalled a folktale she told him when he was about Alex's age. The story is actually a variant of a well-known oral tale that folklorists call "The Gifts of the Little People."[2] The story circulated in the Culebra Creek area in the 1930's, when Joe Taylor's family lived in that part of the valley; Juan B. Rael collected a variant from Felix Esquivel in San Pablo in 1930.[3] A comparison of the tale Joe Taylor remembered hearing from his mother and the one told by Felix Esquivel reveals how Beatriz Mondragón may have made a distinctive contribution to her son's moral vision. Below is my English translation of the story Joe Taylor recalled hearing from his mother in Spanish.

This one is about these two neighbor women. And one of them had a big heart and was a good person and saw the good in everything. She was a good woman, and the other was sort of a cheat, a trickster, and she was looking for whatever she could get. Well, that neighbor woman saw everything other people did and wanted to do it too. They lived in this town, in this little hamlet, and one of them went out one day and went about gathering plants—spinach and flowers and this and the other thing. And there were some people singing. She heard some women's voices singing. Let me tell you before going any further, each neighbor woman had a hump on her back, and one of them heard these voices singing. And when she got there, the witches were singing. And it was so beautiful to hear the witches singing that she started to sing with them. She joined them. And the witches saw right away that she was a modest person, a good person, and they accepted that woman. "All right. Yes, you've come with good intentions and without any idea of doing us any harm." And to do something nice for her, they removed the woman's hump. And this woman, oh, she was so happy. She went back to town. She told her neighbor, "Do you know what?" She said, "I went to this place. There were these women. They were singing beautifully. And I started to sing with them, and they liked it so much," she said, "they did me the big favor of removing my hump."

"Yes," the other one said. "Exactly where are they?"

And she said, "Well." She told her where the witches were. But the next day, the other one put on her cape and went there and looked for where the witches had been. The witches that were singing. Oh, she came upon some women singing to see if they would accept her too. But the witches saw she was a trickster, a woman with bad intentions. And when they stopped singing, when they saw what kind of person the other woman was, they gave her another hump. They put the hump on her they had taken from the other one. So then she went back to town with two humps.

The version Joe Taylor recalled hearing from his mother and the one Felix Esquivel told Juan B. Rael reveal two very different moral messages. Joe Taylor's story stresses the importance of having a big heart that is free from the corrupting influence of greed and envy. Felix Esquivel made a very different point, as he told of two hump-backed men who do not personify good or evil. One man does not have a bigger heart and better intentions than the other, and neither one is a trickster (*pícaro*). One man happened to hear witches utter the phrase, "Lunes y martes y miércoles tres," to which he replied,

"Jueves y viernes y sábado seis." The witches rewarded him by removing his hump and he returned to the other humpback man, reporting what had taken place. The second man approached the witches and heard the same phrase, but replied incorrectly, "Jueves y viernes y sábado seis, y domingo siete." The witches did not like his reply and gave him a second hump.[4]

I do not know what Felix Esquivel meant in 1930, and one will never know exactly how Beatriz Mondragón told her version of the same tale to Joe Taylor when he was a young boy. It is possible, even likely, that Joe Taylor changed the story to fit his current moral vision, in which he attributes corruption to envy and greed. However, it is also possible that his mother contributed to his moral education by telling him the story in her own particular way. He and his older sister, Cordi, declared she was a moral leader in their family. He said she **set good examples. She set very good examples. She never cussed. She used to get mad at us once in a while, but she never hit us and she'd reason with you. She'd advise you. She'd cradle you in her arms. And those were good examples of a loving mother to her kids. She was there when you needed her.** Joe Taylor's sister recalled (in Spanish): **She was the one who taught us religion the most. Sometimes it seems she taught it to us too well because I became very frightened. She told us the end of the world was coming. It was going to go up in flames.**

Sin and Sexuality

Joe Taylor made clear on many occasions that he was brought up with a strong sense of sin. In one of our recent conversations, he explained that his mother and other women taught him about sin by way of their handling of infantile sexuality.[5] We touched upon this subject when discussing the episode in *Alex and the Hobo* where Alex witnessed the hobo and China about to enact the primal scene. In our conversation, Joe said: **The hobo went into that house with China, and they committed the sin of adultery. Probably adultery or whatever it is. Alex could not imagine his parents doing that, even though they gave birth to four people or five people. He didn't know what act his parents committed, or not committed, to conceive a** child. Know what I mean? Did you ever get the meaning of that in the story? He placed the hobo on the same level as his parents. He couldn't imagine his parents doing anything like that. Right? Well, this is what I'm trying to say. A kid grows some and he does not, for one minute, imagine his parents going through the acts of whatever they have to do to conceive a child. Right?

Even though it's technically not a sin.

Even though it's not a sin. I'm not saying it's a sin. I'm saying the act. The act that you go through. It could have been an act in the eyes of the parents. But he didn't know that. He didn't know where he came from. Or his sisters and his brothers came from. He only knew that it was a sin for the hobo and that lady to go ahead and do that same thing here. You place your parents on this high pedestal or classify them equal to or below God, that they cannot sin. They're sort of perfect people. And the love that you have for them is what they preach to you. But you're not aware of that. Your grandparents gave you good examples. "Don't do this, *mi hijito.* Don't do that. That's bad. No [te] hagas físico." If we would sort of touch ourself in a private part, "No [te] hagas físico." That's the word that they used to use. I never had a grandfather to know, but it did come from my grandfather and it did come from my mother and it did come from my aunts because they were churchgoing people.

Contrasting Parenting Styles

As we focused on his transition from the world of his mother to that outside of the home, he recalled how Beatriz was different from Anastacio. He recalled his mother as a women who attempted to protect him by sometimes stopping his father from beating him, by discouraging his friendship with boys of whom she did not approve, and by expressing her strong dislike of alcohol. By contrast, he recalled his father as a harsh disciplinarian but also an intermediary agent who helped him make the transition to the world outside of the home.

About his mother stepping in to prevent his father from beating him, he said: **My dad was very strict in some cases and he'd want to hit us for just anything. And she'd step in the way. She'd step in front of him, as big and as mean as my dad was. Not mean, really, but** strict in his ways. She'd just stand up to him and wouldn't let him hit us. He would back down. He'd probably just slap us around a little bit but not as bad as he would because he was like six-feet-two and weighed two hundred and some pounds and when he hit, he hit. Mom was not a very tall woman. She wasn't a tall woman. Probably about five-two maybe.

He illustrated the contrasting parenting roles of his mother and father with the case of his friendship with an older boy named Gene, the model for James in *Alex and the Hobo.* He recalled how his mother was protective of her son and sometimes did not approve of his choice of friends. Anastacio was less critical of his friendship, but he could be a very harsh disciplinarian.

Gene was a real, live character. I had to have been ten, eleven years old. Maybe I was younger than that because I met Gene from the time we came to this town in forty-three. My parents didn't like Gene. My dad didn't see as much fault in Gene as my mom did. My mom just strictly did not like Gene. And she strictly did not like us hanging around. We'd just come into a new town, and here is her brood, here is her family. She's got to protect her family. We're country people coming over here. We're not streetwise.

Gene got me to go fishing with him, and I didn't want to go. But the only the reason I went with him was because he had lunch meat and weenies. And that was a treat for us. And I went with him, and I didn't come home. And they couldn't find me. And my parents didn't know where I was. And then somebody told my dad that they had seen me go there with Gene, or they knew there was a favorite place where we used to go fish. And my dad went looking for me. And, when he found me over there, man, he brought this big old willow and he whipped me all the way from the river home.

Like James in *Alex and the Hobo,* Gene came to a tragic end. One night he was over here, and they used to play poker, and he was in with the big boys. And there was this guy and he had his truck outside. And I think Gene found the keys inside this truck and he went and took this truck and he went out of town. Right there by Bountiful he flipped it over and he got killed. And I was at the age where I

couldn't picture death and I couldn't picture Gene dead. And then having to go on over there and view him in his coffin.

Alcohol

The death of Gene was a grim symbol of the danger in the world outside the home. James in *Alex and the Hobo,* like Gene in Joe Taylor's historical memory, was a transitional figure through whom Alex moved away from the protected world of his mother. Alex felt a mixture of anguish and curiosity as he left the world of his mother, befriended James and the hobo, and entered the sometimes frightening, violent, and corrupt world of adults.

Joe Taylor might have used alcohol as a poetic device to convey the anguish of entering this dangerous world because his mother had strong feelings about drinking. Alex was frightened of drunks and avoided them when he saw them in his path. *Alex and the Hobo* contains powerful imagery to describe Alex's reaction when, on his way to find Milo, he comes across some men drinking out of a wine bottle near the railroad tracks. **The hair on the back of his neck seemed to stand on end, his heart beat a mile a minute, chills ran down his back, and goose bumps covered his whole body.**

Joe Taylor explained that his mother hated drinking because of what it had done to the men in her family. **My mom didn't like alcohol because alcohol in a sense was in our family from a long, long time ago. I think my grandfather used to drink excessively. My grandfather Taylor on my dad's side. But I didn't know much about my grandfather on my mom's side except that I don't think that he was a drinker or a smoker. But alcohol has played a part in the lives of not only the Taylors but the Mondragóns too. And my mom was a Mondragón through her dad.**

I asked about Beatriz Mondragón's reaction to the Saturday night brawls in Antonito. **She was right here in town when she would see all these drunks and people and she just did not like alcohol. Oh, she said different things. "It's shameful, it's disgraceful. I hope you guys never [drink]. I hope you can learn a lesson by what you're looking at . . . that alcohol has no place in your life. Look at that guy, he's** drunk. **His poor children are suffering and the lady has to go on over to the bar and take money from him.** She comes out of there with a black eye because the guy hit her because she was over there taking his money to provide for the family."

Joe Taylor's recollections of the drunken brawls on Main Street are tinged with his mother's dislike of alcohol as well as his Chicano awareness and the class consciousness that he developed while working for the union. He attributed the chaotic world of drinking to the poverty that in other conversations he blamed on greedy employers who exploited their workers.

It was very sad to see these things and they happened every day. They happened every payday. They happened every week. It was not a thing that happened once and again. It was something that happened every [payday]. And when you find an area that's a depressed area, you find more alcohol. And this was a depressed area over here. It has been. Even today it is the second poorest county in the United States.[6]

He used his memory of Anastacio's moderate drinking to depict in his story how a boy might make the transition from the world of the mother to that of the father without falling into violence and chaos. In *Alex and the Hobo,* Tomás, Alex's father, occasionally took a drink in his barbershop but did not get drunk. Anastacio and Tomás were alike in that both men drank only moderately, although in all other respects they had very different personalities. **My dad was not an alcoholic. My dad used to drink a beer a day. Could you even consider or think of a man that can only drink a beer a day and that's it? Other guys, they're alcoholics. But my dad drank a beer a day. And sometimes, what I mean by a beer a day, I don't mean out of the bottle. I mean he'd go on over there and have one glass of beer like eleven o'clock in the morning, maybe one in the evening. Maybe three glasses of beer a day. But I never saw my dad drunk in all the years that my dad was in existence. He died at the age of eighty-four, and I never saw him drunk.**

Nevertheless, it was difficult for Joe Taylor to drink moderately, particularly with so much exposure to alcohol when he was a young farmworker on the valley's western side. He started drinking when offered wine while working out in the fields, and he struggled with alcoholism until 1977, when he quit drinking entirely. He and Dennis "Hoot" Harlen organized a local chapter of Alcoholics Anonymous in Antonito. They meet weekly in the local Catholic church, and they encourage other members of their community to stop drinking. Joe Taylor's work for AA is an example of his loyalty to his mother.

Alex's Transition to Manhood

Joe Taylor's description of Alex's first steps toward manhood accords with the memory of his own transition from the world of his mother to the world outside the home. When making that transition, Alex had to break from his mother, which Joe Taylor represented with food imagery, associated in his commentary with his mother's love. He also described in his story how Alex was able to break from the mother and move into the world outside the home with "phallic gifts" associated with the hobo and his father. Making the transition to manhood, however, was not without inner conflict and anxiety, which Joe Taylor represented with food and body imagery.

Early on, Alex was confronted with a food-related opposition between his mother and hobos in general. When still in El Rito, Alex saw his mother become frightened when a hobo appeared, asking for a meal. She had heard stories that hobos steal children. So she fed the hobo—to deny anyone food is extraordinarily rude in her culture—but did not invite him into her kitchen, site of familial commensalism.

The connection between food and family/home was evident in two other food-related events in the story. The first was the trip to the Sánchez ranch to fetch the ewe. Alex went with his family in a borrowed pickup truck to bring the ewe back to town, where his father butchered the animal, and everyone in the family cooperated in preparing *burruñates,* a dish made of sheep intestines that Joe Taylor loved to eat as a child. The second food-related event was the pleasant Fourth of July trip to visit Alex's grandmother in El Rito, where he experienced the connection between familial love and eating. **The grandparents had set up tables under the cottonwood trees near the apple orchard in their yard, where the families would gather to eat watermelons, cakes, pies, and every kind of meat, including sausages,**

roasts, and hams. Food and familial love go together. At this same reunion, Alex was reunited with his beloved grandmother, whom he
had missed very much during his time in Antonito. His grandmother's
greeting shows how special he is in her eyes, how much like his
father: **"And you, my Alejandro, there's no mistake in your looks.
You're the image of your father!"** Alex tagged along, following her
wherever she went.

As Alex took his first steps toward manhood, moving away from
his mother (and grandmother) and toward the hobo, he temporarily
left the commensalism of his family home. His mother expected all
members of her family to observe a regular dinnertime (except for
Alex's older brother, Lupe, who was on the verge of manhood). Joe
Taylor recalled his mother saying: **I don't run a restaurant. And you
are going to come to eat, you're going to come on time or you're not
going to eat [No corro un restaurante. Y van a venir a comer, van a
venir a tiempo o no van a comer].** He elaborated: **At one time there
were nine of us in the family. And you went to eat because if you
weren't there, you didn't eat because there was nothing left over.
And those times were hard.**[7]

Alex appeared unable to enjoy the food prepared by his mother for
the family's repast and follow the hobo at the same time. He had to
give up one to have the other, and in the poetic language of a story,
Joe Taylor made the point that a boy must break from his mother
to become a man. Alex was already late for supper after he and Gil
were playing in the stockyards. He was on his way home, already late,
when he spotted the hobo. **He had seen him before and was fascinated by the man. Yet he could not explain why. He decided to follow him. He would find out who he was, where he lived, where men
like him come from, and what being a hobo was like.**

The attitudes of Alex's parents toward the hobo reflect their different claims on their son's loyalty. Alex's mother had told him that hobos steal children, while Alex's father maintained that the hobo was
a decent man. **"He's a quiet man and stays pretty much to himself.
I've never seen him looking for trouble,"** Alex's father said. Alex's
father was a more remote, but important, intermediary agent who
helped his son move from the world of women to that of men.

In yet another passage involving food, Alex reconciles his loyalties to his mother and his friendship to the hobo. Alex's father persuaded his mother to let Alex go fishing with the hobo. Both his mother and the hobo provided Alex with food, which they ate together after fishing the San Antonio River, south of town. At this point in the story Alex receives the first phallic gift, a fishing pole rigged by the hobo. Alex accepts the pole as he is drawn further into the hobo's confidence and into the world of men, represented by Milo's secret, hidden cave. Milo teaches Alex how to bait his hook because the boy is **new at fishing,** a reference to being new at entering the world of masculinity. That world is filled with secrets that men keep from women; the secrecy of masculinity appears in the story as Milo shows Alex his secret cave. However, in order for Alex to enter the secret world of men, he has to recover from his revulsion at seeing the hobo and China about to enact the primal scene. Alex's recovery is his first step in coming to terms with male sexuality, which loving women had taught him was a source of shame.

Fishing with the hobo is the necessary stage for Alex to take a definite and heroic step toward manhood by coming to the rescue of an innocent man. Alex knew the hobo was innocent of killing China because he had seen the bookkeeper run out of the murdered woman's house. Alex witnessed a mob dragging the bleeding and innocent hobo to the Antonito city jail in a scene Joe Taylor described as like the Stations of the Cross leading up to Christ's crucifixion. A little later, Alex learned of Greg's plot to burn down the jail and kill the hobo in order to close the case. Alex decided he could not go to his family for help because they admired the marshal, who was in cahoots with Greg, and would not believe Alex if he told them what he knew. Moreover, Alex had lied to his parents repeatedly so he could spy on the hobo, and he feared his parents' punishment. Feeling caught in a trap, Alex had nightmares and was comforted by his mother, who **held him close to her bosom and comforted him.** Her bosom, of course, is the part of her body she had used to provide food and comfort to Alex as an infant.

Alex could not return to an unconflicted past, and so he took matters into his own hands and decided to free the hobo from his prison while the town was being distracted by the Labor Day carnival. Alex made the one-mile trip from Antonito to Conejos at night, passing through the cemetery, where he heard the screams of La Llorona. Alex was filled with fear, **gagging until there was nothing left in his stomach**. To vomit while taking a step toward proving his manhood was the logical opposite of eating a hearty meal in the bosom of his family.

To be a hero, Alex needs to accept or take another phallic gift, this time in the form of the crowbar he uses to free the hobo from the Conejos County jail. The crowbar is associated with his father, as made evident in the following passage. **He [Alex] remembered seeing a big padlock on a chain holding the door of Milo's cell. In the movies, he'd seen crowbars used to force locks open. He knew his father had a crowbar in the shed near his house. Making sure Gilbert was not around, he headed into the alley, where he found the crowbar in the shed.** After successfully removing the padlock, Alex makes sure to return the crowbar, an act that represents his respect for his father.[8]

Thus, *Alex and the Hobo* is at its base the story of a young man's journey to manhood. At the same time, however, the story is fundamentally concerned with the imperiled nature of Mexicana women: the crime that forms the central dramatic moment is China's murder. Joe Taylor addressed this subject in his commentary, and he also arranged interviews with people from the valley to speak in their own words about the dangers to which Mexicana women have been exposed. Excerpts from two of these interviews are presented in the following chapter.

CHAPTER 8

WOMEN IN PERIL

Joe Taylor links the fate of his culture to the fate of women. He described how his culture, like his moral vision, depends on church-going women like Beatriz Mondragón, who teach their children the concept of sin and stress the importance of having a big heart. He described, in the poetic language of his story, how the class system of Antonito, which is based on greed, threatens women and, by extension, his culture. China died at the hands of a greedy and corrupt Mexicano man who made his living by handling money.

The class system is a threat to Joe Taylor's culture because it enables men and women who do not have big hearts and who have questionable morals to abuse their power and take advantage those who are weaker and more vulnerable. Joe Taylor arranged for me to interview men and women on the western side of the valley so that they could describe in their own words how and why women are in peril. In this chapter I present excerpts from two interviews, one with a man and the other with a woman. Both described how their daughters were in peril because of witches who intended to harm them. Witchcraft is a system of belief with long antecedents in the Southwest that explains misfortune. The particular witchcraft beliefs of the man and the woman Joe Taylor arranged for me to interview are probably an amalgam of Native American and Spanish culture.[1] Many of the original Mexicanos who settled along the banks of Culebra Creek and the Conejos River were and still are Penitentes, who believe there is an intense struggle between good and evil.[2] In Joe Taylor's view, witches are evil because they are in league with the devil, they do not have pure hearts, they are envious, and they are greedy. They personify the inverse of the values he learned in his father's *zapatería* and at his mother's knee.

Belief in witchcraft prevailed before the Anglos arrived in force with the coming of the railroad in the late 1800's. Joe Taylor explained that witches tend to be Mexicanos, they have been around for a long time, and they tend to inhabit the llano rather than the mountains, where Anglos have built their vacation homes. The subject of witchcraft came up in our dialogue when he asked me to define cultural anthropology. Paraphrasing Geertz, I explained that it is the study of culture, which consists of the inherited ways a people make sense of their experience.[3] Joe Taylor responded by telling me that I had to learn how witchcraft victims draw from their culture to interpret what has gone wrong in their lives.

Their testimonies revealed how they have experienced pressure from the class system that developed on the western (Antonito) side of the valley. Some of their experiences have been disturbing and frightening. In the language of social science, their testimonies reveal how they have reacted to Anglo-Saxon hegemony and poverty.[4] Hegemony, according to Raymond Williams, is a notion combining the concept of culture, as a system of meaning, with the Marxist idea of class ideology.[5] Marxists contend that meaning depends on one's position in the class structure, but the production of meaning, in Williams's terms, is "in the hands of those who control the primary means of production."[6] Therefore, those in subordinate classes must struggle to maintain an independent consciousness.[7]

The two people whom Joe Taylor arranged for me to interview described in dramatic language how they are struggling with symbols as well as with poverty. I identify them with the pseudonyms of Pedro and Juana to protect their anonymity.

The "Psychological Vampire"

Pedro's testimony appears first. He described his encounter with a diabolical Anglo miner who proposed to exchange a mine with rich veins of gold and turquoise for Pedro's adolescent daughter.[8] Pedro eventually rejected the offer but only after experiencing a great deal of confusion that left him with a headache. The pain in his head is a palpable expression of his particular struggle to maintain his own independent consciousness. Joe Taylor started the conversation by bringing up the subject of the "psychological vampire," a term he learned from Pedro's late father, who applied it to the Anglo miner. Pedro then spoke softly with a mixture of Spanish and English.

Había este hombre que vivía aquí [There was this man who lived here] up in the mountains. And he was a gold miner. And he was like a hermit. He'd stay up there all year and all winter and all summer and I met this man through a friend of mine. Well, I got to know the viejito [little old man] pretty, pretty well. And he had a gold mine up here by Summitville. And he took me up there one time to go and see it. And he had three different mine shafts. And there was like veins of turquoise and veins of gold and all kinds of stuff in that mine. While we were up there, me dice [he says to me], "¿Qué quieres? [What do you want?] I can do anything for you," me dijo [he told me]. "I can let you see aliens. You want to see aliens?" I told him, "Na."

"Don't you want to see Sasquach?"

Le dije, "No" [I told him, "No"].

Luego [Then], "If you want to see any of these things I can make it happen for you. They come from the fourth dimension," me dijo [he told me].

And, well, I got to know him pretty good, and we used to invite him over here for dinner with us. He was already in his late seventies. And he was sitting here, we were talking, and one of my little girls comes up to him and gives him a little medallita [religious medallion]. He gets it and he looks at it and he tells us, "What you doing with this crud?" Y lo tiró [And he threw it].

So that started making me think about him. And one day, when I was down at my dad's, I was staring into the fireplace. He was talking. And I was thinking to myself, "I wonder if the viejo me embrujó [old man bewitched me] or something. Or the diablo hizo [devil did] something." He [the miner] turns around and looks at me and he goes, "Get that stupid stuff out of your head. Stop thinking like that. There ain't no evil around here," me dijo [he said to me]. Like he knew like what I was thinking, you know. And he used to tell me, "I don't have to get off my chair to kill anybody. I can kill anybody from

right here where I sit." He told me, "I know hypnosis. I could hypnotize you and show you different things and this and that." And, it's not that I didn't believe him, pero tenía metal [but he had metal, i.e., money or power].

Pedro explained that he watched the diabolical miner hypnotize a friend with a tape recorder. You could hear [the miner] talking to somebody but you couldn't hear nobody talking back. He was, like, having a conversation with somebody. And after the tape finished playing and stuff, I asked him about it. And he goes, "Yeah. I was with Elvis Presley. I was his buddy cruising around." This and that.

Pedro came to the Anglo miner's immoral proposal. My oldest daughter had a lot of hair on her back. And he tells me, "Bring her over here for three days, and I'll take the hair off of her back. I'll hypnotize her and take the hair off her back."

This is when all these funny things started happening. He wanted me to leave her there. And I told him, "No."

"I'll give you this gold mine." He started breaking [out] all kinds of papers that the government estimated it.

And le dije [I said to him], "No, no, no, no."

Y se enojó [And he got angry]. So I came back and I told him, "I don't want you comin' around with me and my family anymore."

And he started sending me some pretty nasty letters. In fact, I still have 'em. And he got real mad and he goes, "You people from C——, you think you guys can do whatever you want. You watch, I'm going to bring a whole bunch of rockers down here and we're going to tear this town apart."

What I got out of it was that the spirit of the diablo was in him. And he wanted me to give him my love in return for this gold mine. Well, my oldest daughter was born on Valentine's Day. On February fourteenth. And here was the diablo tellin' me, "You give me your love, and I'll give you this gold mine." And he told me, "I ain't got much time left. And my family died in a car accident a long time ago, and I don't want the government to get a hold of this gold mine and I want to find a family. Somebody I can give it to before I die." I wonder if this man's not the diablo [devil] or something like that, and he's giving me a real wicked look. Like if he knew what I was thinking.

And then all of a sudden I'd get a real sharp pain on my head. My head would hurt.

Joe Taylor thinks the term "psychological vampire" is apt for describing the predicament of many Mexicanos in the San Luis Valley. The psychological vampire drains a person's energy and personifies the way Anglo domination is bleeding the life out of Mexicano culture. The term captures the process of hegemony, by which the members of a subordinate class struggle to maintain their independent consciousness. Pedro was confused over what was right and wrong. He acknowledged earlier that he had been going through a lot of "spiritual head trips," that appeared to be symptoms of his struggle against hegemony. The miner could get into his head, read his thoughts, and tempt him with images from American popular culture. The miner's ability to hypnotize his victims is a special case of the Anglos' control of meaning by virtue of their ownership of the means of production. The miner offered Pedro a glimpse of aliens and Sasquatch from the Fourth Dimension, which Pedro knew from watching the *X-Files,* a very popular television show among Mexicanos and Anglos alike in the San Luis Valley. The Anglo's mine is near Summitville, a symbolic location because it represents the greedy exploitation of the valley's natural resources. Summitville is the name of a mine high in the San Juans that recently poured tons of heavy metals into the Alamosa River, killing all of the fish and poisoning the drinking water.[9] The Summitville mine is an example of the kind of exploitation that Joe Taylor had in mind when he wrote the essay "Goodbye to My Beautiful San Luis Valley." Pedro rejected the diabolical miner's illicit proposal, so his daughter is safe for the time being.

Juana's Testimony

Juana told a different story. Her daughter, she said, is not safe because she is running wild. Juana believed that she and her family fell under the spell of witches when she temporarily lived in Antonito. She made five points, to which I shall return at the conclusion of her testimony. First, her daughter flaunted the older generation's customs of courtship and marriage. Second, Juana found evidence of witchcraft, to which she attributed her daughter's wild behavior, her son's attempted suicide, and her husband's drinking. Third, she discovered that Antonito is a powerful center of witchcraft and believed that three neighbor women had put a spell on her. Fourth, the family problems she attributed to witchcraft began when her husband, a migrant farmworker, lost his comparatively well-paying job. Fifth, she interpreted her deteriorating family life as part of the coming apocalypse. I have translated and edited Juana's testimony to bring out the main points. Interested readers can find her unedited testimony in the original Spanish in the appendix.

Juana's Daughter

Now it's my daughter. Oh, my daughter! Where is she? I don't sleep all night. Nor do I the next day. I feel like I'm dying. The girls of today want more freedom. They [don't think] like I did. They don't talk the way I was raised. Right? "You can't go out after dark because you'll get a bad reputation or something like that."

And I waited [for marriage]. Right? You don't want a bad reputation. And the girls of today, they don't care. They say, "Let them say what they want. I'm going out. I'm going out. And on top of that, my friends won't talk. And my friends have [freedom] to go out, and their mothers let them."

And my sons aren't like that. Like my son is fourteen and he's always home. He helps me in the yard and he isn't interested in going out. And the girls want to. "I'm going out. I'm going to walk over to a friend's. I'm going out . . ."

I don't know. I don't know if it's today's generation or what. But what the girls do seems bad to me.

I ask: What happened to honor?

Juana: It isn't important to them. It's like [they're] saying no one waits. They say that these are the nineties. They want to know what they're getting into. One used to say, "I don't want to sleep with a boy before getting married—Right?—because I want to be a virgin when I go to the altar." Like how I got married. My husband went and asked for me and he had to kneel and ask my grandfather because he brought me up to believe [my husband should] say, "I intend to marry your daughter." Or "Would you let me marry her?"

I left the house in white. Now it doesn't matter what color they wear when they marry. Of if they're virgins or not virgins. Like it's not important to them. Right? They just say, "Well, these are the nineties, and we want to know what we're getting into." Right? Trying out a boy or not doesn't matter to them today. I look around today at a lot of girls and see a lot of young pregnancies. And they don't stop at one. Even if they suffer, they don't stop at one. They have two, three. And like I had six. Because he was my husband, he came from a family of just three. So he wanted a big family to have the family he always wanted. Right? And then they won't let you have just one, like what Joe says, that they're very macho here. Right? They won't let you take a pill or take care of yourself the way you can take care of yourself today. Young people today just do it. It's 'cause they know they can get help with the Welfare system. Sometimes that's why they do it. The kids have one, two, three different daddies. That's the bad thing. It's a shame but the youth of today are lost. And then if bad things happen to them, well, God knows.

Evidence of Witchcraft

Juana identified the cause of her plight as witchcraft, the evidence for which was dolls she found in her son's bedroom. She attributed to the dolls not only her daughter running wild, but also her son's attempt to kill himself and her husband's recent drinking.

Oh, those dolls I told you about! I found them inside of a white envelope. I opened it, and there were six little dolls. Two males and four females. And that is what I have. See? And I took them to that woman [a curer or *curandera*], a woman in Alamosa. The little female [dolls] had dresses, and the male [dolls] had pants. She put them in alcohol. She burned them. And they were different colors. So when she put out the fire, everything was red. The alcohol was red. And I asked her, "Why is it red and not different colors?" Because there were a lot of colors.

She said, "The red is blood." She said, "You're going to see blood in your house." And [the woman in Alamosa] did the cleansing with the egg. All over my body. She rubbed the egg all over my body and then she asked me, "Do you want to know if the diagnosis is bad?"

155

I told her, "Yes." [After the egg exploded and she determined it was because of witchcraft] I asked her, "Why did it do that?"

She said, "Because it made the person angry. Because you came here." She said, "But you have to come back." And oh, I didn't go. I didn't go back again. And she didn't do that again because they say that when she cures someone, she gets very sick. A person who cures gets sick because she takes the sickness the other person has.

Then I came home. She said, "Put crosses on your doors." Right?

Then I came home and went to the hospital. They put me in the hospital. The next day when I left, my son grabbed a knife and was going to kill himself. He was going to cut himself. So then I grabbed the knife, and he pulled on it, and it got me. And there was a whole lot of blood. You could see a lot of blood. And he left. Right? And he just made it to the stop sign and he fell over. And he said, "I'm going to kill everyone," he said. Then he returned, and I put the kids in the car and took off. And he said, "Why are you putting crosses around?" He was very angry. I told him that the day before I had found some dolls in his room. I asked him, "Are you doing something bad?"

And he said to me, "No." He said, "A woman here in Antonito," he said, "gave them to me."

I asked him, "What for?"

He said, "So I could talk to them when I felt sad or depressed." He said, "So I could talk to them. Those dolls give me my peace."

I asked him, "But why the coincidence that there are the four females and two males in the family?"

He said, "I don't know." Right?

But I've seen a lot of changes. I'm a believer. But I didn't used to believe. And I believe it because of the things that have happened in my life, with my children, with my husband. I used to be very active. Do you know what I mean? Not anymore. I'm always tired. I don't want to do anything. And before I . . . Oh, my yard was very beautiful. With its garden. And all that. And now it isn't. It's all dried up.

Antonito as the *Rabo de Brujas*

Juana explained how she learned from a *curandera* that Antonito is the *rabo de brujas* in the San Luis Valley. The word *rabo* literally means "tail" or "handle" of "a skillet or dipper," but it also refers to the child born after twins, who has extraordinary powers.[10] Joe Taylor interpreted *rabo* to mean the stem or stalk of a plant. *Brujas* means "female witches," and so *rabo de brujas* is a metaphorical expression referring to a powerful center of female witchcraft.

I went with this woman [a *curandera*]. She's old now. Right? She's old. And she asked me if I was from here. Her husband is from here. And she asked me, "Do you know," she said, "where the witches are?"

I told her, "No."

She wondered, "Why did you move to Antonito?"

I told her, "My husband."

She said, "Don't you know it's a *rabo de brujas*?"

I said to her, "No."

She said, "There are a lot of witches there." She said, "San Luis, Saguache, and Del Norte." She said, "The ones in Saguache are the youngest. And those in Del Norte are like children. Right? The youngest who practice it. But those in Saguache," she said, "teach the ones in Del Norte. And the ones in Antonito," she said, "they're old. They're older people." She said, "That's the most powerful center of witchcraft."

From a *curandera* in Monte Vista, Juana learned that three of the older female witches in Antonito are probably responsible for her problems.

Three weeks ago I went to Monte Vista, and another woman [also a *curandera*] told me, she said, "There are three people who are doing bad things to you." The bad thing is that where I live, where I rent, they say that family is bad. And I've wanted to move from there [Juana's house in Antonito]. Find another house. And I can't. Something always happens. I don't have the money when I need it. And I go the next day, and the house I want is rented. Right? And they say they're bad people. I don't know. And they told me that the woman who owns the house does bad things. And she won't let us leave. And then this other woman, that I told you about, started coming to my house, she'd come and just go in. There's her and this other one, but I don't know.

Juana's Husband

However, Juana also mentioned that the symptoms of her witchcraft appeared at about the same time that her husband lost his job in Arizona and started to drink heavily.

My husband earned six hundred dollars a week with the job he had. He'd go to Arizona. He'd go to Center. Suddenly there wasn't any work. They didn't even tell him it was going to end. They just told him, "There isn't any more." We don't know why. Nothing. Now my husband, he drinks. He used to drink every weekend. And now he drinks every day. He has to drink a lot every day. And he didn't used to drink like that. It got to where he wrecked his car by driving drunk.

Juana's Apocalyptic Vision

Juana is the member of a small Protestant denomination whose apocalyptic vision she evoked at the conclusion of her narrative.[11]

We're seeing the last of the final days. There's also another thing. The diseases. It says it all in the Bible that we're going to see sons killing fathers, fathers killing sons. Or fathers abusing children. It's all happening. Life is hard.

Interpreting Juana's Narrative

In talking with Joe Taylor, Juana wondered why she was the victim of witchcraft. He suggested that the witches acted out of envy.

Juana: **As I told you, I keep myself busy just with my kids. [And] taking care of the house. Making dinner for my husband and my children. I don't go out visiting in other houses like that, saying I'm going to see a friend. I don't have any friends. I'm just in my house. Right? And I can assure you that I don't do anything bad to anyone for anyone to do a bad thing to me.**

Joe Taylor: **It isn't because you have acted badly. It's that they envy you.**

Juana: **Because we were living very well.**

Joe Taylor explained that envy comes from greed and is another example of corruption. Witches who act out of envy and greed have been around for a long time, but Juana's and Joe Taylor's particular conversation about how Antonito witches have tried to destroy Juana's family points to how the class system is destroying the Mexicano community from within. The idea that a witch, motivated by envy and greed, would use diabolical supernatural power to make Juana's daughter run wild, her son try to kill himself, and her husband lose his job and turn to drink reminds me of Joe Taylor's metaphor about crabs in the bucket, which refers to the envy among Mexicanos in Antonito that prevented them from acting to protect their ethnic and class interests.

If one takes Juana's narrative together with Joe Taylor's story and commentary, Antonito emerges as a place with a history of Mexicanos turning against each other because of class oppression and racial discrimination. Juana recently learned that Antonito is the *rabo de brujas,* a powerful center of female witches. Earlier, Joe Taylor described how Mexicanos fought with each other at dances and on the street because of exploitation and discrimination. Added to this picture is alcohol, which Joe Taylor linked to poverty when he explained the drunken brawls on Main Street in the 1940's and 1950's. **When you find an area that's a depressed area, you find more alcohol, and this was a depressed area over here.**

The churchgoing women who laid the foundation of Joe Taylor's moral education have struggled with these problems for many years in the valley. Both Juana and Joe Taylor's mother abhorred drinking. Juana's mention of the apocalypse at the conclusion of her narrative links her in another way to Beatriz Mondragón, who taught her children an apocalyptic vision that frightened Joe Taylor's sister. To be sure, Juana belongs to a Protestant church, and Beatriz Mondragón was a devout Catholic. Nevertheless, the two women turned to an apocalyptic religious doctrine to hold their families and their lives together, perhaps because they were involved in similar struggles to maintain their cultures on the Anglo-Mexicano frontier.

However, they appear to be losing that struggle for many different reasons, primarily hegemony. Joe Taylor made a direct reference to hegemony after I turned off the tape recorder by remarking that Juana's daughter was flaunting the honor code because she had become Americanized. His use of the word "Americanized" came from his father's distinction between two categories of people he knew in the San Luis Valley. There were the Mexicanos, or speakers of Spanish, and the Americanos, who spoke English. To become Americanized means, of course, to adopt the ways of the Americanos and become less Mexicano. For Joe Taylor and the people who visit his secondhand shop, being Mexicano means speaking Spanish, having a big heart, and adhering to the customs of courtship, marriage, and family life of an earlier generation.

Alex and the Hobo

Juana's testimony is linked to Joe Taylor's *Alex and the Hobo* through the figure of La Llorona, whose legend was circulating at the time of China's murder and Alex's heroic rescue of the hobo from the Conejos County jail. Joe Taylor offered his interpretation of La Llorona's legend based in part on what he learned in the Chicano studies class he took at Adam State College in 1977.

Coronado came to this county. Right? In the days when Spain came to the United States. One of those conquistadors arrived and married an Indian woman and he had children with this Indian woman. Right? But when he finished, ended with things here, he went back, back to Spain. And he didn't want to take the Indian woman and the children he had with her.

Juana: **And this Indian woman was very sad, very hurt.**

Joe Taylor: **And she went and drowned her children she had with this conquistador. And from that point on, she has been heard crying. And from there came the story of La Llorona.**

In some respects, Juana is like La Llorona because she too is grieving for her children, although she did not attempt to drown them. Her daughter could easily become another La Llorona if she falls into the clutches of a greedy man like Coronado or the diabolical miner who offered to exchange his mine for Pedro's daughter. There is a long historical chain between Coronado and the Summitville miner that includes all of the corrupt men and women who have abused their power and taken advantage of those who are weak and vulnerable. Pedro's and Juana's narratives and Joe Taylor's story and commentary reveal some of the ways that Mexicana women have suffered under the oppressive social and economic system that developed on the western side of the valley.[12] His sister, who was the model for Olivia, burst into tears when she read her brother's story. She is now sixty-seven years old, and Joe Taylor said that she still weeps when recalling how *ricos* and powerful Anglos subjected her to their unwanted sexual advances and yet called her "ugly" because she was brown.

CHAPTER **9**

 **CONCLUSION**

Alex Martínez is an authentic hero that Joe Taylor carved out of his culture and his experience at a particular point in San Luis Valley history. Alex is a boy with a deep conscience who lost his innocence as he learned about sin and corruption in his community. He faced a complicated moral dilemma as he worried about his family, struggled with guilt, and tried to figure out what was right and wrong. At a crucial moment, he realized that he had to *act* to save his friend. **Alex, moved by the sight of his brutally beaten friend, whom he knew was innocent, suddenly knew that his loyalty to Milo had to mean something if he were to be a man.** Alex is among the brave men and women in literature, at "any time and in any country,"[1] who have taken risks for an ideal or a principle.

Alex took a risk because **that is the way his parents wanted him to be raised, and that is the way the Church wanted him to be raised.** Joe Taylor had in mind his own churchgoing mother, who taught him about sin, and his cobbler father, who on many occasions confronted the corrupt officials in his community. Joe Taylor wove his concepts of sin and corruption, which are part of his culture, into his story from his position in his social structure.[2] He wrote as a man, as the son of a cobbler, and as a worker in Antonito's class- and ethnically stratified world.

Joe Taylor explained how his ideas of sin and corruption developed as he moved from the world of his mother to that of his father. He recalled the different ways that his parents contributed to his moral education. His mother taught him about sin while giving him love and comfort, and his father taught him about corruption. However, he also recalled how the moral education he received at his mother's knee meshed with what he learned in his father's *zapatería*. Beatriz Mondragón and Anastacio Taylor encouraged him to have a big heart, both by example and through stories. In *Alex and the Hobo,* Beatriz Mondragón's alter ego gave food to the tramp in El Rito as well as being generous within her family. And Anastacio Taylor, Joe Taylor recalled, gave fish to anyone in the town who wanted it. The cultural legacies from his parents include folktales he still holds in his memory, albeit changed to incorporate lessons he learned much later. From his mother, he heard "The Gift of the Little People," which dramatizes the value of having a big heart. From his father, he heard "Juan Chililí Pícaro," which taught him to be a man of his word and to avoid playing the rich man's game. Anastacio Taylor may have told "Juan Chililí" with an "independent" and perhaps "insubordinate" view of his community, reminiscent of artisans in the early English labor movement.[3]

Anastacio Taylor was heroic in standing up to corruption, but he owned no land, he possessed very little money, and he had to send his children out to work in the fields.[4] While working in those fields, Joe Taylor lost some of his innocence as he learned about sex, drinking, and stealing. He also ran into contractors who exploited their workers by paying them by the row or the half-sack, whichever was to their advantage. He still thinks of their exploitation as corruption and sin. From his position as a farmworker, he developed the seeds of a class consciousness that germinated during his union years, when he worked for the perlite plant south of town. His awareness came later on, and he was moved to create an authentic hero by drawing on his culture. After reading *Bless Me, Última,* he realized that he too could carve fiction out of his historical memory.

At the time Joe Taylor created Alex Martínez, the Mexicanos of the San Luis Valley had been experiencing Anglo-Saxon domination for more than a century. Joe Taylor revealed his opposition to hegemony when, in *Alex and the Hobo,* he contrasted his authentic hero to the cardboard heroes in the Hollywood Westerns of his youth. The Hollywood cowboy was the North American counterpart to the Mexican macho, that man who was full of bravado and who first appeared in Mexican ballads of the revolutionary period. The cowboy of film and dime-store novels enjoyed great popularity in the United States between the world wars.[5] Américo Paredes noted that North Americans added the six-shooter to his equipment, the rest of which derived from Mexicano tradition. The six-gun, Paredes noted, was one of the technological innovations that enabled the Anglo-Saxon pioneers to conquer the West.[6] The North American cowboy was usually an Anglo-Saxon who proved his superiority in fights against the darker macho bad guys, often Mexicans and Indians.[7]

When he was the age of Alex, Joe Taylor frequently saw the Hollywood cowboy in the feature films and serials shown in the Antonito cinema. He contrasted his authentic hero of Alex Martínez to the cardboard cowboy of Hollywood Westerns by mentioning the almost never empty six-gun. He wrote: **The bad guy finally ran out of bullets after he shot at least twenty times from a "six-shooter." The hero fired as many rounds but he still had some bullets left in his gun and he shot and killed the bad guy to end the movie.** Writing *Alex and the Hobo* was an act of resistance by which Joe Taylor rejected the cowboy as part of his "lived system of meanings and values."[8] In his story, he had Alex use going to the movies as a ruse so he could carry out his heroic rescue of the hobo from the Conejos County jail.

However, Alex is not the only authentic hero in Joe Taylor's story. The other is the hobo, a mysterious character from another country (Austria) whose native language is not English or Spanish, a man who lives by himself. The hobo turns out to be a spy for the U.S. government who earns a medal of valor in recognition of his heroism during World War II. Joe Taylor's story ends when Alex receives a package containing that medal, which is proof of the hobo's authenticity as a hero. In my conversations with Joe Taylor about editing his story, he insisted that I keep his ending, and after thinking about his life and story I am beginning to understand why.

Alex needs the hobo as an ally because being an authentic Mexicano hero is not sufficient for contending with hegemony. One interpretation of Joe Taylor's story is that Mexicanos need allies from outside of their class and ethnically stratified world in their effort to hold on to their culture, keep their families together, and protect their women from peril. The hobo is such a heroic ally and has a medal to prove it. He is an outsider and is beyond or above the class pyramid dominated by Anglos that Joe Taylor believes is destroying his culture. Like Christ, the hobo is blamed for a crime he did not commit and is dragged through the streets of Antonito in a scene that reminded Joe Taylor of the Stations of the Cross. The victim of the crime is a Mexicana who was violated and murdered by another member of the Mexicano community who, like the *lambe* and Pontius Pilate, turned against those he should have felt a moral obligation to protect. Greg was in the business of selling insurance, which has the ostensible purpose of protecting those who are vulnerable. However, in Joe Taylor's view, true protection is not bought or sold; it comes only by creating relationships through exchange in the manner of the *granjeador*.

There is an important exchange of gifts between Alex and the hobo that creates an alliance in the *granjeador* tradition. The hobo gives Alex a fishing pole, his first masculine tool. Alex saves the hobo's life by breaking him out of the Conejos County jail, and the hobo sends Alex his medal of valor. The exchange of masculine gifts is essential for a boy to take his first steps toward manhood. Although there is no specific quid pro quo, there is the implication that the exchange between the two heroes might continue as each one gets into a scrape and needs the support of the other. I think Joe Taylor has found his own superhero allies, who have encouraged him to pick up the pen and write about his own experiences in an effort to record his culture and resist hegemony. His most important allies are the union movement and the Chicano movement, which, like the hobo, came from outside of the San Luis Valley. Like the hobo, they provided him with gifts—decades of labor relations law and models for writing, like *Bless Me, Última*—that enabled him to act on the masculine moral vision he traced to his mother and father by writing *Alex and the Hobo.*[9] Joe Taylor's story and his account of how he created it are valuable because they reveal his meaning of history. He became visible by writing about his experiences after a lifetime of seeing and hearing so much from the Anglo-Saxon point of view. To become visible is to exercise what Renato Rosaldo has called cultural citizenship,[10] a step Latinos are taking to become full members of their society while maintaining their distinctive cultural heritage.[11]

This book is an experiment. Joe Taylor wrote the story, and I used his oral (and written) commentary to construct a bridge to his readers so that they might understand more deeply his historical allusions. That bridge was constructed out of the words in our dialogue, in which Joe Taylor clarified the implicit and sometimes taken-for-granted meaning of *Alex and the Hobo*. I am constantly learning more about Joe Taylor from our conversations, which have continued right up until the final revisions of this book. On our last visit, it slipped out that he was an acolyte and a fullback in Antonito between 1943 and 1955. An acolyte (*monacillo*) is a boy who serves mass in church,[12] and a fullback is the player on a football team who blasts through the defenses of the opposing team. The traces of both acolyte and fullback are in Joe Taylor's story and in his account of how he created it out of his experience. He takes his religion seriously, he has a deep sense of sin, and he uses his strength to promote the interests of the Mexicano community. He acquired these qualities in his family and his church, and he applied them to the union, to the Chicano movement, and to writing *Alex and the Hobo*.

Juana's Witchcraft Testimony

This appendix contains the text of Juana's witchcraft testimony in the original Spanish and in English translation. Juana learned Spanish from her father, now deceased, who was born in Chihuahua, Mexico. Her speech differed from that of other Spanish speakers in the San Luis Valley who have had no immediate connection with Mexico. For more information on San Luis Valley vocabulary and grammar, consult the dictionaries by Rubén Cobos (1983) and Luis Trujillo (1983) and linguistic studies by Craddock (1976), Bowen (1976), and Hensey (1976). See also Charles Briggs's (1988) study of meaning linked to the speaking context.

Juana's Testimony in Spanish

¡Ay las monitas esas que le dije! Las encontré en un sobre blanco cerrado. Y lo abrí y eran seis monitos. Dos hombres y cuatro mujeres. Y es lo que yo tengo. ¿Ves? Y los llevé con esa mujer, una mujer en Alamosa. Tenían vestidos las mujercitas y pantalones los hombres. Ella los echó alcohol. Los quemó. Y eran de diferentes colores. So cuando apagó todo era rojo. El alcohol era rojo. Y le dije, "¿Porqué es rojo y no de muchos colores?" Porque eran de muchos colores.

Dijo, "Lo rojo es sangre." Dijo, "Vas a ver sangre en tu casa."

Entonces yo me vine. Dijo, "Pon cruces en tus puertas." ¿Verdad? Entonces, yo me vine para la casa y me fuí al hospital. Me metieron en el hospital. Otro día cuando salí, mi hijo agarró un cuchillo y se iba a matar. Se iba a cortar. Entonces yo agarré el cuchillo y le jaló él y me tocó. Y hubo mucha, mucha sangre. Mucha sangre se vió. Y él se fué. ¿Verdad? Y llegó no más a stop sign y se volteó. Y dice, "Les voy a matar a todos," dice. Entonces él se regresó y yo subí a todos los niños en el coche y me fuí. Y él dijo, "¿Porqué pones cruces?" Él está muy enojado. Le dije, ayer unas monas las hallé en el cuarto de él. Le dije, "¿Tú estás haciendo mal?" Y me dijo, "No." Dijo, "Una mujer aquí en Antonito," dijo, "me las dió a mí."

Le dije, "¿Para qué?" Dijo, "Para que yo platicara con ellas cuando yo me sintiera triste o deprimido." Dijo, "Que yo platicara. Esos monitos me dan a mi paz."

Y le dije, "¿Pero qué casualidad que son cuatro mujeres y dos hombres los que están en la familia?" Dijo, "Pero yo no sé." ¿Verdad?

Y esa señora, fuí con esa señora [de Alamosa] y agarró un blanquillo. Y empezó a limpiar. Como dice. Empezó a limpiar así. Y lo echó en un vaso de agua. Como con tanta agua así. Y ese huevo. Psst. Explotó. Y le dije, "¿Qué significa eso?" Dijo, "Es que es brujería."

Pero hace como tres semanas fuí a Monte Vista y otra mujer me dijo, dijo, "Son tres personas las que están haciendo mal."

Ahora mi esposo, él tomaba. Tomaba cada fin de semana. Y ahora toma todos los días. Tiene que tomar mucho todos los días. Y él no tomaba. Hasta que ha chocado donde anda tomando. Lo malo es que donde yo vivo, donde yo rento, dicen que esa familia es mala. Y yo he querido salirme de ahí. Agarrar otra casa. Y no puedo. Algo siempre pasa. Que no tengo el dinero en ese día. Y voy otro día y ya está rentada la casa que yo quiero. ¿Verdad? Y dicen que la gente es mala. No sé. Y me dijeron que la dueña de esa casa practica así cosas malas. Y que ella no nos deja salir de allí. Y luego esa otra señora, que le digo que empezó a ir a mi casa, ella iba y se metía no más. Ésa y ésta otra pero no sé yo. Pero sí he visto mucho cambio. Yo lo creí. Porque yo no creía. Y yo lo creí porque las cosas que están pasando en mi vida, con mis hijos, con mi esposo. Antes yo era muy activa. ¿Sabes? Ahora no. Siempre me mantengo cansada. No quiero hacer nada. Y antes yo . . . Ooh mi yarda era muy bonita. Con jardín. Todo. Y ahora no. Muy seco. ¿No? Y me hizo esa limpia que le dije con el huevo. Todo el cuerpo. Ella pasó el blanquillo por todo mi cuerpo y luego me dijo, "¿Quieres ver lo resultado de que si está mal?"

Y le dije, "Sí."

Le dije, "¿Por qué hizo eso?"

Dijo, "Porque a la persona le dió coraje. Porque tú viniste aquí." Dijo, "Pero tienes que volver a venir." Y ay, yo no fuí. Yo no fuí para allá otra vuelta. Y ahí ella no hace eso porque dice que cuando ella cura alguien, ella se enferma mucho. Que una persona que cura se enferma porque agarra como la enfermedad que tiene la persona. Mi esposo ganaba seis cientos dólares a la semana en un trabajo que él tenía. Iba a Arizona. Iba a Centro. De repente ya no hubo trabajo. Que ni le dijeron se acabó. No más le dijeron, "Ya no hay." No supimos porque. Nada. Y ahora está ganando dos cientos pesos. Pero empezó cuando lo desocuparon, empezó con noventiocho pesos a la semana. Mucho cambio. ¿No?

Como yo le digo yo me mantengo no más con mis niños. Cuidando mi casa. Dándole comida a mi esposo y a mis hijos. Yo no salgo a entrar en casas así, decir voy con una amiga. No tengo amigas. Yo no más en mi casa. ¿Verdad? Y digo yo no le hago mal a nadien para que me hagan un mal. ¿Verdad?

Joe Taylor: No es eso que haces mal. Es que te tienen envidia.

Juana: Porque vivíamos muy bien. Y ahora pues ven que él toma. ¿Verdad? Y eso trae problemas porque siempre está uno alegando. Yo diciéndole, "No debes de hacer eso. Y mira que esto te puede pasar. No hagas eso. No tomes tanto."

Y él se enoja. Y dice, "No. Tú no me mandas. El hombre hace lo que quiere." O algo así. ¿Verdad?

Fuí con una señora. Ya esa señora es grande. ¿Verdad? Mayor. Y me dijo que ella era de aquí. Su esposo era de aquí. Y dijo, "¿Tú sabes," dice, "donde están las brujas?"

Le dije, "No."

Dice, "¿Para qué te cambiaste para Antonito?"

Le dije, "Mi esposo."

Dice, "¿No sabes que está el rabo de las brujas?"

Le digo, "No."

Dice, "Allí hay muchas brujas." Dice, "San Luis, Saguache y Del Norte." Dice, "Los de Saguache ya están más joven. Y los del Del Norte ya son como plebe. ¿Verdad? Más chicos que practican. Pero los de Saguache," dice, "les enseñan a los del Del Norte. Y los de Antonito," dice, "ya son grandes. Personas de edad ya." Dice, "Allí es el rabo de la brujería." Y dice, "Que los martes escuchas ellas. Hoy es martes," dijo ella. Me está diciendo ese día.

Ahora mi hija. ¡Oh mi hija! ¿Dónde andará mi hija? No duermo en toda la noche. Otro día pos ya tampoco. Y siento que me estoy acabando. Las muchachas hoy en día quieren más libertad. Ellas no piensan, como antes yo, no se decían, como yo me crié. ¿Verdad? "No puedes andar afuera después de que obscurezca porque agarras mal nombre o algo así."

Y nosotros, bueno yo—¿verdad?—se conserva uno así. ¿Verdad? No quiere reputación. Y las muchachas de hoy en día, a ellas no les importa. Dicen, "Que digan lo que digan. Yo voy a ir. Yo voy a ir. Y al cabo mis amigos no hablan. Y mis amigos tienen esto que ellos pueden andar y que sus mamás los dejan."

Y los muchachos no. Como mi niño tiene catorce años y él está en casa siempre. Él me ayuda en la yarda y no le interesa salir. Y las muchachas ellas quieren, "Que voy. Pero voy a caminar a mi amigo. Voy . . ."

No sé. No sé será la generación de hoy en día o que será. Pero se me hace mal así de las muchachas.

Taggart: ¿Qué ha pasado con la honra?

Juana: Ya no les importa. Ya es como decir no se conserva. Ellas dicen que son las noventas. Que quieren saber a que van a entrar. Como uno antes decía, "Yo no voy a andar con un muchacho antes de casarme— ¿verdad?—porque yo quiero ser virgen cuando yo vaya al altar." Como yo me casé. Mi esposo fué y me pidió y tuvo que hincarse y decirle a mi abuelito porque él me crió a decir, "Yo me voy a casar con su hija. ¿O usted me deja casar con ella?"

Yo salí de blanco. Ahora no les importa que color se casen. O si son vírgenes o no son vírgenes. Como que no les importa. ¿Verdad? Ellas no más dicen, "Pues son las noventas y queremos saber a que vamos a entrar." ¿Verdad? Tratar el muchacho o no les importa hoy en día. Yo veo a muchas muchachas que hay mucho embarazo entre la juventud, de hoy en día. Y no paran en uno. Aunque ellas sufren, no paran en uno. Sí tiene dos, tres. Y como yo tuve seis. Porque él que fué mi esposo, él fué de una familia de tres no más. So él quiso una familia grande para agarrar a tener la familia que él siempre deseaba. ¿Verdad? y luego no dejaban que uno, como dijo él [Joe], que [son] muy machos acá. ¿Verdad? No dejaban que uno tomara pastillas o que se cuidara como hay ahora que se puede cuidar. La juventud de ahora no más lo hace. Y eso, eso que con el sistema de Welfare, saben que pueden agarrar ayuda. A veces por eso lo hacen. Tienen uno, dos, tres y de diferentes papás. Es lo malo. You know. Es una lástima pero la juventud de hoy en día está perdida. Y luego si les hacen mal, pues [sabe] Dios. Pero estamos viendo los últimos de los últimos días. También es otro. Las enfermedades, todo que dice la Biblia que vamos a ver hijos matando a padres, padres matando a hijos. O padres abusando de hijos. Todo eso está pasando. La vida está difícil.

English Translation

Oh those dolls I told you about! I found them inside of a white envelope. I opened it, and there were six little dolls. Two males and four females. And that is what I have. See? And I took them to that woman, a woman in Alamosa. The little female [dolls] had dresses, and the male [dolls] had pants. She put them in alcohol. She burned them. And they were different colors. So when she put out the fire, everything was red. The alcohol was red. And I asked her, "Why is it red and not different colors?" Because there were a lot of colors.

She said, "The red is blood." She said, "You're going to see blood in your house."

Then I came home. She said, "Put crosses on your doors." Right? Then I came home and went to the hospital. They put me in the hospital. The next day when I left, my son grabbed a knife and was going to kill himself. He was going to cut himself. So then I grabbed the knife, and he pulled on it, and it got me. And there was a whole lot of blood. You could see a lot of blood. And he left. Right? And he just made it to the stop sign and he fell over. And he said, "I'm going to kill everyone," he said. Then he returned, and I put the kids in the car and took off. And he said, "Why are you putting crosses around?" He was very angry. I told him that the day before I had found some dolls in his room. I asked him, "Are you doing something bad?"

And he said to me, "No." He said, "A woman here in Antonito," he said, "gave them to me."

I asked him, "What for?"

He said, "So I could talk to them when I felt sad or depressed." He said, "So I could talk to them. Those dolls give me my peace."

I asked him, "But why the coincidence that there are the four females and two males in the family?"

He said, "I don't know." Right?

And that woman, I went to that woman [in Alamosa], and she took an egg. And she started to clean me. As they say. She started to clean me [by passing the egg all over my body]. And she put it in a glass of water. With this much water. And that egg went pssst. It exploded. And I asked her, "What does that mean?"

She said, "It means it's witchcraft."

But three weeks ago I went to Monte Vista, and another woman told me, she said, "There are three people who are doing bad things to you."

Now my husband, he drinks. He used to drink every weekend. And now he drinks every day. He has to drink a lot every day. And he didn't used to drink like that. It got to where he wrecked his car by driving drunk. The bad thing is that where I live, where I rent, they say that family is bad. And I've wanted to move from there. Find another house. And I can't. Something always happens. I don't have the money when I need it. And I go the next day, and the house I want is rented. Right? And they say they're bad people. I don't know. And they told me that the woman who owns the house does bad things. And she won't let us leave. And then this other woman, that I told you about, started coming to my house, she'd come and just go in. There's her and this other one, but I don't know. But I've seen a lot of changes. I'm a believer. But I didn't used to believe. And I believe it because of the things that have happened in my life, with my children, with my husband. I used to be very active. Do you know what I mean? Not anymore. I'm always tired. I don't want to do anything. And before I . . . Oh, my yard was very beautiful. With its garden. And all that. And now it isn't. It's all dried up. Right? And [the woman in Alamosa] did the cleansing that I told you about with the egg. All over my body. She rubbed the egg all over my body and then she asked me, "Do you want to know if the diagnosis is bad?"

I told her, "Yes."

[After the egg exploded and she determined it was because of witch-craft] I asked her, "Why did it do that?"

She said, "Because it made the person angry. Because you came here." She said, "But you have to come back." And oh, I didn't go. I didn't go back again. And she didn't do that again because they say that when she cures someone, she gets very sick. A person who cures gets sick because she takes the sickness the other person has. My husband earned six hundred dollars a week with the job he had. He'd go to Arizona. He'd go to Center. Suddenly there wasn't any work. They didn't even tell him it was going to end. They just told him, "There isn't anymore." We don't know why. Nothing. And now he's earning two hundred dollars. But he started when [before] they fired him, he started with ninety-eight dollars a week. A big change. Right?

As I told you, I keep myself busy just with my kids. [And] taking care of the house. Making dinner for my husband and my children. I don't go out visiting in other houses like that, saying I'm going to see a friend. I don't have any friends. I'm just in my house. Right? And I can assure you that I don't do anything bad to anyone for anyone to do a bad thing to me. Right?

Joe Taylor: It isn't because you have acted badly. It's that they envy you.

Juana: Because we were living very well. And now they see that he drinks. Right? And that brings problems because one is always quarreling. I am saying to him, "You shouldn't do that. And look, this could happen to you. Don't do that. Don't drink so much."

And he gets mad. And he says, "No. You don't tell me what to do. A man does what he wants." Or something like that. Right?

I went with this woman. She's old now. Right? She's old. And she told me that she was from here. Her husband is from here. And she asked me, "Do you know," she said, "where the witches are?"

I told her, "No."

She asked, "Why did you move to Antonito?"

I told her, "My husband."

She said, "Don't you know it's a powerful center for witches [rabo de las brujas]? I said to her, "No."

She said, "There are a lot of witches there." She said, "San Luis, Saguache and Del Norte." She said, "The ones in Saguache are the youngest. And those in Del Norte are like children. Right? The younger who practice. But those in Saguache," she said, "teach the ones in Del Norte. And the ones in Antonito," she said, "they're old. They're older people." She said, "That's the most powerful center of witchcraft." And she said, "You can hear them on Tuesdays. Today is Tuesday," she said. She was telling me that very day.

Now it's my daughter. Oh, my daughter! Where will she be about? I don't sleep all night. Nor do I the next day. I feel like I'm dying. The girls of today want more freedom. They don't think like I did. They don't talk the way I was raised. Right? "You can't go out after dark because you'll get a bad reputation or something like that."

And we, or I—right?—you waited [for marriage]. Right? You don't want a bad reputation. And the girls of today, they don't care. They say, "Let them say what they want. I'm going out. I'm going out. And on top of that, my friends won't talk. And my friends have [freedom] to go out, and their mothers let them."

And my sons aren't like that. Like my son is fourteen and he's always home. He helps me in the yard and he isn't interested in going out. And the girls want to. "I'm going out. I'm going to walk over to a friend's. I'm going out . . ."

I don't know. I don't know if it's today's generation or what. But what the girls do seems bad to me.

Taggart: What happened to honor?

Juana: It isn't important to them. It's like [they're] saying no one waits. They say that these are the nineties. They want to know what they're getting into. You used to say, "I don't want to sleep with a boy before getting married—right?—because I want to be a virgin when I go to the altar." Like how I got married. My husband went and asked for me, and he had to kneel and ask my grandfather because he brought me up to [believe my husband should] say, "I intend to marry your daughter. Or would you let me marry her?"

I left the house in white. Now it doesn't matter what color they wear when they marry. Or if they're virgins or not virgins. Like it's not important to them. Right? They just say, "Well, these are the nineties, and we want to know what we're getting into." Right? Trying out a boy or not doesn't matter to them today. I look around today at a lot of girls and see a lot of young pregnancies. And they don't stop at one. Even if they suffer, they don't stop at one. They have two, three. And like I had six. Because the man who was my husband, he came from a family of just three. So he wanted a big family to have the family he always wanted. Right? And then they won't let you have just one, like what [Joe] says, that [they're] very macho here. Right? They won't let you take the pill or take care of yourself the way you can take care of yourself today. Young people today just do it. And that, that is because they know they can get help with the Welfare system. Sometimes that's why they do it. [The kids] have one, two, three different daddies. That's the bad thing. You know. It's a shame, but the youth of today are lost. And then if bad things happen to them, well God [knows]. But we're seeing the last of the final days. There's also another thing. The diseases, everything the Bible says, that we're going to see sons killing fathers, fathers killing sons. Or fathers abusing children. It's all happening. Life is hard.

Notes

1. Introduction

1. My understanding of how he created his story came from his "oral literary criticism" (Dundes 1966), which I recorded between 1998 and 2002.

2. See John Comaroff and Jean Comaroff (1992: 39–44, 155–178) for the inscription of colonialism on the body and the body as a construct in Western social thought from Durkheim to Foucault.

3. See Rosaldo (1997: 37) and Lamott (1994: 9) on writing to become visible.

4. V. Simmons (1979: 43–48).

5. My account of the Mexicanos' settlement of the Culebra Creek and Conejos River comes from V. Simmons (1979: 43–47), who notes that the Sangre de Cristo and Conejos land grants had very different histories. While both were originally created by the Mexican government, the original grantees of the Conejos land grant were Mexicano families who had come from a number of communities in northern New Mexico, including Taos, El Rito, Rio Arriba, Rio Colorado, and Abiquiu (V. Simmons 1979: 43). V. Simmons (1979: 47) noted that Charles Beaubien, who by 1848 had gained possession of the Sangre de Cristo land grant, encouraged Mexicanos to settle the Culebra Creek area right after the Treaty of Guadalupe Hidalgo. The narrators of oral histories that I collected in the valley declared that their ancestors settled along the Culebra River because they needed land and water. Some may have been driven from northern New Mexico by Anglo pressure coming in from the south. See V. Simmons (1979: 79–83) for a description of the legal and political process by which Anglo-Saxons acquired the bulk of the land in the Conejos and Sangre de Cristo land grants.

6. V. Simmons (1979: 91) and Petty (1997).

7. T. Rivera (1987, 1988).

8. Olivares (1989: 9–10, 73–74).

9. Anaya (1972).

10. See Radin (1963: 1), Kluckhohn (1945: 79), and Dwyer (1982 [1987]: 271).

11. See Paredes (1977 [1993]: 73–110), Rosaldo (1989: 25–45, 153–175), and Limón (1989, 1994).

12. Comaroff and Comaroff (1992).

13. Deutsch (1987).

14. The qualities that make *Alex and the Hobo* a valuable cultural document are different from those that critics use to judge "literature" as art. Raymond Williams (1977 [1992]: 45–54) interpreted the meaning and the history of the term "literature" in a way that has a particular bearing on Joe Taylor's story. Williams explained that the modern concept combines a sense of "the 'artistic' and the 'beautiful'" with the notion that fiction bears "imaginative truth." The modern concept originated in the Renaissance and developed as a reaction to the demands imposed on the human condition by the Industrial Revolution. Critics of "literature" developed standards for judging aesthetic merit based on criteria of "taste" and "sensibility," which were "unifying concepts in class terms." The notion that aesthetic standards are related to a class system based on a particular mode of economic production helps to place Joe Taylor's story in a broader perspective. As the son of a cobbler and a worker, he wrote from a different class position than the one that produced those standards that some might use to judge his story. *Alex and the Hobo* is nevertheless a work of fiction that contains a powerful "imaginative truth" about being a Mexicano boy on the cusp of manhood in the 1940's.

15. See Briggs (1988: 59–99) for an account of northern New Mexican historical discourse in a conversational context.

16. Cited in Linger (1993: 3).

17. Diana Tey Rebolledo (1994: xx) coined the term "narrative strategies of resistance" for the ways in which Fabiola Cabeza de Baca's stories marked Mexicano culture in the New Mexican landscape. The term also applies to Joe Taylor's writing.

18. See Counihan (1986: 7) on Antonio Gramsci's definition of the organic intellectual. Limón (1994: 26–35) applied the term to John Gregory Bourke, who wrote about Mexicanos in the Rio Grande basin from a different class position. Zavella (1997) and Limón (1994) have drawn attention to the importance of understanding social location in the presentation of Mexicano culture.

19. Briggs (1988: 92–99).

20. Rael (1957, vols. 1 and 2).

21. Rosaldo (1989: 153–175) relates an incident involving Geertz (1968: 152–153), who was working with a young Javanese man who told him "myths and spells" and asked to borrow the anthropologist's typewriter so that he could write. When Geertz asked for the machine back, he hurt the informant's feelings, ending their relationship. Rosaldo (1989: 175) contended that "power relations" got in the way of Geertz's understanding of why the young man wanted to be a writer.

22. See Paredes (1977 [1993]), Dwyer (1982 [1987]), Clifford and Marcus (1986), Clifford (1988), Limón (1989, 1994), Rosaldo (1989).

23. Lawless (1992) wrote about women preachers in Missouri who read her book and did not agree with her interpretation that they were heroically subverting patriarchy. They did not have a feminist consciousness and preferred to describe themselves as responding to the call of God. I did not experience a similar conflict with Joe Taylor, probably because he had already developed class and ethnic consciousness before we began our collaboration.

24. See Taggart (1997, 2002) and Counihan (1999, 2002).

25. Geertz (1973: 5).

26. Marx (1964 [1993]: 112).

27. Robert Stoller (1985) emphasized the role of the father in the boy's transition from the world of the mother. Nancy Chodorow (1978), building on the work of Stoller and others, argued that the father can build up relational capacities in his son. Relational capacities include the ability to be empathetic and have a sense of connection to others. I tested Chodorow's argument with a comparative study of Spanish and Nahuat men. See Brandes (1980), Gutmann (1996), and Limón (1989) for important studies of Hispanic masculinity. (Taggart 1997).

2. Alex and the Hobo

1. "Gilbert" is a pseudonym for Joe Taylor's boyhood friend of another name.

2. China in northern New Mexican and southern Colorado Spanish means "woman with curly hair" (Cobos 1983: 46).

3. Sociedad Protección Mutua de Trabajadores Unidos (see Sánchez 1971).

3. The Valley

1. See J. Rivera's (1998) historical study of acequias in the Upper Rio Grande basin.

2. See Cobos (1983: 43).

3. V. Simmons (1979: 130-132).

4. V. Simmons (1979: 96).

5. See Weigle (1976: 31-47). Weigle (1976: 162-163, 270) notes (165) that the number of stations varied until 1731, when Pope Clement XII established them at fourteen. Weigle identifies the fourteen stations as (1) Jesus is condemned to death by Pilate; (2) Jesus is made to carry the cross; (3) Jesus falls the first time; (4) Jesus meets his blessed mother; (5) the cross is laid on Simon of Cryene; (6) Veronica wipes the face of Jesus; (7) Jesus falls the second time; (8) Jesus speaks to the women of Jerusalem; (9) Jesus falls the third time; (10) Jesus is stripped of his garments and receives gall to drink; (11) Jesus is nailed to the cross; (12) Jesus dies on the cross; (13) Jesus is taken down from the cross; (14) Jesus is laid on the sepulcher.

6. See Weigle (1976: 162-270).

7. See Appadurai (1988), Rodman (1992), Basso (1996), and Stack (1996) for studies of the different meanings of place.

8. Joe Taylor's contrast between El Rito and Antonito is an example of what Margaret Rodman (1992: 644) calls a multilocal conception of place, where "regional relations between lived spaces are developed through infusing experience in one place with the evocation of other events and other places."

9. V. Simmons (1979: 43-44, 46-48).

10. V. Simmons (1979: 135).

11. Swadesh (1966: 92). In 1900 the Mexicanos of Antonito organized the first of eight Colorado branches of the Sociedad Protección Mutua de Trabajadores Unidos (S.P.M.D.T.U.) to fight Anglo discrimination (Sánchez 1971; Deutsch 1987: 26, 222).

12. V. Simmons (1979: 79-83).

13. V. Simmons (1979: 44-46).

14. Peña (1998a: 9, 1998b: 275-291), Peña and Martínez (1998: 154), R. Wilson (199: 1-4).

15. *Rocky Mountain News,* July 13, 2002.

4. Awareness

1. See John Comaroff and Jean Comaroff (1992: 65) for the different ways that ethnic awareness and class consciousness can sustain, mask, reinforce, and refract each other.

2. González (1999: 249–250).

3. For example, Juanita González of Costilla, New Mexico, told the story of "El Baile de los Tecolotes" to Juan B. Rael in 1930 (Rael 1957, 2:600–602). See Griego y Maestas and Anaya's (1980: 142–151) bilingual version of Juanita González's story. In 1940, Vicente López of Antonito told Rael (1957, 2:587–589) a tale of a neophyte attending a witches' sabbat by flying through the air, probably on the back of a *tecolote*.

4. George Foster (1960–1961, 1965) declared that Mexican peasants have an image of the limited good based on envy. In a subtle but complicated argument, he contended that land and other resources are in fact limited but that Mexican peasants in the village of Tzintzuntzan also developed a worldview of the limited good that was part of their system of meaning or culture. Taussig (1980: 13–14) took issue with Foster and argued that narratives about envy are filled with allusions to the narrators' struggles with capitalism.

5. Linger (1993: 3).

6. Comaroff and Comaroff (1992: 156).

7. Gramsci as interpreted by Williams (1977 [1992]: 110).

8. Linger (1993: 3).

9. *Valley Courier,* August 29, 1978.

10. *Valley Courier,* December 20, 1979.

11. *Valley Courier,* February 27, 1980.

12. Thomas Weaver (1965: 167–187) provided a detailed account of a factional dispute over a school in a community in northern New Mexico. In this case, the teachers did not go on strike, but there are some parallels with the Antonito case, one of which was family loyalty or nepotism.

13. Pseudonyms.

14. A pseudonym.

15. A pseudonym.

16. Lorence (1999: 25–26). *Salt of the Earth* was made in 1952 by director Harold Biseman, Academy Award–winning writer Michael Wilson, and producer Paul Jerrico. Biseman became one of the Hollywood Ten, and the film was blacklisted after an eleven-week run in Los Angeles (Lorence 1999: 113–147). See also Wilson and Rosenfelt (1978).

17. Joe Taylor's remark reveals how the history of labor relations in the Antonito area differs from that in other parts of southern Colorado and northern New Mex-

ico, where unions played an important role during much of the twentieth century. From 1913 to 1935, there was continued labor unrest in the Southwest (Kern 1983: 6–7; Deutsch 1987: 116). The United Mine Workers were involved in a bitter strike against the Colorado Fuel and Iron Company that resulted in a massacre when National Guard troops fired on a tent colony in Ludlow, Colorado, on April 20, 1914 (Deutsch 1987: 103–105). Ludlow is across the Sangre de Cristo Mountains and to the east of El Rito. The Liga Obrera de Habla Española (Workers' League of Spanish Speakers), an affiliate of the Industrial Workers of the World, organized workers in the Upper Rio Grande in the 1920's (Deutsch 1987: 173). The United Cannery, Agricultural, and Packing and Allied Workers of America (UCAPAWA), an affiliate of the Congress of Industrial Organizations, was involved in the Greeley area farmworkers' strike of 1932 (Deutsch 1987: 171).

5. Social Structure

1. Deutsch (1987).
2. Sánchez (1971) and Deutsch (1987: 26, 222).
3. Deutsch (1987: 26, 119, 121, 126, 137, 174–175, 182).
4. Deutsch (1987: 28–29).
5. Counihan (2000: 2).
6. Deutsch (1987: 28–29).
7. Cobos (1983: 79, 84) and Trujillo (1983: 121) list *huero/a* and *güero/a* as the San Luis Valley and northern New Mexican Spanish terms for "Anglo-American." Trujillo (1983: 121), who is from Conejos, prefers *huero/a*.
8. Petty (1997).
9. See Counihan (2002) for a Spanish-speaking woman's account of the class structure of Antonito.
10. Mexicano courtship and marriage and the supporting moral discourse are similar but not identical to those of Spain. The similarities include a concern with a woman's premarital chastity, an expectation to ask a woman's parents for her hand in marriage, and the tendency to marry in the same class (Pitt-Rivers 1961 [1966]; Price and Price 1966a, 1966b; Collier 1987; Taggart 1990: 17–76). However, the Mexicanos of Antonito use terms of moral discourse differently. For example, "honor" has more to do with being a man or woman of his or her word than with premarital or marital chastity.
11. See Counihan (2000).

12. The *lambe* is a character in Joe Taylor's commentary that reveals his meaning of history. See Comaroff and Comaroff (1992: 25) for a description of similar characters from other cultures.

13. Vigil (1988).

14. *Yerba* or *hierba* has a number of different meanings in addition to marijuana. See Cobos (1983: 177) and Trujillo (1983: 194).

15. See Broyles-González (1994). See Villarreal (1970) and Mazón (1984 [1995]) for other descriptions and interpretations of *pachucos*.

16. See Limón (1994: 167–183) for an interpretation of violence at dances in south Texas. A fight at a dance led to the famous Sleepy Lagoon trial of 1943 in Los Angeles, in which twenty-two members of the Thirty-eighth Street gang were tried, convicted, and eventually acquitted of killing José Díaz (Romo 1983 [1994]: 166–167, Mazón 1984 [1995]).

6. Anastacio Taylor

1. Thompson (1963 [1966]: 17, 155–156, 157). Thompson noted that in many towns "the actual nucleus from which the labour movement derived ideas, organization and leadership, was made up of such men as shoemakers, weavers, saddlers, harness-makers, booksellers, printers, building workers, small tradesmen and the like" (193). Cobblers appeared in early pro-union demonstrations (427) and were among those protesting the infamous Combination Acts (501). The Combination Acts, passed in 1799–1800 and repealed in 1824, protected the privileges of the aristocracy by codifying existing anti-trade-union laws and prohibiting all combinations, or workers' associations (181, 239, 504).

2. Thompson (1963 [1966]: 503, 523).

3. Cobos (1983: 77).

4. Mauss (1967).

5. This particular definition comes from Cobos (1983: 41).

6. In folklorists' classification, this story is Tale Type 328, "The Boy Steals the Giant's Treasure," and has appeared in the oral tradition of English as well as Spanish speakers in the United States (Baughman 1966: 8; Rael 1957, vol. 2: 367–375; J. Espinosa 1937 [1969]: 87–90). The Spanish variants that circulate in the San Luis Valley most closely resemble a story that de Llano Roza de Ampudia (1975: 145–148) collected in Asturias. See also similar stories from Cáceres (Curiel Merchán 1944: 352–358) and Cádiz (de Larrea Palacín 1959: 179–181). The tale also ap-

pears in a different form in collections from Mexico (Robe 1973: 261–266, 464–477; Wheeler 1943: 366–372), and the Spanish-speaking Caribbean (Andrade 1930: 57–58).

7. In the original transcription, I recorded Joe Taylor as saying, "Ya me ha mandado a Desilú," which I translated as "He's already sent me to Desilú." I interpreted this phrase to mean that the king had sent Juan Chililí Pícaro on several long and meaningless journeys—as if he had sent the hero to Desilú Production Studios in Hollywood, California. However, Joe Taylor did not recognize this phrase four years later and suggested that we use instead "Ya me estoy cansando que me traiga de pendejo," which he translated as "I'm getting tired of him making an ass out of me."

8. Trujillo (1983: 153).

9. See Trujillo (1983: 40, 115).

10. Rael (1957, 2:375–377, 367–372).

11. V. Simmons (1979: 82–83).

12. Broyles-González (1994).

7. Beatriz Mondragón

1. Stoller (1985) found that primary transsexuals, boys and men who are anatomically males but want to be women, do not break their exceptionally close symbiosis with their mothers because they had extremely passive fathers. Stoller concluded that fathers have the task in gender socialization of breaking the mother-son symbiosis by drawing their sons into the world of men. Stoller's interpretation of gender socialization assumed that masculinity is culturally defined differently than femininity. Gilmore (1990) found that there are few if any truly androgynous cultures in the world.

2. This is Tale Type 503 (Aarne and Thompson 1961 [1987]: 170–171).

3. Rael (1957, 2:188–189).

4. Rael (1957, 2:189–190) recorded another version, similar to the one told by Felix Esquivel, from Cleofilas Jaramilla of Santa Fe.

5. The relationship between sin and the handling of infantile sexuality is a major theme in psychoanalytic theory. Freud (1923–1925, 1940 [1989]) argued that a boy develops his sense of sin, or his superego, when he enters the Oedipal phase of his development and desires to possess his mother and banish his father. Faced with threats of castration perceived as coming from the father, he gives up his conscious desire to possess his mother and identifies with his father's moral authority.

The boy's desire for the mother becomes an unconscious urge he does not or cannot express in language (Freud 1900 [1978], 1940 [1989]: 29–44; Roheím 1992: 5). The unconscious has been an extremely controversial concept from the very beginning of the psychoanalytic movement. More recently, scholars sympathetic with those who have been oppressed have argued that Freud's theory has been used against them and to force them to conform to Anglo-Saxon patriarchal norms. Some Chicano scholars (Paredes 1977 [1993]: 73–110; Limón 1989) direct some of their strongest criticisms toward psychoanalytic studies of "Mexican-American" culture on the Texas-Mexican border. Moreover, some feminist scholars find Freud to be "the enemy" because he supports the status quo and is "bourgeois and patriarchal" (Mitchell 1974 [1995]: xv, 5). Cultural anthropologists such as Clifford Geertz (1973) oppose any psychoanalytic theory because it can yield explanations of behavior that are in conflict with the way individuals give meaning to their experience, frequently through language. However, Mitchell (1974) argues that feminists should use Freud's theory to understand their oppression. Moreover, ignoring sexuality in a study of masculinity is foolish, as Alan Dundes (1993 [1994]) argued in his critique of Geertz (1973: 412–453). Joe Taylor had the courage to bring up the subject of the handling of his own infantile sexuality when responding to an earlier draft of this manuscript. His commentary on how his loving mother and grandmother responded to autoeroticism illustrates an enduring insight from psychoanalytic theory; children internalize the concept of sin when their parents show them love as well as disapproval (see Freud 1961 [1989]: 92; Spiro 1987: 137).

6. Conejos is actually the second poorest county in the state of Colorado, with a per capita income of only $12,050, according to U.S. Census figures for 2000. Neighboring Costilla County, which includes San Luis and El Rito, is the poorest county in the state. Costilla and Conejos have remained the two poorest counties in Colorado since the time of *Alex and the Hobo*.

7. Joe Taylor described the daily diet of his childhood: **Most of the meals were repeated every, every day. Like fried potatoes and beans and tortillas and chiles. Those were repeated every day. They were broken only maybe on Sundays when you might have had something else like maybe chicken or something different. But most of the days the meals were pretty much the same. Gravy and potatoes and beans and tortillas and spinach, if it was the season for it.**

8. I thank Sue Carter for reminding me of the phallic gifts that Alex received from the hobo and his father.

8. Women in Peril

1. See M. Simmons (1974 [1980]). Rael (1957, 2:190–192, 587–589) recorded accounts of witches' sabbats in the San Luis Valley in 1930 and 1940. The tales are special cases of narratives that circulate widely in the Mexicano world. See A. Espinosa (1910), Robe (1980: 395–396).

2. Louise Burkhart (1986: 35) noted that the Franciscan theologians in sixteenth-century Mexico handled the problem of evil in two main ways, one of which was a "flirtation with dualism within an overarching monotheism."

3. Geertz (1973: 89) actually wrote that culture "denotes an historically transmitted pattern of meanings embodied in symbols, a system of inherited conceptions expressed in symbolic forms by means of which men communicate, perpetuate, and develop their knowledge about and attitudes toward life."

4. Evans-Pritchard (1937), Taussig (1980), Comaroff and Comaroff (1993: xiv), and Bastian (1993) describe how narratives about the devil and witchcraft are connected to social and economic problems that develop under specific historical circumstances.

5. Williams (1977 [1992]: 108–114); Geertz (1973: 5).

6. Williams (1977 [1992]: 109).

7. Williams (1977 [1992]: 109–111).

8. See Nash (1979) for an important account of the devil in the conceptual system of Bolivian tin miners.

9. *High Country News*, January 19, 1998. For tales of lost mines on the eastern side of the valley, see Campa (1963).

10. Cobos (1983: 143).

11. Juana is a member of one of the small evangelical congregations in the San Luis Valley.

12. See Taggart (1983) for another example of men representing their oppression and threats to their culture in narratives about women. Nahuat men in Mexico depict women in oral narratives in different ways depending on the degree to which they are dominated by Spanish-speaking Mexicans.

9. Conclusion

1. Paredes (1977 [1993]: 216).

2. Pat Zavella (1997: 188) reminds us that the representation of culture varies for subjects depending on their position in the social structure.

3. E. P. Thompson (1963 [1966]: 503, 523).

4. José Limón (1994: 76–94) used Marxist theory to explain why class position is important for understanding presentations of masculinity.

5. I draw here on Américo Paredes' (1977 [1993]: 215–234) essay, "The United States, Mexico, and *Machismo*."

6. Paredes (1977 [1993]: 225).

7. Paredes (1977 [1993]: 225).

8. Williams (1977 [1992]: 110).

9. I thank Sue Carter for suggesting that the depiction of the hobo as an authentic hero is related to Joe Taylor's struggle with Anglo-Saxon hegemony in the San Luis Valley.

10. Renato Rosaldo (1997: 37) quoted Anne Lamott (1994: 9), who said that writing grows out of "our need to be visible, our need to be heard."

11. W. Flores and Benmayor (1997: 2). Examples of cultural citizenship range from strikes (W. Flores 1997) to aesthetic productions (R. Flores 1995, 1997).

12. Trujillo (1983: 140).

Bibliography

Aarne, Antti, and Stith Thompson
1961 [1987] *The Types of the Folktale: A Classification and Bibliography.* Helsinki: Academia Scientiarum Fennica.

Anaya, Rudolfo
1972 [1994] *Bless Me, Última.* New York: Warner Books.

Andrade, Manuel J.
1930 *Folk-Lore from the Dominican Republic.* New York: American Folklore Society.

Appadurai, Arjun
1988 "Introduction: Place and Voice in Anthropological Theory." *Cultural Anthropology* 3: 16–20.

Basso, Keith
1996 *Wisdom Sits in Places: Landscape and Language among the Western Apache.* Albuquerque: University of New Mexico Press.

Bastian, Misty
1993 "'Bloodhounds Who Have No Friends': Witchcraft and Locality in the Nigerian Popular Press." In *Modernity and Its Malcontents,* edited by Jean Comaroff and John Comaroff, 129–166. Chicago: University of Chicago Press.

Baughman, Ernest W.
1966 *Type and Motif-Index of the Folktales of England and North America.* The Hague: Mouton.

Boggs, Ralph S.
1930 *Index of Spanish Folktales.* Helsinki: Academia Scientiarum Fennica.

Bowen, J. Donald
1976 "Structural Analysis of the Verb System in New Mexican Spanish." In *Studies in Southwest Spanish,* edited by J. Donald Bowen and Jacob Ornstein, 93–123. Rowley: Newbury House.

Brandes, Stanley
1980 *Metaphors of Masculinity: Sex and Status in Andalusian Folklore.* Philadelphia: University of Pennsylvania Press.

Briggs, Charles L.
1988 *Competence in Performance: The Creativity of Tradition in Mexicano Verbal Art.* Philadelphia: University of Pennsylvania Press.

Broyles-González, Yolanda
1994 *El Teatro Campesino: Theater in the Chicano Movement.* Austin: University of Texas Press.

Burkhart, Louise M.
1986 *The Slippery Earth: Nahua-Christian Moral Dialogue in Sixteenth-Century Mexico.* Tucson: University of Arizona Press.

Campa, Arthur L.
1963 *Treasure of the Sangre de Cristos: Tales and Traditions of the Spanish Southwest.* Norman: University of Oklahoma Press.

Chodorow, Nancy
1978 *The Reproduction of Mothering: Psychoanalysis and the Sociology of Gender.* Berkeley: University of California Press.

Clifford, James
1988 *The Predicament of Culture: Twentieth-Century Ethnography, Literature, and Art.* Cambridge: Harvard University Press.

Clifford, James, and George E. Marcus, eds.
1986 *Writing Culture: The Poetics and Politics of Ethnography.* Berkeley: University of California Press.

Cobos, Rubén
1983 *A Dictionary of New Mexico and Southern Colorado Spanish.* Santa Fe: Museum of New Mexico Press.

Collier, George
1987 *Socialists of Rural Andalusia: Unacknowledged Revolutionaries of the Second Republic.* Palo Alto: Stanford University Press.

Comaroff, Jean, and John Comaroff
1992 *Ethnography and the Historical Imagination.* Boulder: Westview.
1993 Introduction to *Modernity and Its Malcontents,* edited by Jean Comaroff and John Comaroff, xi–xxxvii. Chicago: University of Chicago Press.

Counihan, Carole

1986 "Antonio Gramsci and Social Science." *Dialectical Anthropology* 11 (1): 3–9.

1999 *The Anthropology of Food and Body: Gender, Meaning, and Power.* New York: Routledge.

2000 "'I Wanted to Go My Way': Class, Gender, and Cultural Citizenship in a Spanish-American Woman's Life History." Paper presented at the annual meeting of the American Anthropological Association, San Francisco.

2002 "Food as Women's Voice in the San Luis Valley of Colorado." In *Food in the U.S.A.,* edited by Carole Counihan, 197–304. New York: Routledge.

Craddock, Jerry R.

1976 "Lexican Analysis of Southwest Spanish." In *Studies in Southwest Spanish,* edited by J. Donald Bowen and Jacob Ornstein, 93–123. Rowley: Newbury House.

Curiel Merchán, Marciano

1944 *Cuentos extremeños.* Madrid: Consejo Superior de Investigaciones Científicas.

de Larrea Palacín, Arcadio

1959 *Cuentos gaditanos I: Cuentos populares de Andalucia.* Madrid: Consejo Superior de Investigaciones Científicas.

de Llano Roza de Ampudia, Aurelio

1975 *Cuentos asturianos: Recogidos de la tradición oral.* Oviedo: Editorial la Nueva España.

Deutsch, Sarah

1987 *No Separate Refuge: Culture, Class and Gender on an Anglo-Hispanic Frontier in the American Southwest, 1880–1940.* Oxford: Oxford University Press.

Díaz-Barriga, Miguel

2000 "Cultural Citizenship." Lecture delivered at Millersville University, Millersville, Pennsylvania.

Dundes, Alan

1966 "Metafolklore and Oral Literary Criticism." *The Monist* 60 (1): 505–516.

1993 [1994] "Gallus as Phallus: A Psychoanalytic Cross-Cultural Consideration of the Cockfight as Fowl Play." In *The Cockfight: A Casebook,* edited by Alan Dundes, 241–282. Madison: University of Wisconsin Press.

Dwyer, Kevin

1982 [1987] *Moroccan Dialogues: Anthropology in Question.* Prospect Heights, Ill.: Waveland.

Espinosa, Aurelio M.
1910 "New Mexican Spanish Folklore: Myths, Superstitions, and Beliefs." *Journal of American Folklore* 22: 395–418.

Espinosa, José Manuel
1937 [1969] *Spanish Folk-Tales from New Mexico.* New York: American Folk-Lore Society.

Evans-Pritchard, E. E.
1937 *Witchcraft, Oracles, and Magic among the Azande.* Oxford: Clarendon.

Flores, Richard
1995 *Los Pastores: History and Performance in the Mexican Shepherd's Play of South Texas.* Washington, D.C.: Smithsonian Institution Press.
1997 "Aesthetic Process and Cultural Citizenship: The Membering of a Social Body in San Antonio." In *Latino Cultural Citizenship: Claiming Identity, Space, and Rights,* edited by William V. Flores and Rina Benmayor, 124–151. Boston: Beacon.

Flores, William V.
1997 "Mujeres en Huelga: Cultural Citizenship and Gender Empowerment in a Cannery Strike." In *Latino Cultural Citizenship: Claiming Identity, Space, and Rights,* edited by William V. Flores and Rina Benmayor, 210–254. Boston: Beacon.

Flores, William V., with Rina Benmayor
1997 "Introduction: Constructing Cultural Citizenship." In *Latino Cultural Citizenship: Claiming Identity, Space, and Rights,* edited by William V. Flores and Rina Benmayor, 1–23. Boston: Beacon.

Foster, George
1960–1961 "Interpersonal Relations in Peasant Society." *Human Organization* 19: 174–178.
1965 "Peasant Society and the Image of Limited Good." *American Anthropologist* 67: 293–315.

Freud, Sigmund
1900 [1978] *The Interpretation of Dreams.* New York: Random House.
1923–1925 "Some Psychical Consequences of the Anatomical Distinctions between the Sexes." In *Standard Edition of the Complete Works of Sigmund Freud,* vol. 19, edited by James Strachey, 248–258. London: Hogarth.
1940 [1989] *Outline of Psycho-Analysis.* New York: Norton.
1961 [1989] *Civilization and Its Discontents.* New York: Norton.

Geertz, Clifford

1968 "Thinking as a Moral Act: Ethical Dimensions of Anthropological Fieldwork in New States." *Antioch Review* 28 (2): 139–158.

1973 *The Interpretation of Cultures.* New York: Basic Books.

Gilmore, David D.

1990 *Manhood in the Making: Cultural Concepts of Masculinity.* New Haven: Yale University Press.

Gonzáles, Manuel G.

1999 *Mexicanos: The History of Mexicans in the United States.* Bloomington: Indiana University Press.

Griego y Maestas, José, and Rudolfo Anaya

1980 *Cuentos: Tales from the Hispanic Southwest.* Santa Fe: Museum of New Mexico Press.

Grimm, Wilhelm, and Jacob Grimm

1944 [1972] *The Complete Grimm's Fairy Tales.* New York: Pantheon.

Gutmann, Matthew C.

1996 *The Meanings of Macho: Being a Man in Mexico City.* Berkeley: University of California Press.

Hansen, Terrence Leslie

1957 *The Types of the Folktale in Cuba, Puerto Rico, the Dominican Republic, and Spanish South America.* Folklore Studies 8. Berkeley: University of California Press.

Hensey, Fritz

1976 "Toward a Grammatical Analysis of Southwest Spanish." In *Studies in Southwest Spanish,* edited by J. Donald Bowen and Jacob Ornstein, 93–123. Rowley: Newbury House.

Kern, Robert, ed.

1983 *Labor in New Mexico: Unions, Strikes, and Social History since 1881.* Albuquerque: University of New Mexico Press.

Kluckhohn, Clyde

1945 "The Personal Document in Anthropological Science." In *The Use of Personal Documents in History, Anthropology, and Sociology,* edited by L. Gottschalk, C. Kluckhohn, and R. Angell, 79–173. New York: Science Research Council.

Lamott, Anne

1994 *Bird by Bird: Some Instructions on Writing and Life.* New York: Anchor.

Lawless, Elaine J.

1992 "I was afraid someone like you . . . an outsider . . . would misunderstand": Negotiating Interpretive Differences between Ethnographers and Subjects." *Journal of American Folklore* 105: 302–314.

Limón, José E.

1989 "Carnes, Carnales, and the Carnivalesque: Bakhtinian Batos." American Ethnologist 16: 471–486.

1994 *Dancing with the Devil: Society and Cultural Poetics in Mexican-American South Texas.* Madison: University of Wisconsin Press.

Linger, Daniel

1993 "The Hegemony of Discontent." American Ethnologist 20: 3–24.

Lorence, James M.

1999 T*he Suppression of "Salt of the Earth": How Hollywood, Big Labor, and Politicians Blacklisted a Movie in Cold War America.* Albuquerque: University of New Mexico Press.

Marx, Karl

1964 [1993] *The Economic and Philosophic Manuscripts of 1884.* New York: International Publishers.

Mauss, Marcel

1967 *The Gift: Forms and Functions of Exchange in Archaic Societies.* New York: Norton.

Mazón, Mauricio

1984 [1995] *The Zoot Suit Riots: The Psychology of Symbolic Annihilation.* Austin: University of Texas Press.

Mitchell, Juliet

1974 [1995] *Psychoanalysis and Feminism: Freud, Reich, Laing, and Women.* New York: Vintage.

Nash, June

1979 *We Eat the Mines and the Mines Eat Us: Dependency and Exploitation in a Bolivian Tin Mine.* New York: Columbia University Press.

Olivares, Julian

1989 Introduction to *The Harvest,* by Tomás Rivera, 9–24, 73–86. Houston: Arte Público.

Paredes, Américo

1977 [1993] *Folklore and Culture on the Texas-Mexican Border.* Austin: CMAS Books.

Peña, Devon G.

1998a Introduction to *Chicano Culture, Ecology, Politics: Subversive Kin,* edited by Devon G. Peña, 3–21. Tucson: University of Arizona Press.

1998b "A Gold Mine, an Orchard, and an Eleventh Commandment." In *Chicano Culture, Ecology, Politics: Subversive Kin,* edited by Devon G. Peña, 249–277. Tucson: University of Arizona Press.

Peña, Devon G., and Rubén O. Martínez

1998 "The Capitalist Tool, the Lawless, and the Violent: A Critique of Recent Southwestern Environmental History." In *Chicano Culture, Ecology, Politics: Subversive Kin,* edited by Devon G. Peña, 141–176. Tucson: University of Arizona Press.

Petty, Hazel Bean

1997 "Early Settlements of Southern Conejos County." *San Luis Valley Historian* 19: 5–29.

Pitt-Rivers, J. A.

1961 [1966] *The People of the Sierra.* Chicago: University of Chicago Press.

Price, Richard, and Sally Price

1966a "Noviazgo in an Andalusian Pueblo." *Southwestern Journal of Anthropology* 22: 302–322.

1966b "Stratification and Courtship in an Andalusian Village." *Man* (n.s.) 1: 526–533.

Radin, Paul

1963 *Autobiography of a Winnebago Indian.* New York: Dover.

Rael, Juan B.

1957 *Cuentos españoles de Colorado y Nuevo Méjico.* Vols. 1 and 2. Stanford: Stanford University Press.

Rebolledo, Diana Tey

1994 Introduction to *We Fed Them Cactus,* by Fabiola Cabeza de Baca, xiii–xxxii. Albuquerque: University of New Mexico Press.

Rivera, José A.

1998 *Acequia Culture: Water, Land, and Community in the Southwest.* Albuquerque: University of New Mexico Press.

Rivera, Tomás

1987 . . . *y no se lo tragó la tierra/. . . And the Earth Did Not Devour Him.* Houston: Arte Público.

1988 *The Harvest.* Houston: Arte Público.

Robe, Stanley H.
1973 *Index of Mexican Folktales*. Folklore Studies 26. Berkeley: University of California Press.
1980 *Hispanic Legends from New Mexico: Narratives from the R. D. Jameson Collection*. Folklore and Mythology Studies 31. Berkeley: University of California Press.

Rodman, Margaret C.
1992 "Empowering Place: Multilocality and Multivocality." *American Anthropologist* 94: 640–691.

Roheím, Géza
1992 *Fire in the Dragon and Other Psychoanalytic Essays on Folklore*. Princeton: Princeton University Press.

Romo, Ricardo
1983 [1994] *East Los Angeles: History of a Barrio*. Austin: University of Texas Press.

Rosaldo, Renato
1989 *Culture and Truth: The Remaking of Social Analysis*. Boston: Beacon.
1997 "Cultural Citizenship, Inequality, and Multiculturalism." In *Latino Cultural Citizenship: Claiming Identity, Space, and Rights,* edited by William V. Flores and Rina Benmayor, 27–53. Boston: Beacon.

Sánchez, Frederick
1971 "A History of the S.P.M.D.T.U." *San Luis Valley Historian* 3: 1–16.

Simmons, Marc
1974 [1980] *Witchcraft in the Southwest: Spanish and Indian Supernaturalism on the Río Grande*. Lincoln: University of Nebraska Press.

Simmons, Virginia McConnell
1979 *The San Luis Valley: Land of the Six Armed Cross*. Boulder: Pruett.

Spiro, Melford E.
1987 "Social Systems, Personality, and Functional Analysis." In *Culture and Human Nature: Theoretical Papers of Melford E. Spiro,* edited by Benjamin Kilborne and L. L. Langness, 109–144. Chicago: University of Chicago Press.

Stack, Carol
1996 *Call to Home: African Americans Reclaim the Rural South*. New York: Basic Books.

Stoller, Robert
1985 *Presentations of Gender.* New Haven: Yale University Press.

Swadesh, Frances León
1966 "Hispanic Americans on the Ute Frontier from the Chama Valley to the San Juan Basin 1694–1960." Ph.D. diss., University of Colorado.

Taggart, James M.
1983 *Nahuat Myth and Social Structure.* Austin: University of Texas Press.
1990 *Enchanted Maidens: Gender Relations in Spanish Folktales of Courtship and Marriage.* Princeton: Princeton University Press.
1997 *The Bear and His Sons: Masculinity in Spanish and Mexican Folktales.* Austin: University of Texas Press.
2002 "Food, Masculinity, and Place in the Hispanic Southwest." In *Food in the U.S.A.,* edited by Carole Counihan, 305–314. New York: Routledge.

Taussig, Michael
1980 *The Devil and Commodity Fetishism in South America.* Chapel Hill: University of North Carolina Press.

Thompson, E. P.
1963 [1966] *The Making of the English Working Class.* New York: Vintage.

Trujillo, Luis M.
1983 *Diccionario del Español del Valle de San Luis del Colorado y del Norte de Nuevo México.* Alamosa: O and V Printing.

Vigil, James Diego
1988 *Barrio Gangs: Street Life and Identity in Southern California.* Austin: University of Texas Press.

Villarreal, José Antonio
1970 *Pocho.* New York: Anchor.

Weaver, Thomas
1965 "Social Structure, Change, and Conflict in a New Mexican Village." Ph.D. diss., University of California, Berkeley.

Weigle, Marta
1976 *Brothers of the Light, Brothers of Blood: The Penitentes of the Southwest.* Albuquerque: University of New Mexico Press.

Wheeler, Howard T.
1943 *Tales from Jalisco Mexico.* Philadelphia: American Folk-Lore Society.

Williams, Raymond
1977 [1992] *Marxism and Literature.* Oxford: Oxford University Press.

Wilson, Michael, and Deborah Silverton Rosenfelt
1978 *Salt of the Earth.* New York: Feminist Press and City University of New York.

Wilson, Randall K.
1999 "'Placing Nature': The Politics of Collaboration and Representation in the Struggle for La Sierra in San Luis, Colorado." *Ecumene* 6 (1): 1–28.

Zavella, Pat
1997 "Reflections on Diversity among Chicanas." In *Challenging Frontiers: Structuring Latina and Latino Lives in the U.S.,* edited by Mary Romero, Pierrette Hondagnew-Sotelo, and Vilma Orti, 187–194. New York: Routledge.

Index

Aarne, Antti, 184n.2
abuelo, 80
acequia, 75, 179n.1
acolyte, 166
Adam State College, 4, 90
álamo, 133
Alamosa, 84
alcohol: mother's dislike of, 141, 143–144; poetic device as, 143–144
Alcoholics Anonymous, 145
Alex and the Hobo, time of, 5
allusion, forms of, 5–6
altos, los, 132
Anaya, Rudolfo, 4, 90, 178n.9, 181n.3
Anglo-Saxons: arrival of, 3; callousness of, 85–86; corruption of, 110; cowboy as, 163–164; nativism of, 104; prejudice of, 98–101; psychological vampire as, 150–153; racism of, 104; settlements of, 84; sexual harassment by, 161
Antonito: El Rito and, 82–87; settlement of, 3, 84; as witchcraft center, 159. *See also* Conejos Land Grant, Conejos River
Antonito Classroom Teachers Association (ACTA), 92
Appadurai, Arjun, 180n.7
apocalyptic vision, 140, 158, 159
artemisia (sagebrush), 76
Asturias, 183n.6
authors, ethnicity of, xi–xii

balls of fire, 22–23, 75, 87
Basso, Keith, 180n.7
Bastian, Misty, 186n.4
Baughman, Ernest W., 183n.6
Bayard, New Mexico, 101
Beaubien, Charles, 86, 177n.5
Benmayor, Rina, 187n.11
birth control, 155
Biseman, Harold, 181n.16
Blackmore, William, 86
Bless Me, Última, 4, 90, 163, 165
body, 177n.2
Bountiful, 142
Bourke, John Gregory, 178n.18
Bowen, J. Donald, 167
Brandes, Stanley, 179n.27
Briggs, Charles L., 167, 178nn.15,19
Broyles-González, Yolanda, 134, 183n.15, 184n.12
Bureau of Land Management (BLM), 78
Burkhart, Louise, 186n.2
burruñates, 23–24, 145

Cabeza de Baca, Fabiola, 178n.17
Cáceres, 183n.6
Cádiz, 183n.6
caló, 115
Campa, Arthur L., 186n.9
capitalism: greed and, 87–88; views on, 87–88
caporal, 111
Carter, Sue, 185n.8, 187n.9

Center, 158
chamiso pardo, 76
change, 84
chastity, 182n.10
Chávez, César, 93, 134
Chicano: attitude toward, 91; awareness of, 91, 144; scholars, 5; term,
use of, 91
child care, 118, 136–137
china, 179n.2
Chodorow, Nancy, 179n.27
Christ, 62, 147, 165
class: courtship and, 109–110; divisions
of, 104; ethnicity and, 97–101; marriage and, 107–110; mobility, 107–
108; system of, 115, 149
class consciousness, 7; development
of, 94–96; among English workers,
121; resistance to, 91
Clifford, James, 179n.22
cobblers: English, 183n.1; independence of, 121–122; shop of, 118–119
Cobos, Rubén, 167, 179n.2, 182n.7,
183nn.3,5,14, 186n.10
cofradías, 81
Collier, George, 182n.10
colonization, 8
Colorado Education Association (CEA),
92
Colorado Fuel and Iron Company,
182n.17
Comaroff, Jean, 5, 177n.2, 178n.12,
180n.1, 181n.6, 183n.12, 186n.4
Comaroff, John, 5, 177n.2, 178n.12,
180n.1, 181n.6, 183n.12, 186n.4
Combination Acts, 183n.1
Conejos, town of, 182n.7
Conejos County, 185n.6
Conejos Land Grant, 3, 85, 177n.5
Conejos River, 149, 177n.5; settlement
of, 2–3, 84
Congress of Industrial Organization
(CIO), 182n.17

contractor: abuse by, 112; definition of,
111; ethnicity of, 111
cooking, 137–138
cops, corruption of, 120–121
Córdova, New Mexico, 7
corruption: definition of, 6–7; examples
of, 110, 120–121; greed as cause of,
88; innocence and, 6; learning
about, 120–121; *ricos* practicing,
110; sin and, 6, 88
Costilla, New Mexico, 181n.3
Counihan, Carole, xii, 1, 4, 9, 11, 73,
109, 178n.18, 179n.24, 182nn.5,9,11
courtship: changes in, 153–155, 170–
171, 174–175; class and, 109–110;
dances and, 109–110; honor in, 109;
practices of, 109–110; in Spain,
182n.10
cowboy: ethnicity of, 164; Hollywood
films of, 163–164
Craddock, Jerry R., 167
crops, 111
Culebra Creek, 133, 138, 149, 177n.5;
settlement of, 2–3. *See also* El Rito
cultural citizenship, 166, 187n.11
culture, 150, 186n.3
curandera, 155, 157, 167–170, 171–173
Curiel Merchán, Marciano, 183n.6
cuzco, 123

dances: courtship and, 109–110; fights
at, 117, 183n.16
daughters, 137
De Herrera, Pete, 92, 116
De Herreras, 85
de Larrea Palacín, Arcadio, 183n.6
de Llano Roza de Ampudia, Aurelio,
183n.6
Del Norte, 84, 85, 157
Deutsch, Sarah, 5, 104, 178n.13,
180n.11, 182nn.1–4,6,17
dialogue, 8
Díaz, José, 183n.16

Díaz Barriga, Miguel, xii
diet, 185n.7
discrimination, 105–106
drinking: explanation of, 144–145; father's moderation in, 144; mother's dislike of, 143–144; poverty and, 144–145, 158. *See also* alcohol
Dundes, Alan, 177n.1, 185n.5
Durango, 85
Durans, 85
Durkheim, Emile, 177n.2
Dwyer, Kevin, 178n.10, 179n.22

eating: rules regarding, 145–146; in speech, 133; symbolism of, 133. *See also* food
El Rito, 132, 137, 145, 163; comparison to Antonito, 82–87; early home in, 73; food production in, 83–84; kinship in, 83; memories of, 82–84; leaving, 122; settlement of, 84. *See also* Culebra Creek
El Teatro Campesino, 134
employers, attitudes of, 85–86
envy, 91, 181n.4
Espinosa, Aurelio, 186n.1
Espinosa, José Manuel, 183n.6
Esquivel, Felix, 132, 138, 139, 140, 184n.4
estranged labor, 10
ethnic consciousness, 7; class and, 97–101; resistance to, 91
ethnic divisions, history of, 104
ethnicity: of authors, xi–xii; class and, 97–101
ethnic tension: in football, 106–107; history of, 104–106; in Great Depression, 104
ethnic terminology, 2–3, 91
Evans-Pritchard, E. E., 186n.4

father: child care by, 118, 136; in contrast to mother, 141–143; fighting

corruption, 118, 120–121; generosity of, 122–124; independence of, 121–124; as model, 118; respect for, 120
feeding, meaning of, 137
field boss: abuse by, 112; definition of, 111; empathy of, 112; ethnicity of, 111; *lambe* as, 114–115; power of, 112; role of, 111; sexual harassment by, 112. *See also caporal, mayordomo*
Figgen, Kathy, xii
fights, 106–107, 115–117
fish: cooking of, 137–138; distribution of, 123, 137
Flores, Richard, 187n.11
Flores, William V., 187n.11
folktales
—Tale Type 124A "Pigs Build House of Straw, Sticks, and Iron," 89–90
—Tale Type 328 "The Boy Steals the Giant's Treasure": distribution of, 183n.6; El Rito version of, 133; text of, 124–129
—Tale Type 503 "The Gifts of the Little People," 163, 184n.2; text of, 138–139
food: in daily meals, 185n.7; mother's love and, 137; rules of, 146; in speech, 133; story image of, 145–148; symbolism of, 9
foreman, 114–115. *See also caporal, mayordomo comerse,* 133
Foster, George M., 181n.4
Foucault, Michel, 177n.2
Franciscans, 81, 186n.2
Freud, Sigmund, 184–185n.5
friendship: and kinship, 109–110; and marriage, 109–110

gang violence, 116–117
Garcías, 85

Geertz, Clifford, 150, 179n.21, 179n.25, 185n.5, 186nn.3,5
gender relations, 5
geography, 107. See also space
gift exchange, 123–124. See also granjeador
Gilmore, David D., 184n.1
Gilpin, William, 86
Gonzáles, Manuel G., 181n.2
González, Corkey, 93
González, Juanita, 181n.3
Gramsci, Antonio, 7, 91, 178n.18, 181n.7. See also hegemony
grandes, los, 132
grandfather, 136
granjeador, 134, 165: definition of, 123; gift exchange as, 123
grantee, 84
Great Depression, 104
Great Lakes Carbon (GrefCo), 94
greed, 7: corruption and, 88; sin and, 88; spirits of, 75, 87–88
Griego y Maestas, José, 181n.3
grievance, 98–101
Guadalupe–Hidalgo, 3
güero/a, 182n.7. See huero/a
Gutmann, Matthew C., 179n.27

Harlen, Dennis "Hoot," 145
hegemony, 159–160; definition of, 91, 150; personification of, 153; resistance to, 163; witchcraft and, 150; writing against, 165
Henry, T. C., 85
Hensey, Fritz, 167
hero, 148; definition of, 162
hierba, 183n.14. See also yerba
High Country News, 186n.9
Hispanos, emigration of, 85
historical imagination, 5. See also Jean Comaroff, John Comaroff
history, meaning of, 165
honor, 109, 154, 170, 174, 182n.10

huero/a, 105, 111, 182n.7

income, per capita, 185n.6
Industrial Workers of the World (IWW), 182n.17
infantile sexuality, 184–185n.5
innocence, 6

Jacobin, 121
Jaquez, José María, 84
Jaramilla, Cleofilas, 184n.4
Jaramillo, Phil, xii
Jerrico, Paul, 181n.16

Kern, Robert, 182n.17
kinship: in El Rito, 83; marriage and, 109–110; in strike, 103
Kiowa Hill, 77
Kiowas, 77
Kluckhohn, Clyde, 178n.10
Ku Klux Klan, 104

labor: gender organization of, 136; history of, 181–182n.17; social organization of, 111
la calle de los ricos, 107
La China, 75
La Jara, 84, 111
La Llorona, 79, 148, 160
lambe, 102, 135, 183n.12; attitude toward, 114; definition of, 114; derivation of, 114; ethnicity of, 114; example of, 115; field boss as, 114; folktale character as, 134; foreman as, 114–115; greed as cause of, 114; Pontius Pilate as, 165
Lamott, Anne, 177n.3, 187n.10
land grant: Conejos, 3, 85, 177n.5; Sangre de Cristo, 3, 177n.5
land speculators, 84–85
Lawless, Elaine, 9, 179n.23
Liga Obrera de Habla Española, 182n.17

limited good, 181n.4
Limón, José, 178nn.11,18, 179nn.22,27, 183n.16, 185n.5, 187n.4
Linger, Daniel, 178n.16, 181nn.5,8
literature, 178n.14
llanero, 73
Lobato, Cecilia, 132–133
Lobatos, 75
London Corresponding Society (LCS), 121
López, Vicente, 181n.3
Lorence, James M., 181n.16
Luceros, 85
Ludlow massacre, 182n.17
luminaria, 80

machismo, 187n.5
macho, 113, 155, 171, 175. *See also* Matthew Gutmann
magic mountain, 76
Manassa, 84
manhood, 6
Manifest Destiny, 2, 5
Mansfield, John, 94
Marcus, George E., 179n.22
marijuana, 116; term for, 183n.14
marriage: class in, 107–110; friendship in, 109–110; kinship and, 109–110; reasons for, 109
Martínez, Rubén O., 180n.14
Marx, Karl, 10, 150, 179n.26
Marxist theory, 187n.4
masculinity: acquiring, 136; of father, 118; food and, 145–148; phallic gifts of, 145–148; respect in, 117; sexuality and, 147, 185n.5; theories of, 10, 184–185n.5, 187n.4
Mauss, Marcel, 123, 183n.4
mayordomo, 111. *See also* field boss
Mazón, Mauricio, 183nn.15,16
menudo, 23
mestizo, 3, 81
metemal, 130

metote, 130
Mexican, 2–3
Mexicanos: anger among, 115; definition of, 2–3; fights among, 115–117; images of, 133; Mexicans and, 2–3; origins of, 3
Mexican Town, 107
México, 107
Mitchell, Juliet, 185n.5
monacillo, 166
Mondragón, Beatriz, death of, 10
Mondragón, José Inez, 122
Montevista, 84, 85
moradas, 81
moral complexity, 7
moral vision, 7
Morgan, John, 79
Mormons, 79
mother: child care by, 136; contrast to father, 141–143; cooking by, 137–138; love of, 137; moral lessons from, 138–140; protecting children, 142–143; religion taught by, 140
multilocal, 180n.8

Nash, June, 186n.8
nativism, 104

Olivares, Julian, 177n.8
Olmos, James, 116
oral literary criticism, 177n.1
oral narratives. *See* folktales
organic intellectual, 7
Ortiz, Manuel, 105

pachucos, 183n.15; definition of, 115–116; gang of, 116; speech of, 116
packers, 111
Pai, Lou, 86
Paine, Thomas, 122
palabra, 124, 134
Paredes, Américo, 164, 178n.11, 179n.22, 185n.5, 186n.1, 187nn.5–7

patrón, 131
pelegartero, 130
Penitentes, 81, 149
Peña, Devon G., 180n.14
perlite; definition of, 94; mine, 94; processing plant, 94
Petty, Hazel Bean, 177n.6, 182n.8
pícaro, 130, 133–134, 138–139
pickers, 111
picket lines, 102–103
Piñon Hills, 75
Pitt-Rivers, J. A., 182n.10
poplar, 133
poverty: and drinking, 144; and witchcraft, 150
power, symbol of, 133
prejudice, 98–101
Price, Richard, 182n.10
Price, Sally, 182n.10
primal scene, 30–31, 140–141
psychoanalytic theory, 184–185n.5
psychological vampire, 7, 150–153

rabo de brujas, 156–157, 159
racism, 104
Radin, Paul, 178n.10
Rael, Juan B., 8, 132, 139, 178n.20, 181n.3, 183n.6, 184nn.3,4,10, 186n.1
railroad, arrival of, 3, 84
Raza Unida Party, 10, 90–91, 94
Rebolledo, Diana Tey, 178n.17
reciprocal ethnography, 9
relajo, 134
relationality, 179n.27
religion, teaching of, 140
respect, 117, 120
rica, courtship of, 109–110
ricos: in Antonito, 107; corruption among, 110; definition of, 104–105; folktale image of, 131, 134; history of, 104–105; sexual harassment by, 110, 161

Rivera, José A., 179n.1
Rivera, Tomás, 4, 177n.7
Robe, Stanley H., 184n.6, 186n.1
Rocky Mountain News, 180n.15
Rodman, Margaret C., 180nn.7,8
Roheím, Géza, 185n.5
Romero, Mary, xii
Romo, Ricardo, 183n.16
Rosaldo, Renato, 166, 177n.3, 178n.11, 179nn.21–22, 187n.10
Rosenfelt, Deborah, 181n.16
Ruybal, Lionel, 92, 93, 116

sagebrush, 76
Saguache, 157
Salt of the Earth, 101, 181n.16
Sánchez, Frederick, 179n.3, 180n.11, 182n.2
Sanford, 84, 111
Sangre de Cristo land grant, 3, 177n.5
San Luis, town of, 80, 157
San Luis Valley Southern, 79
San Pablo, 81, 132, 133, 138
Santa Fé, 85
school strike, 92–94
Segura, Antonia, 137
sexual harassment: example of, 110, 113–114; metaphor of, 110–111; in story, 26, 110–111
sexuality: infantile, 185n.5; learning about, 6; masculinity and, 185n.5; sin and, 140–141, 184–185n.5; in story, 26, 30–31; symbolic importance of, 147
sibling tie, 110, 137
Simmons, Marc, 186n.1
Simmons, Virginia, 177nn.4–6, 180nn.3,4,9,10,12,13, 184n.11
sin: greed and, 88; innocence and, 6; learning about, 6, 11, 138, 140–141; sexuality and, 140–141, 184–185n.5; theory of, 184–185n.5
sinvergüenza, 130

sisters, 110, 137
six-gun, 164
Sleepy Lagoon, 183n.16
social stratification, 104
South Conejos County School Board, 92, 94
space, 82, 107
Spiro, Melford, 185n.5
S.P.M.D.T.U., 179n.3; dances in, 109–110; history of, 104, 180n.11
Stack, Carol, 180n.7
Stations of the Cross, 62, 80, 147, 180n.5
Stoller, Robert, 179n.27, 184n.1
storyteller commentary, 129–132
stratum endogamy, 107–110
strike, 92–94, 102–103
Summitville disaster, 153
Swadesh, Frances León, 85, 180n.11

Taggart, Beatrice, xii
Taggart, James M., 179nn.24,27, 182n.10, 186n.12
Taos, 84
Taussig, Michael, 181n.4, 186n.4
Taylor, Anastacio, death of, 10
Taylor, Jack, 86
Taylor, José Inez: birth of, 4; languages of, 3–4
Taylor, Zachary, 86
Taylor ranch, 86–87
Teamsters, 96
Ten Commandments, 6
terrorism, 85
Thompson, E. P., 121–122, 183nn.1,2, 187n.3
Thompson, Stith, 184n.2
"Three Little Pigs, The," 89–90
Tijerina, Reies López, 93
transsexuals, 184n.1
truck driver, 111–112
Trujillo, Luis M, 167, 182n.7, 183n.14, 184nn.8,9; 187n.12

typewriter incident, 179n.21

unconscious, 185n.5
union: election of, 96; history of, 181–182n.17; joining, 94–95; opposition to, 101–103; role in, 94–103
United Cannery, Agricultural, and Packing and Allied Workers of America (UCAPAWA), 182n.17
United Mine Workers, 95, 182n.17
Utes, 76, 84

Valley Courier, 92, 181nn.9–11
Velazquez, Leonard, xii
Vigil, Cornelio, 84
Vigil, James Diego, 115, 183n.13
Villarreal, José Antonio, 183n.15

Weaver, Thomas, 181n.12
web of meaning, 10
Weigle, Marta, 180nn.5,6
Wheeler, Howard T., 184n.6
Williams, Raymond, 150, 178n.14, 181n.7, 186nn.5–7
Wilson, Michael, 181n.16
Wilson, Randall K., 180n.14
witchcraft: antecedents of, 149; classification of, 156–157; cleansing of, 76; culture in, 150; definition of, 149–150; diagnosis of, 155–156; economics of, 150, 159; envy in, 149–150, 158–159; ethnicity of, 150; evidence of, 155–156; greed in, 149–150; hegemony and, 150; Penitentes and, 149; places of, 75, 150; psychological vampire as, 7, 150–153; sabbat of, 181n.3, 186n.1; testimony of, 150–160, 167–175
witches' mountain, 76
work, organization of, 111–112
workers: categories of, 111; exploitation of, 7

writing: cultural citizenship as, 165–166; inspiration for, 90–91; reason for, 1–3; resistance as, 165

yerba, 116, 183n.14

zapatería, 118–119
Zavella, Pat, 178n.18, 186n.2
zoot suit, 115–116
Zoot Suit, 116